Indian Christianity and Its Public Role

Indian Christianity and Its Public Role

Socio-Theological Explorations

Editor
Gnana Patrick

Department of Christian Studies
University of Madras, Chennai

&

Christian World Imprints
New Delhi

First Published in 2019 by

Department of Christian Studies
University of Madras
Chepauk, **Chennai-600005**
gpatrick@unom.ac.in
http://www.unom.ac.in
Phone: +91 9444825175; 9790825175

&

Christian World Imprints
Christian Publishing & Books from India
H-12 Bali Nagar, **New Delhi-110015**
info@christianworldimprints.com
www.ChristianWorldImprints.com
Phone: +91 11 25465925

ISBN: 978-93-5148-345-8 (HB)
ISBN: 978-93-5148-346-5 (PB)

Printed in India.

Contents

Preface

Indian Christianity is facing up to a new phase in its bi-millennial existence. It is a phase wherein it increasingly becomes self-conscious, aware of its identity and role, and gets involved or participates in 'public' concerns or roles. It is a phase distinct and different from earlier ones, whether pre-colonial or colonial eras, when Indian Christianity was less self-conscious of its identity but more spontaneous in involvements. Today not merely its minority status in terms of numbers, but also its religio-cultural practices and social involvements are being problematized, called into question, and debated in the public realm.

It is necessary that Indian Christianity grows in its publicness in a healthy way. Growing in publicness would imply that Indian Christianity takes effort to become aware of its place in the Indian public, and be involved heart and soul in the processes of the Indian public. The term 'public', in a fundamental sense, would connote, as Hannah Arendt suggests, 'being seen and heard' by different others across space and time. Though it sounds something very ordinary, the normativity involved in this experience is radical, because it would mean not 'extending a privateness' into a public, in the name of being public; it would rather be a radical virtue analogical to 'sitting around a table', not falling over others, and maintaining one's distinct identity and location. The table which separates different others but yet brings them into communicative relationship is perhaps a potent symbol of the public. Such a deep sense of being public is carried further into specific connotations, when it relates itself to such emergent categories called 'public religion', 'religion in the public sphere', 'public theology', and the like. The term is present in these phrases with its rich and varied connotations: first of all, it relates itself to the political process, in a very broad sense, i.e., partaking of the process of decision-making for common good or public life; secondly, it stands for certain discursivity / communicative action, found in the relatively independent space between family, economic systems, and states (and some scholars distinguish it from the sphere of civil society as well); thirdly, though it differentiates itself from family, economy and state, it debates or reasons about them, by way of contributing to creation of public opinion to eventually and effectively impact upon the political praxis; and there are many other context-dependent connotations too. As ours is a participatory world in which increasing quantum of people participate in various spheres of life - be it science, technology, medicine, culture, education, religion, etc., they participate immensely in politics too, the sphere of decision-making for public life or common good. And therefore it is but a relevant concern to see that Indian Christians too participate in public life creatively, meaningfully and liberatively.

By way of exploring and propounding this concern, a national consultation was organized by the Department of Christian Studies at the University of Madras in February 2018. Some of the salient papers presented in the seminar are brought together in this volume for wider readership. The papers explore from various disciplinary perspectives Indian Christianity in relation to public concerns. There are papers, written from perspectives of social sciences, which explore the sociological status of Indian Christianity, along with its commitment for empowerment of marginal cultures, educational contributions, etc. There are others written from theological perspectives, exploring the prospects of doing public theology, as a manner of inspiring to participate in the political processes of this country, to participate effectively in debates while formulating and implementing public policies. There are also papers which deal with such important questions of religious pluralism, inter-religious, inter-disciplinary dialogues, etc., to enrich the quality of Indian civil society.

The national consultation, which gave the inspiration and resources for this volume, was made possible because of the participation of scholars who reflected upon various facets of this concern; I am deeply grateful to them. My sincere thanks to Vice-Chancellor Prof. Dr. P. Duraisamy and Registrar Prof. Dr. R. Srinivasan of the University of Madras for their dedication in their service to the University, and thereby inspiring us to be similarly dedicated. I thank my colleague Dr. K. James Ponniah for his cooperation to organize the consultation, our office-administrator Ms. Majella Fernando and our office-assistant Mr. Vinayaga Murthy for taking good care of the administration of the Department. I take this opportunity to express my gratitude to the Institute of Missiology, MISSIO, Aachen, Germany, for providing a timely financial grant which helped us to successfully organize the consultation. Finally, I wish to convey my thanks and appreciation to Mr. Sudhanshu Kanda of the Christian World Imprints for contacting me, and doing a fine work of publication.

Gnana Patrick
05 February 2019

Introduction: Indian Christianity in the Public Realm

Gnana Patrick
University of Madras

Experience of religion in our contemporary world is unique in many ways. One among them is unmistakably the way it is being experienced in the public realm. By 'public realm', I mean the spaces addressed as state, political society, public sphere, and civil society. Presence of religion in these spaces has become consequential in terms not merely of external political processes, but also of values and visions, moods and motivations, etc., experienced by individuals internally. Whether a state establishes or disestablishes religion, whether and how religious issues or identities are being debated in the institutions of political society, whether public reasoning includes elements of religion, and, whether and how religion become part and parcel of voluntary initiatives are consequential for the governance both of polities and of individual selves today. Our contemporary religious experience has, thus, become one of public religion!

One of the known scholars to reflect about 'public religion' is Jose Casanova, a contemporary sociologist of religion. Based on experiences from countries of the Middle East and Eastern Europe, he argued in a publication titled *Public Religion in the Modern World* (1994) that religion went public in the modern context, falsifying the so-called thesis of secularization and privatization. Later on in

2012, he argued that 'religion going public' was an experience not only of the West, but of the East as well. He cited instances of public religion from different continents, including India, showing how religion became part and parcel of the discursive public, generating public opinion. He spoke of different spaces of the political process – state, political society, and civil society, and of their respective public spheres and public religions: state in its bureaucracy, political society in its legislatures and political parties, and civil society in its institutions between state, family and market, have their public religions. This manner of disaggregating public spheres and public religions is a meaningful way of understanding the phenomenon. We find other scholars of religion too understanding public religion in a similar fashion. For example, in the Indian context, Rajeev Bhargava adopts an approach wherein he speaks about the relationship of religion to politics in terms of ends, institutions and personnel, and law and public policy. Placing it within the framework of 'political secularism', parallel to John Rawls' 'political liberalism,' Bhargava would defend that a secular polity can be in a healthy relationship with civil society (the level of law and public policy), while making a separation at the level of ends (nature of the state) and institutions / personnel (bureaucracy).

I find such an approach helpful to explore the relationship of Indian Christianity to the Indian public realm. Indian Christianity has been relating itself to the various spheres of Indian polity not in a uni-linear and unitary fashion, but in a differential and context-specific manner. Indian Christianity's public role can be understood better with its nuances and complexities when we disaggregate the spheres of involvements. It is a fact that the numerical strength of Indian Christianity in proportion to other religious communities is not very significant, or wielding political powers at that level. It is not, however, to say that Indian Christianity, therefore, is not involved in the process of statecraft or construction of Indian nationhood. Participation of Indian Christians in freedom struggles and their participation in nation-building and national integration during the post-independent era are not insignificant.[1] Looking at it from the

[1] Cf. Mary John, *Indian Catholic Christians and Nationalism – A Study Based on the Official Catholic Journals of the Period 1857 - 1947* (New Delhi: ISPCK, 2011).

reverse pole, the political heat being produced by the phenomenon of conversion at the State level and the series of anti-conversion laws enacted by some regional States of independent India indicate the public religious implication of Indian Christianity. Coming to the sphere of political society, reckoned in terms of participation in political parties or lobbying agencies, despite certain localised power in some North Eastern states, Indian Christianity cannot claim much in terms of being a public religion. However, when it comes to the sphere of civil society, Indian Christianity's participation has indeed been significant. It would do well to take a look at the way Indian Christianity down through the centuries has been present and involved in this sphere.

Christianity and the Indian Discursive Public

Christianity's relationship with the Indian discursive public, a prototype of the civil sphere, has indeed been complex, characterised by processes of involvement, contestation, differentiation, and distinction. Though we do not have many studies focusing on the way Indian Christian community related with the native public during the first fifteen centuries of the Common Era, what emerges as a general opinion today is that it was a multidimensional relationship, interacting with native cultures and religions even while maintaining its distinctiveness. The anecdotal statement made by Placid J. Podipara that Indian Christianity of the time was 'Hindu in culture, Christian in religion and Oriental in worship' conveys the character of the relationship. Being a trading community that had established commercial relations with others and had struck marital ties with the natives, Indian Christians of the time had been to a large extent socio-culturally integrated, but continued to be religiously distinct. As A. M. Mundadan would put it, "[T]he life St. Thomas Christians had been leading till the arrival of the Portuguese spanned two worlds: the geographical, political and social world of Malabar or Kerala (India), and the ecclesiastical world of East-Syrian or the Persian Church..."[2] Though spanning the two worlds, the Syrian

[2] A. M. Mundadan, *History of Christianity in India – Vol. 1: From the Beginning up to the Middle of the Sixteenth Century* (Bangalore: Church History

Christians (St. Thomas Christians) lived their lives more as natives than outsiders, and as Susan Bayly would put it, were "honoured and rewarded" by native rulers on account of their being "warriors, traders and Church notables."[3] The native rulers seemed to have constructed Church buildings and donated lands, finance, etc., to the Syrian Christians. Such a benefaction, as Bayly would narrate, points out to a considerable level of integration of the Syrian Christians with the native community. Moreover, they shared a rich content of religious beliefs and cultural practices with the natives, including their purity-pollution laws.[4] Thus a specific manner of native existence, though sharing in different socio-cultural and political worlds, characterised the lifeworld of Indian Christians from ancient times. It would imply also that they had established a relationality, including a field of communication – cultural, religious, and even political with the native people.

Christianity's relationship with the Indian discursive field became more pronounced during the modern era. Aided by the availability of the inchoate print media, Christian missionaries began to interact with the wider public from the sixteenth century onwards. Catholic missionaries in the southern Tamil region - starting with Henrique Henriques (1520-1600), who introduced the printed Christian literature, to Robert de Nobili (1577-1656) and Joseph Constantine Beschi (1680-1747) who produced varieties of literatures, prose and poetry, had embarked upon public conversations and disputations on religious and philosophical matters. Disputations on religious themes went hand in hand with adaptations of Indic language, symbols, and traditions to express and shape up a native Christian tradition. Literary creations like epics, tales, commentaries, dictionaries, and translations of Indic classics into European languages created a base for early public discursive practices emergent during the seventeenth-eighteenth centuries. This is not to deny the existence of discursive

---

Association of India, 2001), 145.

[3] Susan Bayly, *Saints, Goddesses and Kings – Muslims and Christians in South Indian Society, 1700-1900* (New York: Cambridge University Press, 1989), 243-44.

[4] Ibid., 250-257; Cf. Susan Viswanathan, *The Christians of Kerala* (New Delhi: Oxford, 1993).

forums prior to their introduction by Christian missionaries; the vibrant debating forums of the last Tamil Sangam (circa 400 BCE – 200 BCE), the interreligious dialogical forum run by Akbar as recent as mid sixteenth century CE, the "intensifying religious interactions" during the Mughal period,[5] are good examples of their earlier existence. However, while the latter debating spheres existed more among rulers and experts, the former began to include wider sections of people.

The Protestant missionary presence, beginning with the first Protestant missionary Bartholomew Ziegenbalg who had installed a printing press at Tranquebar and the Serampore trio who had established a printing 'industry' at Serampore during the eighteenth century contributed to the emergence of a printed-literature-based discursive field in the Indian public. The subsequent eventful missionary activities of the classical missionary societies and of the Anglican churches during the nineteenth century contributed multi-dimensionally to the relative strengthening of the discursive public. Translations of Bible into native languages and printing them, and undertaking the 'mission' of imparting modern education to wider sections of Indian population, along with making efforts to do away with discriminatory and oppressive practices in the Indian socio-cultural systems, went a long way in enhancing the Indian discursive public, which, along with the rule of law and the relatively more rationalised administration of the British India, began to grow steadily. Founding of various institutions by 'orientalists' for study of native literatures and printing the Indological classics to circulate them among the public markedly changed the demography of readership in the Indian subcontinent. A process of democratisation of Indian classics, along with the spread of modern mass education, contributed significantly to the emergence of the structures of public communication. It is no less significant a fact that Indian Christianity was a singular contributor to this process.

However, it needs be noted that there were also elements which kept isolating Indian Christians from the wider public. For example,

---

[5] Cf. Vashua Dalmia and Munis D. Faruqui, eds. *Religious Interactions in Mughal India* (New Delhi: Oxford University Press, 2014).

the exclusivist discourse of 'no salvation outside the church', embedded in both the Catholic ecclesiology and the Protestant evangelical proclamation, kept other religiously knowledgeable persons at a distance and vice a versa; the manners, customs, food habits, and other cultural markers of the colonisers with whom Indian Christians were identified with was yet another source of isolation; and, as Chandra Mallampalli has shown, the British rule effectively shifted the Indian Christians to the margins of the Indian public, when it came to the application of laws related to inheritance, property holding, etc.[6] And, finally, the emerging Indian nationalist discourse, though secular in character, made the Indian Christians self-conscious about their identity as a minority amidst a majority.

The post-colonial era has brought forth a different scenario as regards the presence of Indian Christianity in the Indian public. A phase of post-independent national integration, combined with the project of Five-Year plans for development, saw Indian Christians involved enthusiastically in welfare schemes, programmes of poverty alleviation, literacy programmes, disaster management, sanitation, health, and primary / higher / professional education of the Indian population. Spread of the modern education to further layers of Indian population set in a 'silent revolution' as in the words of Christophe Jeffrelot,[7] and Indian Christians came to constitute and bear a distinctively subaltern social identity. Advocacy for civil liberties of the subaltern people, involvement in movements for various social goals, voluntary initiatives for amelioration and eradication of social evils, etc., became important sites of Christian presence. In terms of relationship with other religions, they undertook inter-religious dialogues, study-centres, and ashrams for inter-religious experiences.

All these were done in an ambience of relative spontaneity and freedom! The scenario changed with the political ascendance of the far-right, with its religio-cultural nationalism. As studies show,

---

[6] Cf. Chandra Mallampalli, *Christians and Public Life in Colonial South India, 1863-1937 – Contending with Marginality* (London: RoutledgeCurzon, 2004).

[7] Cf. Christophe Jeffrelot, *India's Silent Revolution – The Rise of the Low Castes in North Indian Politics* (Delhi: Permanent Black, 2003).

violence against Christians[8] has rapidly increased, and conversion has become a thorny issue between those who affirm their Constitutional right for conversion and others who oppose it not merely in debates but also through acts of violence. Majoritarianism in politics has given a hegemonic power to the religious majority in the domains of culture, knowledge, education, and even civil rights, and it has been adversely instrumentalised by a small section that has self-assumed the religious leadership of the majority, by collating an ideology with religion, and this religion with patriotism. Indian Christians, as a result, seem to develop tendencies to 'in-grow', become self-conscious, etc., rather than participating in the public life of the nation. Religio-cultural nationalism of the self-assumed leadership goes to the extent of implicating the Indian Christian identity to be culturally conflictive and politically divisive, with an implied accusation of preventing the Indian nation from emerging into the global world as a united political power; it is as if the patriotism of Indian Christians, along with that of other religious minorities, needed to be proved on a day-to-day basis. One could think of the isolation of Indian Christians also as one suffered by a subaltern identity in a ritual framework of purity and pollution characteristic of the Indian caste-system.

It is time the Indian Christian community stood up, without being despondent about its vulnerability, but as a catalyst that can participate in more substantive and enduring ways in the wider Indian public, in the expansive civil sphere of the nation. One of the well-known Indian Christian statesmen, K. T. Paul, making a mention in his speech about the 'spirit' of Indian Christians during the first Roundtable Conference held in Briton, said:

> ... nor do we feel isolated in point of culture and tradition. We drink from the same founts of literature, art and music, and in fact the most modern tendency of even our religious thought and expression is to relate them, in all loyalty to its past history and tradition, to the categories that are derived from what is characteristically Indian lore... The attitude of

[8] Cf. Sarbeswar Sahoo, *Pentecostalism and Politics of Conversion in India* (Cambridge: Cambridge University Press, 2018).

> our community is thus one of trust and confidence... Our religious life brings us into intimate relations with the life of many nations of the West, and our community is in a peculiar position to appreciate the enormous importance of our country maintaining international relationships on as many lines as possible. We shall fail in our duty if we do not here and now emphasise, what indeed is no new idea to our national leaders, that our Motherland has everything to gain by every tie she makes with other nations, East and West.[9]

Though much removed in time and context from ours, K. T. Paul's capturing of the Indian Christian spirit at the time of the surge of nationalist sentiments in the 1930s seems very relevant today. Paul was a Christian nationalist, did not support the communal electorates, and gave expression to an idea of interactive and integrating existence for Indian Christians. Though duly acknowledging the challenges of being a minority, Paul went ahead to imagine that the Christians were in a unique position, rooted in the Indian cultural heritage on the one hand and opportuned to mediate with the international communities on the other. This is a meaningful viewpoint even today, when extreme cultural nationalist forces are gaining power in the Indian political horizon. Extremely challenging situations do not make Indian Christians less Indian, in spite of the concerted inimical portrayal to be one; and, no acute pain inflicted on them make them less connected with others nationally and internationally. This unique position, imbued with the depth of the Indian 'spirit', is the vantage point from which Indian Christianity has to look upon its identity, religion, culture and its commitment for the Indian democratic nation. It is with this spirit that Indian Christianity is called upon to explore its public role today. Developing a sound 'public theology' is nothing but a meaningful way of living out this public role in the Indian nation.

---

[9] H. A. Popley, *K. T. Paul – Christian Leader* (Madras: The Christian Literature Society, 1987 [originally published by YMCA, Calcutta 1938]), 193-194.

Indian Democracy and Christian Public Theology

Transforming the democratic State into a substantive one, with participatory discursive public spheres, obtains priority for political and public Christian theologies in India today. A substantively participatory democracy is of theological value because of peoples' hopes and aspirations attendant upon such a political vision for India. When a constitutional democracy was born in India, the hopes especially of the subaltern people of India were raised: they began to imagine a political community which would ensure economic equity, social equality, civil liberties, human rights and dignity to all sections of people. Dr. Ambedkar, the chief architect of the Constitution, sought to integrate these transforming hopes in the democratic instrument. The Constitution opened up an agenda for social justice (the affirmative action), embodying the ardent wish and presuming the 'general will' of the people for retributive justice. The focus was on *opening the public* to everyone, beyond ascriptive exclusions. That the Constitution provided for the right of the State to intervene and open up the temples for the subalterns is a case in point. An Indian Christian public theology would then premise itself upon this hope of 'opening the public', opening up the spaces of freedom and opportunities to the excluded.

This, however, brings in the question of the relationship of religion to the secular democratic State in India. 'Can religion be formally related to the secular Indian state?', 'If yes, what is the nature and content of this relationship?' - are relevant questions here, which are being debated around the theme of secularism. It needs straightaway be clarified that what we are concerned about here is 'political secularism', i.e., secularism as a principle to guide political decisions, and not creation of a secular culture or ethos as prevalent in western societies. Donald E Smith, one of the early commentators on the matter, opined that India's success as a secular State depended upon how it performed in terms of 'freedom of religion' (freedom to believe, practise, propagate, etc., including associational practice of religion), 'citizenship' (entitlements for equality and equity), and 'separation of State and religion' (mutual non-interference). He assessed that India stood a fair chance of emerging to be a secular

State. His yardsticks, however controversial and programmatic though, are not irrelevant today, especially when one wishes India to work towards realising the egalitarian values. The independent India, in its initial stages, was rather guided by these inner components of Indian secularism, even while facing serious challenges in terms of the emerging communal forces, including the trauma of partition. These components were not lost sight of even while being totally involved in expounding an Indian specific secularism in the context of the partition and the communal challenge. However, the present-day developments seek to delegitimise the vision of secularism enshrined in the Constitution as pseudo-secularism, brings in serious challenges to the secular democratic State of India. This force, as it has become a ruling dispensation today, seeks not only to dominate the political arena, but also to hegemonise the religio-cultural consciousness of the people of India, by constructing a 'Hindu' identity to be presented in the global arena, while retaining the ascriptive social hierarchy along with the religio-cultural legitimation attendant upon it. Its voice is growing louder, resulting in silencing of minority voices, stifling of civil liberties attendant upon one's citizenship, shrinking of the democratic space of debate and dissent,[10] and relegating ultimately the transforming hopes of the subaltern people to the backyard of politics.

The interpretation of Indian secularism as 'principled distance' by Rajeev Bhargava is rather insightful. He makes an argument that this secularism is different from the western 'laicite' and 'wall of separation' varieties, and best suited for situations of 'deep religious diversities' as in India.[11] Though Bhargava's proposal is relevant, one is left with a question whether the principled distance will be able to keep a *principled* distance under the weight of majoritarian political force and hegemony.

---

[10] Cf. Romila Thapar, *The Public Intellectuals in India* (New Delhi: Aleph Book Company, 2015).

[11] Cf. Rajeev Bhargava, "How Should States Deal with Deep Religious Diversity? – Can anything be learned from the Indian Model of Secularism?" in *Rethinking Religion and World Affairs*, ed. Timothy Samuel Shah, Alfred Stepan and Monica Duffy Toft (Oxford: Oxford University Press, 2012), 73-114.

We need an effective secular principle which neither 'establishes' any religion in any manner at the level of the State, nor get closed up against the contributions of religions. Indian secularism would be tested by the success it achieves in terms of realising the transformative goals of the Constitutional State. The relationship of religion to the State and the public sphere too, therefore, needs to be tested on the touchstone of these transforming goals. As Donald E Smith envisaged, the touchstone of secular democracy is the relative autonomous functioning of citizenship, religion, and State, freed from mutual interference and domination. This triad is the cornerstone of a substantive democracy, which would ensure the realisation of the transformative goals. Citizenship stands for the duties and rights, including the entitlements to freedom from multiple wants; freedom of religion stands for the rights of an individual for choice of religion; and, the State, politically separated from religion, stands for the common good a community is pursuing politically.

Religions need to play appropriate roles in the civil sphere to help humanity nurture a sense of autonomous self along with the spirit of transpersonal relationships characterised by sacrifice, dedication and mutuality, which are the abiding values of democracy. Civil society is the sphere where different religions can come together in an ambience of freedom to work for common good. The strength of religious plurality lies in its ability to be in relationship with others. A 'secular' State provides the space where people as citizens can be related to one another but on a transcendental basis, journeying towards ever greater realisations of common good.

Church in India needs to become a *public body* today. It needs to become public not so much to project itself and its activities as to bear witness to its faith in a transcendent God, whose revelation the community called the Church experienced in the words, deeds, death and resurrection of Jesus Christ, the incarnate God. It was in Jesus Christ this community began to experience the encounter of history and mystery of transcendence in a transforming manner. A call for transformation of relationships, embodying mutuality, creativity and peace, was the core of this encounter. This transforming experience needs to continue through history and Church, as a community, needs to be a catalyst in this. In so doing, the Church finds the liberal democratic institutions of the State and civil society, however fragile and failing though, the most solicitous, and brings itself in participatory solidarity with these institutions to mediate the experience of transforming relationships.

Inasmuch as these institutions are public, the Church body itself is a public. It cultivates the character of publicness within its own body as much as in the wider society. It makes itself a public body, by imbibing the spirit and practice of democracy, doing away with unmeaning hierarchies; it makes itself a public sphere, wherein a 'public reasoning' can take place among the believers; and it makes itself a civil society wherein the spirit of participatory democracy among the community of equals can be cultivated.

It should become public also in the sense of becoming more interactive in the wider public. There are several ways in which it can become publicly interactive. A very unassuming but firmly witnessing way is to bear witness to the Christian values whenever or wherever one holds public offices. Christian subjects, in their embodied personhood, can be the best witness to the transforming values. Another way of becoming public is interacting in 'conversational publics' with the Christian vision of events and issues. Needless to point out to the fact that the Christian voice does not emerge significantly in media publics, at least not proportionate to the education that it has received. Yet another important way, challenging though, is becoming accountable to the wider public in matters public. Churches have the highest level of human resources, individually and collectively; but, what is its output to the wider society? Can we have an auditing of human resources? Similarly, can we institute mechanisms for social auditing, opening ourselves for external examination as to how inclusive and open our communal relationships are? These are questions only to see that the Indian Church becomes truly public, effectively interacting in the public, without burying its head in deep furrows of self-pity and defeatism.

Similar to such 'Public Christianity', there can also emerge 'Public Islam', 'Public Hinduism', and the like. In his article titled, "Religion in Politics and the Politics of Hinduism", written as an introduction to his edited volume on *Political Hinduism – The Religious Imagination in Public Spheres*, Vinay Lal ends the article with a query whether a political Hinduism – a Hinduism that is sensitive to the political goals of establishing justice, citizenship rights, human rights, community rights, development and peace is not possible? He calls it a political Hinduism, which is away from the Hindutva variety of political ideologies, but one that represents the religious aspirations of the majority of Hindus to construct a polity which is deeply democratic and egalitarian. Such Hinduism, according to him, can be shaped up, not so much from the Brahminical religious traditions, but from the religious traditions of the subaltern or marginal people of India. One would be intoned by this to think of the socio-religious movements which arose during the modern era, constructing emancipatory identities for the subaltern people. Can such religious traditions be found today? If yes, they can become the participants of public theological conversations in our country.

This Volume

Propelled by the interest to reflect about the public role of Indian Christianity, a consultation was organised at the University of Madras in February 2018 on a title "Indian Christian Public Theology: Prospects and Challenges." It discussed several concerns relating Indian Christianity to the public realm: though being a numerical minority, the Christian presence in various sites of Indian public life like education, nation-building, development projects, social movements, civil society initiatives, etc., were explored to see whether the Christian presence could be more significant than its number. Strengthening of a substantive democracy, eradication of poverty and caste-discrimination, eradication of ascriptive hierarchies, fostering interreligious dialogue, nurturing a political secularism for the statecraft, interrogating majoritarian cultural nationalism, initiating science-religion dialogue in the civil sphere, and similar concerns were identified as pertinent concerns for a public Indian Christianity. In addition to the perspectives of social sciences, a theological perspective too was integrated, by introducing the concept of public theology, to steer the reflection on Indian Christianity's public role towards future possibilities with a faith-based normative orientation. Papers presented during the conference are brought together in this volume for the benefit of the wider public.

T. K. Oommen, the well-known Indian sociologist, makes an insightful analysis, in his four-part article, of the prospects and challenges facing Christians in India with regard to their public role. Beginning with an observation that speaking of minorities in the Indian context is one of continuing perplexity, Oommen goes into the scenario of the political identification of religious minorities which happened over the decades, giving into multiple political negotiations and considerations, making it a *process of minoritization* as far as the salient minority communities (Muslims and Christians) are concerned. This process goes on even while being resisted by the minorities. The political power of the minorities, especially in the case of Christians, remains muffled due to several factors which keep the community fragmented and inhibited. Geographically dispersed, economically not strong (75 per cent of Christians being rural based), socially ambiguous – being with the dominant even while speaking for the subalterns, denominationally fragmented, racially differentiated, and linguistically diversified, Christians in India seem to lack the power for public roles. What, therefore, becomes not merely viable but more meaningful in terms of a public role is entering into the 'secular forum' along with various minority or minoritized identities, including gender minorities, and rally around the rights of citizenship in our democratic polity. Such a rallying is not against the Indian spirit of secularism, but indeed a manner of strengthening the very secular fabric of India. The nation-state of India, in which recognition of the right of self-determination for different nationalities is becoming part and parcel of the process of democracy, needs to reckon with the rights of minorities, and the minorities themselves need to effectively negotiate with the state. T. K. Oommen's article gives a sociologically sound analysis of the condition of possibilities for Indian Christians to play their public role.

S. M. Michael, an anthropologist, discusses the status of tribal people within the Indian nation. After providing a clarification of the very term 'tribe', Michael goes into the demography of the tribal people in India and into the politics of different other names being given to the tribal people. In spite of according them with multiple names, it is surprising that the Government has not accorded the official status of 'indigenous people' to them. It would amount to, according to Michael, not recognizing their identity in its fullness. Recognising their autonomous identity not merely in name but also in terms of their culture and resisting the present-day tactics of the rightist forces to co-opt them into the 'Hindu' fold are efforts very relevant today. Michael surmises that Christianity, which has involved in several uplift programmes for the tribal people, can be a meaningful source of strength to preserve their identity and freedom.

Mohan Doss profiles the Indian Christian involvement in the field of education. One of the well-known sites of Christian involvement in the civil sphere of Indian nation is formal education. Though a numerical minority, Indian Christianity's participation in building up a nation by forming generations of youth with character and skills for employments is a substantive participation in the life of the nation. In his three-part essay, Doss begins the first part with presenting some contemporary challenges to the mission of education, emerging from the market-driven global world as well as the homogenizing forces at home; in the second part, he gives a history of the Christian involvement in this field to show how Christianity served as a trend-setter in educating the wider public of this nation, ensuring education for the long-excluded identities and communities. In the third part, he goes into the inspiration of Christian faith that continues to motivate the Christian mind to be involved in this service of education. While being appreciative of the Christian role, Mohan does not fail to point out to the not-so positive developments in tendencies emerging within Christianity to commercialize education. It is in empowering the marginalized through education, Mohan reminds us, that Christianity has the continuous legitimacy to be involved in the field.

L. Sahayaraj, in a cogently written essay, discusses the issue of uniform civil code that has become a bone of contention today. Though provided with a uniform criminal code, India has not been able to come up with a uniform civil code, due mainly to the complexity of the issue in a context of innumerable instances, born out of mixed religions, cultures, identities, etc., seeking exceptions to the rule. Though the Indian Constitution under Art. 44 puts forth its vision of creating a uniform civil code, it has not become a reality until now. Interestingly, Indian political parties or forces have shifted stances on this matter. While the Hindu Mahasaba opposed it in the early post-independent period, the rightist forces today are trying to implement it, while the political voice of Indian Muslims are always opposing it due not only to the ambiguity of the plan, but also to the wilfulness of the rightist politics. Indian Christians are not unequivocal on this matter. While the Catholic church at the national level is generally welcoming it with a proviso that it should reflect the 'spirit and mandate' of the Constitution, regional bodies of the Catholic church, say for example, the Tamilnadu Bishops' council is opposing it. Complexity and ambiguity continue to hold sway until today on this matter.

These foregoing four essays look at the context and concerns of Indian Christians from the perspectives of social sciences. Their sociological, anthropological, and legal explorations are treating *some* of the salient concerns of Indian Christianity, and certainly not all of them. They are perhaps some examples for further explorations. The following six essays are public theological explorations, introducing the concept of public theology, looking at its relevance for India, exploring its resonance in social teachings of churches, relating church with state and with the core concerns of democracy, religious pluralism, inter-religious and inter-disciplinary dialogues.

Archbishop Prakash Mallavarapu opines that Indian Christian public theology opens up good possibilities for relevant theologizing in our contemporary world, especially in the Indian context. 'What else can theology be, except being public?' is his question, when he thinks of theology as 'God-talk', which can happen only in a public ambience. In that sense, Christian God-talk becomes a public theology, by engaging with public issues which humanity is facing today. Indian Christianity, along with several other public theologies pursued by Dalai Lama, Buddhist leaders, subaltern leaders, and so on, is called upon to engage with public issues theologically. Pope Francis has set the example through his encyclical, *Laudato Si*, wherein he is involved in doing public environmental theology. We need to take cue from Pope Francis and involve in doing Indian Christian public theology.

P. T. Mathew, in a well written essay, gives a sound introduction to public theology. Spotting a trace of public theology in the early Christian practice of apologetics, and taking an insight from Johannes Baptist Metz, Mathew speaks of the present-day public theology as *apologetics ad extra*, involving in 'rational theological' conversations with others in the wider public on matters of public concern. He writes: "The near absence of theology and theologians from public debates on issues of importance is a matter of concern. Theology needs to wake up from this slumber." He then goes into clarifying the concept 'public', and then into tracing public theology in the biblical fountain to Christian theological literature, leading to contemporary political and public theologies. With a brief introduction to public theologies and theologians emergent in the Euro-American context, Mathew turns his attention to the Indian context, and discusses the probable audience, goals, methods, and content of Indian Christian public theology. Mathew's essays serves as a good introduction to the concept and history of public theology.

Moses Manohar reflects upon the relationship between Christianity and democracy. Tracing the origin of politics to Greek city-states and Plato's philosophy, Manohar points out to the richness of qualitative politics. The Greek political philosophy did speak about such valuable themes as distributive justice, political virtues, etc., but, it did not consider slaves and women to be worthy of being political subjects. The Christian conception of politics, however, stands for certain universality, lending space for the excluded. A good political theology needs to inspire people to value the political ideals of democracy, participation, citizenship, leadership, and so on. Christian political theologies like the liberation theologies, though promoted social involvements, did not propel political participation in constitutional democracies. It is time Christian political theologies, including public theologies, realised the importance of nurturing the ideals of citizenship, democracy, and political participation so as to bring in Reign of God upon earth.

Varghese Manimala unpacks the theme of religious pluralism for our contemporary context. The opening he creates by speaking of religious pluralism neither as unrelated religious plurality nor as variations within basic monistic paradigm comes as a meaningful way of approaching religious pluralism today. He reflects about it as something fundamentally related to the realm of *mythos* rather than that of *logos*, as an experience of religion that comes in different instances. It would mean that no one tradition can claim the totality of religious experience, though each tradition can legitimately claim its uniqueness or singularity. Discussing the stereotypical typologies like exclusivism, inclusivism, interpenetration, and parallelism, Manimala points out, with the help of Raimon Panikkar and others, that pluralism is a horizon which is indispensable for any religious seeker and is something that opens up immense possibilities of religious experiences. Drinking from this fertile soil, humanity can nurture its hopes and aspirations of the future in meaningful ways. Manimala takes care to caution about some pitfalls involved in the understanding as well as practice of religious pluralism. He points out also to some of the basic concerns to which the vision of religious pluralism can meaningfully respond to.

X. D. Selvaraj, after presenting some central teachings from the corpus of the Catholic Social Teachings as well as from the World Council of Churches, avers that they could well be relevant to public theology in today's context. However, as they have been confined to church circles and held as the 'best kept secrets of the Churches,' they remain isolated from public spaces. When those who are inspired by these social teachings go out of the church circles and ally themselves with other socially concerned movements, including secular movements, they do impact upon the public life of the people. Their networking with socially concerned movements will be much enriched when they do 'public theology' on issues of public concern, understood with the help of different disciplines like sociology, history, anthropology, etc. In our Indian context today, public theology has to be the voice of the excluded, i.e., the poor - having been excluded by the market–driven economic systems, the minorities - being excluded by rightist politics like Hindutva, and the Dalits, Tribals and women - being excluded by the dominant.

Peter Susaimanickam, a budding scholar of religion and society, reflects upon the inter-relationship between state and Church. A genuine interaction happens where there is a mutual recognition between two agents. It is, therefore, mandatory that State and

Church should recognize each other's specific domain. State should be democratically secular, and Church should be altruistically prophetic. A dialectics between the two ensures establishment of a just society founded on the accepted values of equality, liberty and fraternity. This article makes an attempt to provide a theoretical framework for an authentic interaction between State and Church. In order to facilitate this interaction, the paper argues in favour of the Recognition Model as against the antagonistic and antiestablishment models. The reason being, the Recognition Model creates openness on the part of the State to interact with religion. In the same way, the Prophetic Church is preferred to the Kingly and the Priestly Church. Only the Prophetic Church can be an extension of the life-giving presence of Jesus in the Indian soil. The paper argues that only an Accommodative Indian Constitutional Secular State is optimal for the interaction with the Church, since it is supportive of different religions. Likewise, the Prophetic Church is presented as the Church which displays its public character opting to protest on the road along with people of other faiths. These distinctive characteristics of both, the State and the Church, will enable the state to maintain a principled distance from every religion in order to promote fundamental values. Thus, the aforesaid interactive framework will ensure that we become truly Indians and truly Christians.

Binoy argues for the meaningful place of theology in the public realm of civil society, and he makes his arguments with special reference to the need of dialogue between science and theology. Binoy writes: "Science is a study of causes and theology is an inquiry into meaning. So science and theology are like different sorts of maps, and both help us to get a better picture of reality because each in its own way represents that reality more or less faithfully. Science and theology are two sides of reality and they complement each other." While such a complementarity is factual, and needs to be fostered, one needs also to beware of the fault line that makes science into pseudo-science and theology into fundamentalism. Binoy takes us back to the history of good sciences in the Indian and international contexts, and calls for a synergy between science and theology for a healthy civil society during our present times.

The volume is, thus, a modest contribution to reflection upon a few aspects of the public role of Indian Christianity today.

Bibliography

Bauman, Chad M. *Christian Identity and Dalit Religion in Hindu India, 1868-1947*. Grand Rapids, Michigan: William B Eerdmans Publishing Company, 2008.

_________ *Pentecostals, Proselytization, and Anti-Christian Violence in Contemporary India*. New York: Oxford University Press, 2015.

Bayly, Susan. *Saints, Goddesses and Kings*.

Bergunder, Michael. *The South Indian Pentecostal Movement in the Twentieth Century*. UK: William B. Eerdmans Publishing Company, 2008.

Brown, Judith M. and Robert Eric Frykenberg, eds. *Christians, Cultural Interactions, and India's Religious Traditions*. Grand Rapids, UK: William B. Eerdmans Publishing Company, 2002.

Copley, Antony. *Religions in Conflict – Ideology, Cultural Contact and Conversion in Late-Colonial India*. Delhi: Oxford University Press, 1997.

Dasgupta, Sudeep. "Gods in the Sacred Market Place: Hindu Nationalism and the Return of the Aura in the Public Sphere." In *Religion, Media and the Public Sphere*, edited by Birgit Meyer, Annelies Moors.

Dienberg, Thomas. "Mysticism and 'Public' Theology – Theoretical Background and Some Theological Reflections." In *Mysticism, Spirituality and Secularism – An Indepth Search for Meaning and Authenticity in a Pluralistic World*, edited by Varghese Manimala, 93 – 111. New Delhi: ISPCK & Hyderabad: HMI, 2015.

_________ "Mystical Experience – Tradition and the Aspect of Resistance and Public Theology." Ibid., 112 – 129.

Dube, Saurabh. *After Conversion – Cultural Histories of Modern India*. New Delhi: YODA Press, 2010.

Farias, Kranti, K. *The Christian Impact in South Kanara*. Mumbai: Church History Association of India, 1999.

Fernando, Leonard and G. Gispert-Sauch. *Two Thousand Years of Faith – Christianity in India*. New Delhi: Penguin India, 2004.

Goel, Sita Ram. *History of Hindu-Christian Encounters*. New Delhi: Voice of India, 1989.

Helund, Roger E. *Quest for Identity - India's Churches of Indigenous Origin: The 'Little Tradition' in Indian Christianity*. New Delhi: ISPCK, 2000.

Jenkins, Richard. *Social Identity*. New York: Routledge, 2008 (third edition).

Joseph, John E. *Language and Identity – National, Ethnic and Religious*. New York: Palgrave Macmillan, 2004.

Katju, Manjari. *Hinduising Democracy – The Vishva Hindu Parishad in Contemporary India*. New Delhi: New Text, 2017.

Kim, Sebastian. "The Church as a Public Body: Exclusion and the Quest for Authentic Community in India." In *Theology in the Public Sphere – Public Theology as a Catalyst for Open Debate,* au. Sebastian Kim, 79 – 108. London: SCM Press, 2011.

Kim, Sebastian C.H. *In Search of Identity – Debates on Religious Conversion in India*. New Delhi: Oxford University Press, 2003.

Maliekal, Jose. *Standstill Utopias? Dalits Encountering Christianity*. New Delhi: ISPCK, 2017.

Mangalwadi, Vishal. *Missionary Conspiracy – Letters to a Postmodern Hindu*. Mussoorie, UP: Nivedit Good Books Distributors Pvt., Ltd. 1996.

Melakandathil, Pius, Joy L.K. Pachuau and Tanika Sarkar, eds. *Christianity in Indian History – Issues of Culture, Power and Knowledge*. New Delhi: Primus Books, 2016.

Oddie, Geoffrey A. *Hindu and Christian in South-East India*. London: Routledge, 2017.

Oommen, T. K. and Hunter P. Mabry. *The Christian Clergy in India – Volume 1 – Social Structures and Social Roles*. New Delhi: SAGE, 2000.

Patil, R. R. and James Dabhi, eds. *Dalit Christians in India*. New Delhi: MANAK Publications Pvt. Ltd., 2010.

Phan, Peter, C. ed., *Christianities in Asia*. UK: Wiley-Blackwell, 2011.

Roberts, Nathaniel. *To Be Cared for – The Power of Conversion and Foreignness of Belonging in an Indian Slum*. New Delhi: Nayayana, 2016.

Robinson, Rowena and Sathianathan Clarke, eds. *Religious Conversion in India – Modes, Motivations, and Meanings*. New Delhi: Oxford University Press, 2003.

Robinson, Rowena and Joseph Marianus Kujur, eds. *Margins of Faith – Dalit and Tribal Christianity in India*. New Delhi: SAGE, 2010.

Robinson, Rowena, ed. *Minority Studies*. New Delhi: Oxford University Press, 2012.

Rouner, Leroy S. ed. *Civil Religion and Political Theology*. Notre Dame: Notre Dame University Press, 1986.

Rowena, Robinson. *Christians of India*. New Delhi: SAGE, 2003.

Sahay, Keshari N. *Christianity and Culture Change in India*. New Delhi: Inter-India Publications, 1986.

Sahoo, Sarbeswar. *Pentecostalism and Politics of Conversion in India*. UK: Cambridge University Press, 2018.

Swarup, Ram. *Hindu View of Christianity and Islam*. New Delhi: Voice of India, 1992.

Thayil, Thomas. *The Latin Christians of Kerala*. Bangalore: Kristu Jyoti Publications, 2003.

Veer, Peter van der. "Religion in South Asia." Annual Review of Anthropology, Vol. 31 (2002), pp. 173-187.

Wilfred, Felix. *Christians for a Better India*. New Delhi: ISPCK, 2014.

Zachariah, K. C. *The Syrian Christians of Kerala – Demographic and Socio-Economic Transition in the Twentieth Century*. New Delhi: Orient Longman, 2006.

PART I

CONTEXT AND CONCERNS

1

Being a Minority: Prospects and Challenges Facing Christians in India to Play their Public Role

T. K. Oommen

Professor Emeritus, Jawaharlal Nehru University, New Delhi

The term 'minority' may denote racial, linguistic or religious categories, but to invoke the term without specifying the category under reference is utterly confusing. For example, the sub-committee on minorities of the Constituent Assembly of India invoked a purely mechanical notion (Ansari, 1996). Thus the Anglo-Indians, the Parsis and the tribes of Assam on the plains with less than 0.5 per cent of the then total population of India were grouped into one category. The second category consisted of communities having more than 0.5 per cent but not more than 1.5 per cent of the total population – the Indian Christians[1] and Sikhs. The third group included Muslims and Scheduled Castes whose population exceeded 1.5 per cent of the total population. Thus religious, racial, caste and tribal groups

[1] It was necessary to specify 'Indian' Christians because there existed 'non-Indian' Christians such as Anglo-Indians and Eurasians who too were Christians.

with differing structures of deprivations were clubbed together into the category of minorities, which is not helpful to understand the prospects and identity challenges of minorities. As the present task is confined to religious minorities it is necessary to provide a feasible categorization of this category of minorities based on both facts and perceptions.

I

Religious minorities in India may be categorized into three, based on the sources of their origin and the consequent deprivations they are subjected to. These are: (1) Religious minorities of Indic origin - indigenous tribal communities, Hindu protestant religions such as Buddhism, Jainism and Sikhism; (2) immigrant religious communities such as Jews, Zoroastrians and those of Baha'i Faith and (3) those religious communities which are perceived as products of colonialism and conquest – Christians and Muslims respectively – but whose followers are mainly converts from local caste groups.

The main source of deprivation of religious minorities of Indic origin is the denial of their identity as religious groups. Thus the first Census of Independent India in 1951, categorized the religion of Scheduled Tribes[2] who did not specifically insist on their religion as non-Hindu, was designated as Hindu. While Jains, Buddhist and Sikhs are identified by their religion in the Indian Census, the Hindu Code Bill[3] lists all of them as Hindus. This legal expansionism dismantles their religious identities which is a major source of their deprivation as religious minorities. However, this legal position is in conformity with the conceptualization of Hindu advanced by the

[2] 'Scheduled Tribes' was the term introduced by the British colonial administration to denote the tribal peoples who claim to be Adivasis or the first settlers of India. But this term made Aryan Hindus who claimed nativity in India uncomfortable and Adivasis were referred to as Vanavasis or forest dwellers. Similarly, the term Scheduled Caste was introduced to refer to those lower caste Hindus who were placed lowest in the five-fold hierarchy and believed to be polluting castes.

[3] The Hindu Code Bill consists of four acts – the Hindu Marriage Act, Hindu Succession Act, Hindu Minority and Guardianship Act and Hindu Adoptions and Maintenance Act. When applied to religious minorities the Bill substantially eroded the social mores of these communities.

Rashtriya Swayam Sevak Sangh (RSS).[4] There is another context in which the status of Indic religious communities is confirmed as Hindus. The Presidential Order promulgated in 1950 was amended in 1954 to extend benefits conferred on to those Hindu SCs who embraced Sikhism (Mazbhis) and in 1990 to those who embraced Buddhism, usually referred to as Neo-Buddhists. All the three measures listed here taken by the State in India to "protect" the religious minorities of Indic origin substantially erodes their identity.

The immigrant religious minorities who came to India to escape religious persecution in their homelands are the Jews, the Zoroastrians and the Baha'is. In the understanding of RSS these immigrants are to be treated as guests and this is true in the cases of Jews and Zoroastrians as they did not proselytize. The number of Jews in India did not exceed 26000 at any point in time and although there is no history of their persecution in India, most of them migrated to Israel in the wake of the Zionist movement to settle down in the territory of Jewish State. The Zoroastrians too remained a tiny religious community in India and their population has been dwindling as they are an insulated religious community; given their strict practice of endogamy many men and women remain unmarried. They are a prosperous urban middle class, not only that the most visible corporate house (the TATAs) belongs to this community but several distinguished lawyers/jurists and physicians of India belong to this community. Of these three immigrant religious communities who settled down in India, only the Zoroastrians are bestowed the status of a religious minority by the National Minority Commission, a body set up by the State in India.

The Baha'is was the last immigrant religious community who came to India in the 1870s. Till the 1950s they remained a tiny group but in the 1960s they launched a conversion project in the Malwa region of Madhya Pradesh and their population swelled to 400,000, the overwhelming majority of converts being Scheduled Castes. This triggered an anti-Baha'i mobilization by RSS and thanks

[4] Cf. V. D. Savarkar, *Hindutva: Who is a Hindu?* (New Delhi: Bharat Sahitya Sadan, 1949).

to State intervention they not only abandoned the conversion project but retreated from public activities.[5]

The two religious minority communities of India which face the wrath of Hindu militants and are subjected to unfavourable State policies are the Muslims and the Christians, the two biggest religious minorities of India. The Muslims count some one hundred and forty million, accounting for 14 per cent of the total population of India. The fact that there are only a dozen countries in the world with 100 million or more population but the Muslim population of India exceeds this and India is among the three most populous Muslim countries in the world, the other two being Indonesia and Bangladesh, should alert us to the fact that to refer to such a huge population as a 'minority' is a misnomer.

Christian community in India is much smaller as compared with Muslims and in Independent India hovered around 2.3 to 2.4 per cent of the total population. But the fact that the presence of both Muslim and Christian is attributed to conquest and colonialism respectively renders them cultural outsiders even as they are political insiders (citizens) is the single most important source of their deprivation. But this perception itself is historically incorrect, as pre-conquest Islam and pre-colonial Christianity existed in India. Be that as it may, Golwalkar pronounced: "In this country, Hindus alone are national, and Muslims and others (read Christians), if not actually anti-national are at least outside the body of the nation."[6] The State policy in Independent India followed this line of thought in that the policy of reservation is not applied to these religious communities when the SCs convert to Islam and Christianity, in contrast to Mazbhi Sikhs and Neo-Buddhists as noted above. Thus not only that Muslims and Christians are the two largest religious minorities in India, but they are subjected to a *process of minoritization*.[7]

---

[5] Cf. W. Garlington, 'The Bahai Faith in Malwa', in *Religion in South Asia,* ed. G.A. Oddie, (New Delhi: Manohar, 1977), 101-18.

[6] M. S. Golwalkar, M.S., *We or Our Nationhood Defined* (Nagpur: Bharat Prakashan, 1939), 56.

[7] Cf. T. K. Oommen, "State Formation, Minoritization and Violence in Postcolonial India", in *Violence Studies,* ed. Kalpana Kannabiran (New Delhi: Oxford University Press, 2016), 120-141.

II

With this short introduction to religious minorities in India, let me focus on Christians and Christianity. First, the size of the Christian population itself is a contested one. While the highest percentage recorded is 2.4 per cent in Indian Censuses, the *World Christian Encyclopaedia* records that the Christian population is 3.9 per cent[8] which is a difference of 1.5 per cent, which translates into 15 millions! The difference is accounted by crypto-Christians, that is, those who are believers in Christianity but they do not report it to State officials which would deprive them of the benefits of the policy of reservation. This means the self-denial of religious identity by some 15 million Christians is a function of State policy which denies equality to all citizens irrespective of caste and religion, a constitutional provision and promise.

In a parliamentary democracy the public presence, political clout and geographical / territorial concentration or dispersal is directly correlated. If a religious minority is concentrated in a specific geographical area the possibility of their representatives getting elected to the legislative bodies would be substantial. In turn this augments their political clout. This is evident when one compares the situation of Sikhs with 1.8 per cent of Indian population with Christians who have 2.4 per cent of the population. Although there are three Christian majority States in India – Meghalaya, Mizoram and Nagaland – their tiny sizes cannot send an adequate number to the legislative bodies. Thus the political bargaining power of Christians is very limited in India. Further the geographical location of Christians too matters.

Nearly 90 per cent of Christians in India are drawn from India's geographical periphery; 65 per cent from the five Southern States –Andhra Pradesh, Karnataka, Kerala, Tamilnadu and Goa. In a region-wise reckoning, Kerala with 20 per cent and Goa with 30 per cent of Christian populations each do make some impact at the State level politics. The second concentration of Christians is in Northeast, but in spite of the three Christian majority states, this

---

[8] Cf. David Barret, ed., *World Christian Encyclopaedia* (Nairobi: Oxford University Press, 1982).

enclave has only 13 per cent of Christians of India. Thirdly, the tribal belt of Chotanagpur has 11 per cent of Christian population. And, the Hindi belt and the Indo-Gangetic plain which together make the power centre of India have only 10 per cent of India's Christian population. Because of this demographic situation the Christians fell between the two stools, while the Muslims with their staggering numbers although widely dispersed and Sikhs with smaller numbers could wield a better political clout as compared with Christians.

The rural-urban disparity is well-known in India and the urban dwellers are privileged in many respects. Given the fact that 75 per cent Christians are rural dwellers, they are engaged in low-prestige occupations and economically poor, the possibility of their getting re-recruited into the category of political elite is scanty. This is not to deny that there is a tiny urban middle class among Indian Christians largely because of the community's engagement with the educational and health sectors. But these are not stepping stones to make a difference in public life, particularly political life. The conventional proclivity of Christians to engage in civil society is also eroding thanks to the restrictions brought in by the government in the flow of foreign funds.

The *World Christian Encyclopaedia* estimated that the Christian denominations in India numbered 286 in the mid-1970s and 330 in the mid-1990s. However, only 260 out of the 330 are identified by name in the encyclopaedia. Further, of these 260, basic data were available only for 148. Only one denomination, namely the Catholic Church had more than eight million members, the exact figure being 8,469,075 in mid 1990s. The Church of South India with 1,555,902, the Orthodox Syrian Church of the East with 1,412,100 and the council of Baptist Churches in North East India with 1,064,990 were the three largest denominations after the Catholic Church with pan-Indian spread, others being regional in their origin. This means an overwhelming majority of Christian denominations are tiny in size. In a country with more than 1000 million population, Christians who make a mere 25 million cannot play a significant public role. But the fact that they are denominationally fractionated makes their public presence indeed insignificant.

While Christians in India are not united into a common public platform, there are three organizations which encapsulate most of the denominations: the Catholic Bishops Conference of India (CBCI), the National Christian Council of India (NCCI) and the Evangelical Federation of India (EFI). But the goals and orientations of these organizations are ecclesiastical and not public in that they rarely conjointly pursue goals which affect the entirety of Christian citizens of India. Denominational splintering is a global phenomenon for Christianity but in those countries wherein they are a minority it is necessary to constitute a public 'secular' forum to fight for citizenship rights provided for in the Constitution of the country. That is, without ignoring or denying the doctrinal and ritual variations of denominations, it is absolutely necessary to function as a socio-political force to pressurize the predatory State and the rapacious market. In this endeavour it is necessary to align with other powerless groups of citizens – women, dalits, adivasis, lower OBCs, transgender, other religious minorities and the like. To enter public life in a democracy - an organizational weapon - is an imperative.

Apart from denominational differences there are linguistic variations among Christians in India. Generally speaking Western Christian countries are anchored to one dominant language – German, French, Italian, Portuguese. Where it is not, as in Great Britain and Spain, linguistic differences persist as illustrated by the Scottish or Welsh problem in the former and the Catalonian problem in Spain. But the Indian situation is qualitatively different. Languages drawn from four language families are spoken in India: Indo-Aryan (73%), Dravidian (25%), Austro-Asiatic (1.5%) and Tibeto-Chinese (0.5%). And, more than 100 mother tongues each of which has 10,000 or more speakers are in existence in India. And, India has no 'official' or 'national' language. The speakers of the most numerous language, viz. Hindi makes for only 38 per cent of India's population even after absorbing some 40 mother tongues into it.[9] The point of interest for the present discussion is that Christians in India do not make a linguistic unity but a linguistic multiplicity and

[9] For details see T. K. Oommen, *State and Society in India* (New Delhi: Sage Publications, 1990), 124-135.

the elective affinity exists among Tamil, Bengali, Maharastrian and such other Christian groups.

Christians in India are differentiated based on race too. There are two kinds of this: one is the product of race-mixture, broadly known as Anglo-Indians, but are also referred to as Luso-Indians, Eurasians, etc., - progenies of Europeans (Portuguese, French, Dutch, English male and Indian female). They are all Christians and English-speaking and usually keep aloof from Indian Christians. The other variety of racially distinct Christians belongs to Northeast India, phenotypically different from the rest of Indians. The Christians of the Christian majority States of India – Meghalaya, Nagaland and Mizoram – although are denominationally linked to the rest of Indian Christians, are racially distinct. These two racially different Christian groups – Anglo Indians and North East Christians – are socio-culturally aloof from the remaining Christians of India.

Christians in India are also differentiated based on India's pernicious caste system which grouped the population into inferiors and superiors. The categories are: Brahmins, Kshatriyas, Vaishyas - the so-called upper castes, the Shudras who are above the pollution line and the "untouchables" who are below the pollution line and the tribals, who are outside the pale of the caste system but often functioned as a bridge-group between those who are above and below the pollution line. While all societies are stratified based on class, gender, age and rural-urban differences, some societies are also heterogeneous due to the presence of racial and cultural (religious and linguistic) complexities. But Indian society is also hierarchical in that the doctrine of creation and the theory of Karma and Re-birth categorise the population into inferiors and superiors. While the Hindu theological prescriptions do not apply to Christians, the prevailing proclivity is to follow these in social life. Thus the Syrian Christians of Kerala and the caste-Hindu converts from other parts of India have formed caste-like structures avoiding commensality and inter-marriages particularly with those converts from ex-untouchables.[10] To mobilize Christians of differing caste

[10] Cf. T. K. Oommen and Hunter P. Mabry, *The Christian Clergy in India: Social Structure and Social Roles* (New Delhi: Sage Publications, 2000).

backgrounds for public action is a formidable task. In fact, divisions into upper caste, OBC, Dalit and Adivasi Christians are so common that forging an all-India Christian community is a Herculean task.

To conclude, Christians in India are stratified based on class, gender and rural-urban backgrounds like Christians everywhere in the world. But they also differ based on races and languages within the same polity as in several cases. Further, they are also vivisected based on their social origins, i.e., caste backgrounds. Thus viewed, the 2.4 per cent Christian population of India, counting some twenty-five to thirty million, are divided into numerous tiny groups. And, intersectionality further complicates the situation with numerous permutations and combinations. Think of Christians who are poor, Dalit, Protestant, Tamil, and female on the one hand and middle class, upper caste, Catholic, Bengali and male on the other. What is common between them is religious identity and Indian citizenship, but they do not share equality, dignity and security. It is unlikely that such a disparate group of Christians in India can be mobilized into collective actions in the public space. What is the way out?

III

I suggest that the shared identity which galvanise Christians in India into collective actions is single citizenship shared by all members of Indian polity and the ideology of 'secularism'. But instead of undertaking an Indian reading of secularism, many including Christians, tend to follow one or another western meanings of secularism. There are at least three connotations of this: (1) separating man and society from the transcendental and divine; (2) institutionalizing rationality through a process of displacing religiosity; (3) relegating religion to the private realm of human activity. The first of these notions is conceptually untenable, the latter two are empirically impossible.

The dualism and dichotomization implied in separating the secular from the sacred is at the root of the persisting confusion in this context. It is important to insist that the sacred is not a quality confined to the religious realm. For example, the national flag is also perceived "sacred", but it belongs to the secular realm. What is important to note is that the sacred object whether it is drawn from the religious or secular context is a symbol. And, symbols can be constructed only by human beings and the meanings of which cannot be understood through sense organs. Symbol making is a process through which meanings are created and attributed to objects, events, persons and entities. Therefore, the effort to establish separate space for the sacred apart from the secular is bound to fail because they are inextricably intertwined. That is, if we want to capture the authenticity of human experience which is holistic and relates to ultimate concerns the sacred and the secular should be viewed in unison.

Secularism is often perceived as the onward march of rationality aided by science and abetted by technology. The scientific temper is believed to be displacing religious beliefs. What happens in reality is that certain aspects wrongly attributed to religion – myths, magic, superstitions – gradually disappear. Confronted by science and technology, religion transforms itself but does not disappear. Because a completely rational human being is a conceptual monster - s/he will not remain sane. Therefore, rationality and religiosity are bound to be viewed as necessary ingredients for a wholesome human existence.

Third, secularism is defined as a process by which religion is relegated to the private realm. This understanding is indicative of a mistaken reading of the very nature of religion as a phenomenon. Individuals can and do practice religion as private entities which do not exhaust religious practices. But the practice of religion is essentially a collective phenomenon. The essential dimensions of religion are belief and ritual; the former needs to be reinforced and the latter re-enacted in the collective context. Therefore, to displace religion (and the sacred) with the secular (and the rational) as well as to privatise religion are empirically impossible.

The western understanding of secular / secularism arose out of the specificity of western empirical situation. The western nation-states are either culturally homogeneous or homogenized. Not only that they are predominantly Christian, but they are usually uni-denominational. All of them have one official / national language and other languages are either uprooted or marginalized (Oommen, 1997). The division of labour between the State and the Church is clear; the former engaging in secular matters and the latter involved in religious matters. None of these apply to India. Indian polity is multi-religious and multi-lingual; there is no official religion and as many as 22 languages are official. There is no Church in Hinduism, the majority religion professed by over 80 per cent of the population and the State often undertakes the function of the Church as reformer of religions of Indian origin. Given these specificities the idea of secularism as enunciated and practiced in the Christian West is inapplicable to India.

As India is utterly multicultural the notions of secularism which is applicable to India are two: (1) the State treats all religions with equal respect and (2) the State keeps equal distance from all religions. And, these are provided for in India's constitution which ought to be accepted by all including religious minorities. As a demographically insignificant minority which is spatially dispersed and internally differentiated based on language, caste, race as well as denominations, the prospect of Christians being mobilized based on their religious identity is bleak. At any rate, to conceptualise a religious collectivity as a political community is communalism, which is antithetical to the very idea of secularism as provisioned in India's Constitution. Therefore, the pathway to enter public action for Christians in India is through secularism and as citizens of the Indian State.

IV

Historically the relationship between States and minorities had passed through three phases.[11] First, the hegemonic phase in colonial and empire States wherein minorities had a subordinated co-existence. The 'national' identity was the identity of the mainstream community religious or linguistic or a combination of the two. Second, the uniformity phase when homogenization of the national population was the acclaimed motto of the nation-state. The minorities surrendered their primordial identities for citizenship - equality either voluntarily and often forcefully. Third, the pluralist phase wherein recognition of several identities and citizenship-equality co-existed. The multi-national States of the socialist-countries and the

[11] Cf. P. Worsley, *The Three Worlds: Culture and Development* (London: Weidenfeld and Nicholson, 1984).

multi-cultural polities of capitalist democracies exemplified this. We are now entering the fourth phase wherein both multi-national and multi-cultural States are becoming democratic and market-driven.

The nation-states abandoned the idea of homogenous polities because of the compulsions of globalization and the consequent turbulence of migration. But the intellectuals of India, a multi-national and multi-cultural polity, which could be more appropriately designated as a 'national state'[12] seem to be clinging to the hackneyed idea of nation-state for they fear being labelled as anti-national and unpatriotic. In this they are abandoning their public responsibility for political expediency.

The doctrine of people's self-determination germane to democracy is not applied to India. The fact is that a conglomeration of nations, without their own sovereign states, co-exists in India. If the nations of India, that is territorially anchored linguistic communities, are to co-exist under one political roof, they should be conceded adequate cultural autonomy. As a corollary to this the religious minorities which are territorially dispersed should also be invested with the required space in the polity to function as responsible citizens without eroding their religious identities. The challenge which is faced by the multi-national federal polity of India and the prospects of religious minorities to prosper within it is to accept an idea of India which is suitable for us. Confucius (BC 551-479) famously pronounced: 'For peace in the Kingdom take good care of definitions'. Alas! We are yet to attempt this in India.

Select Bibliography

Ahmad, Imtiaz. 'Governance and Minorities in India.' In *Minorities of India: Problems and Prospects*, edited by M.A. Jawaid, K.N. Jahangir and Shankar Bose. New Delhi: Indian Council of Social Science Research, 2007.

Ansari, Iqbal A. *Readings on Minorities: Perspective and Documents*, Vol. II. Delhi: Institute of Objective Studies, 1996.

---

[12] Cf. T. K. Oommen, "Nation Building and Diversity" in *Unity in Diversity: Learning from Each Other*, eds. I.R. Watts and R. Chattopadhyay. New Delhi: Viva Books, 2008), 21-36.

Barret, David B (ed). *World Christian Encyclopaedia.* Nairobi: Oxford University Press, 1982.

Deshpande, S. *Dalits in Muslim and Christian Communities: A States Report on Current Social Scientific Knowledge.* New Delhi: National Commission for Minorities, 2010.

Galanter, M. *Competing Inequalities: Law and the Backward Classes in India.* New Delhi: Oxford University Press, 1984.

Garlington, W. 'The Bahai Faith in Malwa', in G.A. Oddie (ed). *Religion in South Asia*, New Delhi: Manohar, 1977.

Golwalkar, M.S. *We or Our Nationhood Defined.* Nagpur: Bharat Prakashan, 1939.

Hasan, Zoya. *Politics of Inclusion: Caste, Minorities and Affirmative Action.* New Delhi: Oxford University Press, 2009.

Job, G. V. et. al. *Re-thinking Christianity*. Madras: Christian Literature Society, 1939.

Kymlicka, Will. *Multicultural Citizenship*. Oxford: Oxford University Press, 1995.

Oommen, T.K. *State and Society in India*, New Delhi: Sage Publications, 1990.

_________. *Citizenship, Nationality and Ethnicity.* Cambridge: Polity Press, 1997.

Oommen, T.K. *Nation, Civil Society and Social Movements.* New Delhi: Sage Publications, 2004.

_________. 'Nation Building and Diversity' in *Unity in Diversity: Learning from Each Other*, I.R. Watts and R. Chattopadhyay (eds), New Delhi: Viva Books, 2008.

Oommen, T.K. and Hunter P. Mabry. *The Christian Clergy in India: Social Structure and Social Roles.* New Delhi: Sage Publications, 2000.

Oommen, T.K. "State Formation, Minoritization and Violence in Postcolonial India", in Kalpana Kannabiran (ed.) *Violence Studies*, New Delhi: Oxford University Press, 2016, pp. 120-141.

Pandey, G. (ed). *Hindus and Others: The Question of Identity in India Today*, New Delhi: Oxford University Press, 1993.

Savarkar, V.D. *Hindutva: Who is a Hindu?*, New Delhi: Bharat Sahitya Sadan, 1949.

Schermerhorn, R.A. *Ethnic Plurality in India*. Tuscon: University of Arizona Press, 1978.

Worsley, P. *The Three Worlds: Culture and Development*. London: Weidenfeld and Nicholson, 1984.

2

Christianity and the Indigenous People in India

S. M. Michael
Director and Professor of Cultural Anthropology
Institute of Indian Culture, Mumbai

Introduction

This paper "Christianity and the Indigenous People in India" is presented in the context of the discussion on "Indian Christianity: Public Theological Exploration." By 'Public Theological Exploration' I understand that the Christian faith in India interacts with public issues and happenings in order to empower and transform the lives of people for dignity, freedom and justice. By this, Christian faith becomes a lived reality in the midst of public events.

With this understanding when we discuss "Christianity and the Indigenous People of India", we cannot take the happenings to the *Indigenous People in India* in isolation. We need to place our subject in the wider context of the happenings in India in terms of its culture, economy and politics. In the past and at the present there are efforts to homogenize India in terms of one culture, one language and one religion. The RSS chief Mohan Bhagwat expressed such sentiments on 24th February 2018 at Meerut, when he said: "As Hindus, we have to unite because the responsibility of this country is upon us."[1] We need to ask 'what is the status of indigenous people in this public discourse of getting united as Hindus'.

Who are the Indigenous People of India?

The UN general assembly in 2007 adopted the Declaration on the Rights of Indigenous Peoples. India, however, is yet to *recognize* tribal people as indigenous. "Until and unless the country recognizes the tribal communities as indigenous peoples, the tribal population will continue to suffer as their rights can't be ensured according to the UN declaration," - said Mr. Phoolman Chaudhary, vice-chairman and Asia representative on the UN Permanent Forum on Indigenous Issues in a seminar for Tribal leaders in New Delhi on Feb. 16-17, 2018. Hence, in the case of India, since the Indian government does not recognize the term "indigenous people", for our practical purposes we can say that the indigenous people of India are the tribals of our country. Intuitively, the tribals of India perceive this and call themselves as "Adivasis" (Primordial Inhabitants). Next to the African Continent, India has the largest concentration of tribal population in the world. There are more than 500 tribal communities in India.[2]

Academic Discussion on the Identity of Tribals of India

The term 'tribe' was adopted by anthropologists from ordinary usage in English. In Medieval English the word 'tribe' indicated 'a primary aggregate of people claiming descent from a common ancestor'. With the advent of colonization, European anthropologists applied

---

[1] Deeptiman Tiwary, "25th Swayamsevak Samagam - RSS chief: Hindus unite, India's responsibility is upon us", *Indian Express.* Mumbai Edition, 2018), 7.

[2] Cf. R. C. Verma, *Indian Tribes through Ages* (New Delhi: Ministry of Information & Publications, Government of India, 1990).

the term 'tribe' to the people who lived in a primitive condition in backward areas and did not know the use of writing. Since then the term 'tribe' has been widely accepted and has been operational as a technical / academic / administrative term. The 'tribal' population is termed also as 'native'/ 'indigenous' population in anthropological literature. Tribal society is referred to also as 'primitive society'/ 'pre-state society'/ 'folk-society', etc.

When it comes to define the term "tribe", there is no generally accepted definition.[3] Etymologically the word 'tribe' derives its origin from the word 'tribuz' meaning three administrative divisions of ancient Rome. The Oxford Advanced Learner's Dictionary defines a tribe as a "group of people of the same race, with the same custom, language and religion who live in a particular area and are often led by a chief."[4] The British applied it to "a population that lived on the periphery of political and administrative life and called them 'Scheduled Tribes' and guaranteed special rights and protection.[5]

But, the study of tribes in India and the perceptions of their identity begin by locating them not just in the social context, but also in cultural, political and religious context of their living. Tribal India lives in the forests, hills and naturally isolated regions; it is known by different names, meaning either the people of the forest in the hills or the original inhabitants. It is believed that they were the earliest among the present inhabitants of the country.[6]

The popular names given for them are: Vanyajati (castes of forest), Vanvasi (inhabitants of forest), Pahari (hill-dwellers), Adimjati (original communities, primitive people), 'Adivasi' (original first settlers), Janjati (folk People), Anusuchitjanjati (scheduled tribes), and so on. Among these terms 'Adivasi' is known most extensively

---

[3] T. B. Naik, "What is a Tribe? Conflicting Definition", in *Applied Anthropology in India*, ed. L. P. Vidyarthi (Allahabad: Asia Publishing House, 1968), 85-86.

[4] Sally Wehemeir, ed., *The Oxford Advanced Learner's Dictionary* (London: Oxford University Press, 2000), 1387.

[5] Francis Pereira, *Faith Tradition of the Kuñrukhar (Uraoñs)* (Delhi: ISPCK, 2004).

[6] L. P. Vidyarthi, *Rise of Social Anthropology in India: A Social Science Orientation* (Delhi: Concept Publishing Company, 1976), 25-26.

and Anusuchitjanjati (schedule tribes) is the constitutional name covering all of them.

Yet, there is an ambiguity in the term 'tribe'. Its evolution is very complex. Sociologists and Anthropologist have not arrived at a unanimous definition of the term. But the most attempted definition took an evolutionary perspective, depicting tribes as backward and primitive. The McMillian Dictionary of Anthropology starts by acknowledging that, "this term has been widely used in anthropology, but there is no general consensus as to its precise definition or appropriate application."[7] Others like L. P. Vidyarthi[8] 'give a host of characteristics, mostly derogative ones denoting primitiveness' that must be fulfilled for a group to qualify as a tribe.

Sumit Guha (2015:50-57) describes that the term 'tribe' is used in Indian Sociology and Political discourse and does not fit the observed characteristics of the people labelled above in any part of the world. He says so because "all over the world tribes have been generally referred to as a strong organisation, often possessing much latent military power"[9] but in India we hardly find the tribes with latent military power (leaving out few retaliation in the name of tribal movements).

But for Virginius Xaxa, "[T]ribe is a society, like all other societies, made up of people with its own boundaries. It is a group of people who belong to a society by virtues and rules which they obey. They have their boundaries which is linguistically, culturally and politically different."[10] Therefore, "they are a distinct group of people, who have a geographical isolation, physical features, simple condition of living, general backwardness to the practice of animism,

---

[7] Symour-Smith, C. *Macmillan Dictionary of Anthropology* (London: Macmillan Press Ltd, 1986), 281.

[8] L. P. Vidyarthi, "Nehru's Approach to Tribal Problems", in – *Applied Anthropology in India*, ed. L. P. Vidyarthi, 1968, 87.

[9] Sumit Guha, "States, Tribes, Caste: A Historical Re-exploration in Comparative Perspective", *Economic and Political Weekly*, 50(46&47), No-21, 2015, 50-57.

[10] Virginius Xaxa, "Transformation of Tribes in India: Terms and Discourses", *Economic and Political Weekly*, June, 12. 34(24), 1999, 1519-1524.

special language, etc."[11] With this he means to say that tribals are culturally different from the mainstream population of India.

Christian Movement among Tribal People

About 104 million people in India are members of Scheduled Tribes, which accounts for 8.6% of India's population (according to the 2011 census). Among them, about 9-10 per cent are Christians. Among the total Indian Christians, the tribals form about 25 per cent.[12]

The causes of their conversion to Christianity are many. Felix Padel, an anthropologist, narrates:

> [T]he main reason may be attributed to the dedication and hard work of the missionaries with some much needed activities like school education and hospital facilities. They also try to change the so-called 'barbaric' customs, besides making them well behaved, 'well dressed and well groomed'. ...This definitely gave a new set of moralities. School education also provided a code of conduct and discipline."[13]

Archbishop Thomas Menamparampil points out that "Christ and His message provided a new vision of life; implanted or strengthened certain values, e.g., a sense of Providence, faith in a loving Father in Heaven, the concept of forgiveness, that of universal brotherhood, the value of suffering, of renunciation."[14] Sebastian Karotemprel confirms the above observation of Archbishop Thomas: "Before the advent of Christianity in the nineteenth century, the

---

[11] Virginius Xaxa, "Tribes as Indigenous People of India", *Economic and Political Weekly*, Dec, 18, 34(51), 1999, 3589-3595.

[12] S. D. Ponraj, *Tribal Challenge and the Church's Response* (Madhupur: Mission Educational Books, 1996), 62 & 159.

[13] As quoted by Sukant K. Chaudhury, "Do Kondh Constitute a Tribe? The Question of Identity," *The Eastern Anthropologist,* Vol. 61, No. 4, October-December, 2008, 473- 483.

[14] Archbishop Thomas Menamparampil, "Stimulating Hidden Potentialities: The Power of the Christian Message", *Impact of Christianity in North East India,* ed. J. Puthenpurakal SDB (Shillong: Vendrame Institute Publications, 1996), 8-15.

tribal world-view was limited to a clan, village or at the most to a particular area of state. Christianity has brought a new world-view to the tribal people not only by exposing them to the Indian nation but also to the international community."[15]

Further studies on conversion movements show that mass conversion of tribals to Christianity is related to the tremendous socio-economic and cultural changes brought about by westernization and modernization. Christianity helped the tribals to meet the newly emerging world.[16] O. L. Snaitang, studying Christianity and Social Change in North East India, finds that Christianity provided a means through which the tribals could accommodate themselves to the changes that were imposed through British administration and the process of modernization it brought with it. In a situation where radical changes were taking place, Christianity provided institutions, a new lifestyle and ideology which protected the tribal society from the danger of detribalization and loss of identity. A new sense of tribal solidarity, which transcended the traditional fragmented order, was created. This was founded over the maintenance of the traditional kinship code, which was the only feature common to the tribals prior to the coming of the British.[17] Group conversion especially corresponded to the mentality of the people, for they were accustomed to act in groups. According to J.W. Picket, mass-movements protected the converts from social dislocation and reduced the danger of westernization.[18]

A renowned anthropologist F. C. Wallace observes that when people's expectations no longer match their experiences, people reorient their cultural codes to another. If the tribal religions do not agree with their everyday experience, and if their worldviews are too

---

[15] Sebastian Karotemprel, Sebastian, "The Impact of Christianity on the Tribes of North East India", *Impact of Christianity in North East India*, ed. J. Puthenpurakal SDB (Shillong: Vendrame Institute Publications, 1996), 16-60.

[16] Nalini Natarajan, *Missionary among the Khasis* (New Delhi: Sterling Publishers, 1997).

[17] O. L. Snaitang, *Christianity and Social Change in North East India* (Shillong: Vendrame Institute, 1993).

[18] J. W. Picket, *Christian Mass Movements in India* (Lucknow: Lucknow Publishing House, 1993, 2nd Indian Edition).

far off from people's experiences and if people find themselves in dire straits, they are likely to change their religion and then change realities to match the new religious ideas of a better world.[19] When tribal religions failed to function very well for the complex necessities of trade in the globalized world, Christianity provided a vision that reoriented the society so that it could transcend the limitations of the kinship system.

Christian tribals are living in the midst of their own tribal communities who practice their indigenous religion. All the same, the problems, difficulties and political processes which go on among the tribals are common to both Christian and other tribals of India.

Tribal Community in the midst of other Communities

Being a part of Indian society, the tribal communities have always co-existed with the general masses / non-tribal people and lived in close vicinity for centuries. Circumstances often drove the tribal people into the quiet corners of the country. After being absolutely cut off from the mainstream, the tribal communities became losers and sufferers as a result of exploitation by the powerful and dominant ruling class. This ultimately led the tribal communities to be overburdened with misery and distress. As a result of the confinement, each tribal community achieved a degree of equilibrium with their ecology and reduced to a state of utter ignorance. Each of the isolated tribal communities developed a specific way of life with a set of typical thought and behavior pattern. These isolated tribal communities were considered to be – 'happy enough in their own world'.

Powerful 'zamindars' began to exploit the tribal people. They conspired with the corrupt officials and forced the tribal people to vacate the land in their possession. Taking an undue advantage of the helpless condition of the tribal people, the traders and money-lenders took every opportunity to exploit them. In this process, the tribal communities completely lost their 'age-old rights on land'. With this, the traditional economy of the tribal communities was

---

[19] As quoted by E. Paul Durrenberger and Suzan Erem, *Anthropology Unbound: A Field Guide to the 21st Century* (London: Paradigm Publishers, 2010), 152.

challenged. As a result of overall exploitation of the isolated forest dwelling tribal communities, there was a great discontent among them. They began to involve in violent revolts and militant struggle in different tribal areas.

Politics of Tribal Identity

There are two major contrasting opinions with regard to the social, cultural and political identity of tribes in India. There is one school of thought who believes that there is no difference between caste and tribe in India.[20] Equally strong opinions are expressed that in India tribals have distinctive culture and they do not belong to the caste system.

Many scholars have presented evidences from the classical, medieval and contemporary sources to demonstrate the tribes of India to be a distinctive category from caste.[21] From an insider point of view several tribal groups identify themselves as "adivasis" or indigenous or most ancient inhabitants of India.

In all the above characteristics, tribes are distinguished from the castes with regard to their cultural practices and social

---

[20] G. S. Ghurye, *The Aborigines, So-Called, and their Future* (New Delhi: Oxford University Press, 1943); Id., *The Scheduled Tribes* (Bombay: Popular Press, 1959); A. Beteille, *Six Essays in Comparative Sociology* (New Delhi: Oxford University Press, 1976); F. G. Bailey, *Tribe, Caste, and Nation: A Study in Political Activity and Political Change in Highland Orissa* (Manchester: Manchester University Press, 1960).

[21] N. K. Bose, *Culture and Society in India* (Bombay: Asia Publishing Co., 1941); D. G. Mandelbaum, "Social Grouping in Man", in *Culture and Society*, ed. H.L. Sapire (New York: Oxford, 1956); F. G. Bailey, "Tribe and Caste in India" *Contributions to Indian Sociolog*, Vol. 5, 7-19, 1961; A. Beteille, "The Definition of Tribe", in *Tribe, Caste and Religion in India*, ed. Romesh Thapar (New Delhi: Macmillian India Ltd., 1981), 7-14; A. Beteille, "The Concept of Tribe with Special Reference to India", *Indian Tribes and the Mainstream*, eds. S. K. Chaudhury and S. M. Patnaik (Jaipur and New Delhi: Rawat Publications, 2008); K. S. Singh, *The Scheduled Tribes* (New Delhi: Oxford University Press, 1994); B. K. Ray Burman, *Tribes in Perspective* (Delhi: Mittal Publications, 1994); Stephen Fuchs, *The Aboriginal Tribes of India* (New Delhi: Macmillan Indian, 1973); Christoph von Fuerer-Heimendorf, *Tribes of India: The Struggle for Survival* (Berkeley: University of California, 1982).

organizations.[22] Tribes are an autonomous group who are having their own distinctive culture and who are not belonging to Sanskritic culture and not members of the Hindu caste system, though a lot of attempts are being made to sanskritize them through the course of Indian history. Their religious worldview is not governed by the Hindu philosophical ideas of karma, dharma, rebirth and moksha. The tribals do not have the Hindu Sanskritic gods in their pantheon. They do not have temples or statues at their original sacred grooves. Thus, conceptually, the following criteria were adopted to characterize a tribal community with such features as geographical isolation, simple technology and condition of living, general backwardness, practice of animism, tribal language, physical features, etc.

Xaxa puts it very clearly that the two divisions within the society were seen because of the social organisations. He says, "[C]aste was treated as a society regulated by the hereditary division of labour, hierarchy, principle of purity and pollution, civic and religious disabilities, etc. whereas, Tribes on the other hand were characterized by the absence of features attributed to caste."[23]

In spite of the distinctive characteristics of the tribes, there is a vigorous attempt to absorb tribals to Hindu caste social structure. Several examples have been given by Arjun Patel[24] and S. M. Michael.[25]

Constitutional Understanding of Tribes

From the above discussion, it is clear that it is very difficult to offer a precise and clear-cut definition of the concept of tribe because the

[22] K. Kamal Misra, "On `Tribe' and `Tribalism'", *The Eastern Anthropologist*, vol. 61, No. 4, October-December 2008, 429-440.

[23] Virginius Xaxa, "Tribes in India", in Das, Veena, ed. *The Oxford India Companion to Sociology and Social Anthropology* (New Delhi: Oxford University Press, 2003), 333-408.

[24] Arjun Patel, "Hinduisation of Adivasis: A Case Study from South Gujarat", in *Dalits in Modern India: Vision and Values* (New Delhi: Vistaar Publications, 1999), 186-212.

[25] S. M. Michael, *Christianity and Cultures: Anthropological Insights for Christian Mission* (New Delhi: ISPCK, 2015), 148-179.

nomenclature is overshadowed by political, religious and economic implications.

According to Article 342 of the Indian Constitution, the President of India, using his / her discretion, schedules certain communities as Tribes eligible for certain governmental benefits. They are called Scheduled Tribes (ST), thus, the term `tribe' has a lot of political connotation. About 8.2% of the Indian populations are officially listed as Scheduled Tribes for the purpose of special benefits of political, economic and educational achievements. However, there are several ethnic groups in India who, by and large, retain cultural background 'analogous' to the officially listed tribes. Ethnicity and cultural identity have emerged as significant social issues for these groups in contemporary India.

The Rights of the Tribals: Three Major Policies

During the course of the development of Indian nationalism, the question of tribal identity sprang up very strongly. Elwin Verrier, though born a British, worked very closely with Gandhi and Nehru and adopted Indian way of living and thinking. He studied and lived with several of the country's little-known tribes. He married a Gond girl and made Mandala as his centre for social work. He is considered to be an authority on tribal culture. He argued that the tribals were the original settlers to this land. They lived with nature and their habits and way of life were conditioned by nature, and they have had their unique cultural characteristics and identity. He argued that when these tribals came into contact with non-tribals, they were likely to shed their good qualities of life and that might lead to their loss of nerve. So, he pleaded that they be kept isolated from the mainline of civilization. The proposition made by Elwin created a debate in India. The Gandhian workers argued that the tribals cannot be kept deprived of the benefits of civilization. Isolation in this case would keep them backward, ignorant, poor and illiterate.

The Hindutva nationalists, on the other hand, have a completely opposite view of tribal identity. They deny a separate cultural identity for tribals. While the tribals identify themselves as "*Adivasi*" (first or ancient inhabitants) of India, the Hindutva ideologues call them as *Vanvasi* (jungle or forest dwellers). They are of the opinion that there is no cultural and religious difference between tribals and Hindu castes. These ideologues receive their inspiration from Indologists and Sanskrit oriented scholars like G. S. Ghurye, the well-known sociologist from Bombay University who called the tribals of India as "Backward Hindus."[26] Actually, Ghurye devoted two long chapters on tribal assimilation in his book *The Aboriginals, So-Called and their Future*. It is the long cherished aim of the Hindutva nationalists to absorb the tribals to Hinduism through an assimilation policy.[27]

Nevertheless, the liberal nationalist leaders who were not very much satisfied with the Elwins' isolation theory and the Ghurye's assimilation theory, added number of provisions in the constitution so as to benefit the welfare of tribal people. They gave the status of scheduled tribe to this people so that they could have reservations in jobs and appointments. The constitution also brought in inhabited areas of tribals for the purpose of special treatment in respect of the administration. By doing so, the Indian constitution had tried to 'integrate' the tribal communities into the thrust of one nation.[28] Thus the theory of integration was taken over by the constitution to define the tribes as scheduled categories.

Article 342 of the Indian Constitution declares that, "the President may specify by public notification tribes or the tribal communities or parts of or groups within tribes or tribal communities which shall for the purpose of this constitution be deemed to be scheduled tribe in relation to that state." Thus, they were duly specified. However, it does not contain the criterion for the specification of any community as scheduled tribe. Xaxa

---

[26] G. S. Ghurye, *Caste and Race in India* (Bombay: Popular Prakashan, 1963), 19.

[27] Arjun Patel, "Hinduisation of Adivasis: A Case Study from South Gujarat", *Dalits in Modern India: Vision and Values* (New Delhi: Vistaar Publications, 1999), 186-212; S. M. Michael, *Christianity and Cultures: Anthropological Insights for Christian Mission* (New Delhi: ISPCK, 2015), 148-179; Selvam, "Sociology of India and Hinduism: Towards a Method", in *Dalits in Modern India: Vision and Values* (New Delhi: Vistaar Publications, 1999), 165-185.

[28] Virginius Xaxa, "Tribes in India", in *The Oxford India Companion to Sociology and Social Anthropology* (New Delhi: Oxford University Press, 2003), 333-408.

observes: "[T]he question of tribes in India is closely linked with administrative and political considerations. Hence, there has been increasing demand by groups and communities for their inclusion in the list of scheduled tribes of the Indian Constitution. That partly explains the steady increase in the proportion of the scheduled tribe in India especially in the period between 1971 and 1981."[29]

Therefore, in the post-independent India, successive governments have continued with the policy of "scheduling" areas, tribes, castes, and other backward classes despite the weaknesses and difficulties embedded in the process. This is primarily because political parties have found that it is easier to win the voters of "Scheduled India" than the voters of mainstreamed India. The scheduled tribes and castes usually have specific demands, and each political party presents solutions to their demands in its campaign in every general election. Thus the meaning of scheduled became very much misused and manipulated for political gains. This also affects and blurs the identity and the economic future of tribals in India.

Hindutva Politics and Tribal Identity

India is a pluralistic country comprising multi-ethnic, multi-lingual, multi-religious and multi-cultural characteristics. But today this notion of Indian reality is under great threat. The Hindutva forces who are in almost all mainline political parties and in the government administrations are increasingly seeking to homogenize the culture of India towards an upper caste, Sanskritic, Brahmanic Hinduism. Anything outside this cultural orbit is denied legitimate existence in Indian society. For example, from ancient times, the tribals have been eating cow meat. But today, the Hindutva forces deny this cultural practice of tribals by enacting laws against their culture.

Immediately after the Independence of India in 1947 and the promulgation of Indian Constitution in 1950, committees were set up for the reorganization of States in the Indian Union. The pleas of several tribals were rejected for their tribal states. The tribal population has been forcefully divided into several states. For

[29] Virginius Xaxa, "Tribes as Indigenous People of India", *Economic and Political Weekly*, Dec, 18, 34(51), 1999, 3589-3595.

example, the Bhil tribes had their own big kingdom in Pre-British India. They are denied a state of their own. They are split in several states where Hindu caste people are the dominant population. Thus, Bhils are found in Rajasthan, Gujarat, Madhya Pradesh and Maharashtra. Culturally, linguistically and politically, the Bhils are divided. How could they think of one cultural community in this condition? Similarly, the Adivasis of Chota Nagpur have been also divided in different states like Madhya Pradesh, Chhattisgarh, Orissa, Jharkhand, Bihar and West Bengal. This is an injustice done to the tribals of India by caste Hindus for their own economic and political advantage which plays out in the exploitation of tribals today in all aspects.

Tribals are the worst Victims of Development Activities

It is a strange paradox that although the tribes inhabit the most resource-rich regions of India, development benefits hardly reach them. They are the worst victims of `development' activities, urbanization and industrialization, and eco-tourism projects. These activities cause involuntary displacement, alienation from the natural resources, cultural disorganization, disengagement with the intense community life, eventually pushing them into abject poverty and squalor.[30] Many tribes in recent times symbolize the most victimized segments of our society caused by land alienation, poverty, indebtedness, industrialization and urbanization. The tribes of India are dejected people who are facing a loss of cultural identity as well as individual identity because of the interest of `the other'.

Tribal Movements

This exploitation of tribals from all aspects of their life has given rise to many big and small, sometimes violent tribal movements. These movements are primarily aimed at protecting themselves from the dominant caste communities.

Tribal movements were not only agrarian but also forest-based. Some revolts were ethnic in nature as these were directed against

---

[30] John H. Bodley, *Tribal Peoples and Development Issues: A Global Overview* (Mountain View, CA: Mayfield Publishing Co., 1988).

zamindars, moneylenders and petty government officials who were not only their exploiters but aliens too. When tribals were unable to pay their loan or the interest thereon, money-lenders and landlords usurped their lands. The tribals thus became tenants on their own land and sometimes even bonded labourers. The police and the revenue officers hardly understand them and help them. On the contrary, they also used the tribals for personal and government work without any payment. All these factors of land alienation, usurpation, forced labour, minimum wages, and land grabbing compelled many tribes like Munda, Santhals, Kol, Bhils, Warli, etc., in many regions like Assam, Orissa, Rajasthan, Madhya Pradesh, Andhra Pradesh, Bihar, and Maharashtra to revolt.

The management of forests also led some tribes to revolt, as forests in some regions are the main sources of their livelihood. The government policies not only deprived the tribals of several forest products but also made them victims of harassment by forest officials. This led tribes in several regions to launch movements.

The establishment of heavy industries, construction of dams and launching of development plans in tribal zones has necessitated displacement of local population. Thousands of tribal families were displaced from their traditional habitats. Money lenders, shop keepers and other caste people's migration to tribal areas have been equally detrimental. Destruction of forests as a consequence of felling trees for industrial purposes has threatened the small communities of hunters and food-gathers.

Those who could take advantage of new economic and educational frontiers were able to better their lot, while a large sections of the tribals, not adequately prepared to deal with new challenges, gradually depressed into poorer sections of the society. Against economic and social disparities, they have raised a collective voice.

The Naxalite movement of the tribals in Bihar, West Bengal, Andhra Pradesh; the agrarian movements of the Gonds and Bhils in Madhya Pradesh and the forest-based movements of Gonds were mainly launched for liberation from oppression and discrimination.

Conflict over the mining of bauxite in Chota Nagpur region has taken a violent turn with killing of three innocent tribal people.

Since 1993, the police have registered 80 criminal cases against the tribal people and activists. On several occasions, the police resorted to lathi charge. Activists were attacked and offices of the resistance movement were destroyed.

Another movement has been started in Keonjhar district of Orissa against mining in the 1990s by the displaced people, particularly tribals. In Keonjhar, the mining activities have led to heavy influx of workers from many parts of the country. The 1990s saw an increase in migration due to geographical and socio-economic reasons, leading to a threat of cultural invasion. Violence of all type increased. Mining has led to indiscriminate deforestation and displacement of inhabitants. The chief slogan of the movement against mining has been "Our lands, our minerals and our rights." The villagers have been harassed by police and implicated in false cases for organising meetings, public rallies and hunger strikes. A number of villagers had been sent to jail in false cases between 1994 to 1999.

There are several other tribal movements related to the problem of their identity. For example, in the North-East, the Bodo and Naga movement are related to this. Ethnic identity takes up political route for raising their interests. In all these separatist movement, uneven development and modernisation, concentration of gains in some area and their non-dispersal to other, and urban- oriented models of growth are the chief causes.

If we take into consideration all the tribal movements, it could be said that the tribal unrest and the resultant movements were mainly movements launched for liberation from (i) oppression, exploitation and discrimination, (ii) neglect and backwardness, and (iii) a government which was callous to the tribals' plight of poverty, hunger, unemployment and exploitation leading to movements due to separatist tendencies.

Inclusive Development as Means to build Peace in the Tribal World in India

Tribals of India are the marginalized communities of India. If we want to integrate them with other communities, then, the only way is that the State and Central governments must prioritize social, economic and political inclusion for rebuilding trust between tribal and other communities.

The tribal culture should be respected; their land and forest rights should be restored. When big industrial companies enter the tribal areas, most of the non-technical jobs should be given to them.

A number of commissions and committees were appointed in the recent past to look into the problems of developments in the tribal areas in the country and they have recommended a number of measures to remove the socio-economic disparity. While these policies are in themselves good, the implementation is the problem. The caste bureaucrats who are coming from caste background do not feel the pain of the tribals. Hence they do not give the importance, these policies deserve for the tribal development. For example, as per the Census of 2011, the literary rate of tribal population is 59%, which is far lower than the rate of all India which is 73%. Similarly, the Gross Enrolment Ratio (GER) for tribals is only 11% as compared to the overall GER ratio of 21% for the country. This is only just one indicator in the disparity of tribals compared to others. Unless they are brought to the full development on par with others, conflict is bound to show its ugly head. Hence, in order to build peace and harmony within India from a tribal perspective, we need an inclusive development of tribals. This is a priority.

Importance of Recognizing Tribals of India as Indigenous People: Christianity and the Indigenous People of India

The core of Christian faith is that we are all "created in the image and likeness of God". This implies that the basic dignity of every human person is a God-given one. Nobody can take away the God-given gift. This basic faith of Christians has manifested itself in all the welfare programmes of the Church towards the empowerment and social uplift of the tribes in India. All the same, today there is so much of invasion of non-tribals in the land of the tribes. They have lost their tribal rights on forest, their land is usurped by the landlords and by multi-national companies. Many tribals are migrating to cities as daily labourers and domestic workers. They are being exploited at the workplace.

In the recently held Seminar on the *Rights of Indigenous People in India* in Delhi on 16-17 February, 2018 at Indian Social Institute, Mr. Phoolman Chaudhary, the Vice-Chairman and Asia representative on the UN Permanent said, "Until and unless the country recognizes the tribal communities as indigenous peoples, the tribal population will continue to suffer as their rights can't be ensured according to the UN declaration." Ashok Bhai Chaudhari, an organizer of the seminar, said they decided to discuss the legal and health rights of tribal people because "ignorance of tribal people on these two has cost them much."

In another meeting held by two tribal bodies based in New Delhi — *Adivasi Ekta Parisad* (indigenous unity forum) and *Adivasi Samanweye* Front, Bharat (indigenous coordination front, India) — where 40 medical doctors and 20 lawyers met to discuss issues like sustainable health care and the constitutional rights of tribal communities in India, Fr Nicholas Barla, secretary of the Indian Catholic bishops' Commission for Tribal Affairs, pointed out that hundreds of cases are "pending against tribal people in courts … even petty cases because of lack of legal awareness."

In addition, the plight of the indigenous people of India is highlighted by the recent report of the Amnesty (2017). It highlighted that India's indigenous communities continue to suffer displacement because of industrial projects, while hate crimes against Dalits remain widespread. More than 6,500 crimes were committed against indigenous people in 2016 and their communities continued to face displacement as the government acquired land for projects such as mining. In September 2017, activists protested Sardar Sarovar Dam in Gujarat state, saying it had displaced some 40,000 families without paying adequate reparation.

The Church has taken up many social uplift programmes in different cities of India. But it is too small and impossible to adequately address the problems of the tribals today. The cultural assimilation policy of certain ideologies and political movements must be resisted with people's movements for their legitimate rights. The Church has to net-work with all people of good-will and social movements interested in the empowerment of the tribals of India. The cultural, economic and political rights of the tribals should be protected for the Indian nation which is rich with many cultures, languages and identities.

Select Bibliography

Bodley, John H. *Tribal Peoples and Development Issues: A Global Overview*. Mountain View, CA: Mayfield Publishing Co., 1988.

Burman, Ray B.K. *Tribes in Perspective.* Delhi: Mittal Publications, 1994.

Fuchs, Stephen. *The Aboriginal Tribes of India.* New Delhi: Macmillan, 1993.

Fuerer-Heimendorf, Christoph von. *Tribes of India: The Struggle for Survival.* Berkeley: University of California, 1982.

Ghurye, G.S. *Caste and Race in India.* Bombay: Popular Prakashan, 1963.

Guha, Sumit. "States, Tribes, Caste: A Historical Re-exploration in Comparative Perspective", *Economic and Political Weekly,* 50(46&47), No-21, 50-57, 2015.

Michael, S.M. *Christianity and Cultures: Anthropological Insights for Christian Mission.* New Delhi: ISPCK, 2015.

Misra, Kamal K. "On `Tribe' and `Tribalism." *The Eastern Anthropologist.* Vol. 61, No. 4, October-December, 2008.

Naik. T.B. "What is a Tribe? Conflicting Definition." In *Applied Anthropology in India,* edited by L.P. Vidyarthi. Allahabad: Asia Publishing House, 1968.

Patel, Arjun. "Hinduisation of Adivasis: A Case Study from South Gujarat", *Dalits in Modern India: Vision and Values.* New Delhi: Vistaar Publications, 1999.

Pereira, Francis. *Faith Tradition of the Kuñrukhar (Uraoñs),* Delhi: ISPCK, 2004.

Singh, K.S. *The Scheduled Tribes.* New Delhi: Oxford University Press, 1994.

Symour-Smith, C. *Macmillan Dictionary of Anthropology,* London: Macmillan Press Ltd, (1986).

Verma R. C. *Indian Tribes through Ages*. Ministry of Information & Publications, Government of India, New Delhi, 1990.

Vidyarthi, L.P. *Rise of Social Anthropology in India: A Social Science Orientation*, Delhi: Concept Publishing Company, 1976.

Wehemeir, Sally, ed. *The Oxford Advanced Learner's Dictionary*, London: Oxford University Press, 2000.

Xaxa, Virginius. "Tribes in India." In *The Oxford India Companion to Sociology and Social Anthropology*, edited by Veena Das, 333-408. New Delhi: Oxford University Press, 2003.

Xaxa, Virginius. "Tribes as Indigenous People of India." *Economic and Political Weekly*, Dec, 18, 34(51), 3589-3595, 1999.

3

Christianity and Education in India

Mohan Doss
Professor, Jnana-Deepa Vidyapeeth, Pune

Introduction

Although Christians are only 2.34% or 29 million of India's population of 1.3 billion, their influence in the field of education is very high. In fact, the number of educational institutions run by Christian Churches gives an impression that the Christians form a higher percentage of the population. For instance, *The Catholic Directory of India 2013* gives the following statistics: Pre-primary Schools 979; Primary Schools 4079; Middle Schools 2123; High Schools 3578: Higher secondary Schools - Junior Colleges - 1782; Vocational Training Centres 681; Degree Colleges 232; Professional Colleges 449 (Kanjrakkatt, 2013). One should add to these numbers also the five Universities. The Christian community has made and continues to make praiseworthy contributions to contemporary India in the field of education.

This paper on 'Christianity and Education in India' consists of three parts. The first part points out to some of the challenges of the present times which have impact on education in India. The second part takes a glance at the past to view Christianity's contribution in the field of education. The final part looks at Jesus for inspiration and points out, some of the pathways, although not exhaustive, to respond to the present situation in the field of education in contemporary times. The paper concludes with the affirmation that Christianity's efforts to provide education to the poor and the downtrodden enabled and enriched the practice of democracy in India.

I

Contemporary Challenges to Education in India

Education in India is at the crossroads today. Education is a means of liberation from ignorance and illiteracy but it has become in the present context of globalization a commercial venture for market forces. In addition, "[E]ducation" that is "meant to be a positive activity for the formation of the learner towards personhood now seems to be becoming a tool in the hands of fundamentalists for injecting the ideals of narrow religio-cultural nationalism and communalism" (Stanislaus 2004, 236).

Globalization

Globalization that is sweeping over our country has provided better modern transportation and communication technologies, compressed the world into a 'global city' and, made humanity deeply aware of its interconnection and interdependence. At the same time, globalization has enabled the developed countries to exploit the poor nations economically and subordinate politically through the processes of privatization and liberalization, which has led to greater misery and poverty for the poor (Stanislaus 2004, 236-237).

Globalization, with its ever expanding wings, is excluding the poor ever more from the immense benefits of contemporary scientific and technological progress. It promotes a homogenizing agenda of the powerful and attempts to destroy the pluralist cultural orientations of the peripheries. Fundamental rights and dignity of the powerless are increasingly and easily violated. In fact, the market forces are reigning supreme and the needs of the poor and the earth are placed on the margins. Globalization is "generating an ever-expanding greed for profit and power, promising an unending material progress, and causing irresponsible exploitation of the rare resources of the earth and polluting the environment" (Stanislaus 2004, 237). All these are affecting the educational system severely today.

Religious Fundamentalism and Cultural Monism

In the contemporary Indian scenario, groups imbibed with a spirit of religious fundamentalism promote *cultural monism*. The motto of this conceptualization is: one nation, one people, and one culture (Golwalkar, 1939). Cultural monism "tends to homogenize entire India under the Hindutva rubrics. It is ringing the death knell of the age-old Indian ethos of religiocultural pluralism and harmony" (Stanislaus 2004, 238). There are other alternative cultural orientations operative in the present scenario, such as cultural pluralism and cultural federalism. They aim to counter cultural monism. The secular forces advocate the former, celebrate the religio-cultural diversity of India and demand the respectful co-existence of different religions and cultures. Cultural federalism is proposed by various regional and linguistic movements which "conceive Indian society as a conglomeration of nations, basically linguistic and tribal entities, a multi-national state" (Stanislaus 2004, 238).

The fourth conceptualization emerges from the underprivileged social strata of the Indian society comprising of the Dalits (16%), the Scheduled Tribes (8%), and the Backward Classes (52%). There have been and are attempts "to mobilize all of them as *dalitbahujans* (oppressed masses) in order to be an alternative political and cultural force to counter the dominating caste hierarchy and institutionalized inequality. This is called cultural subalternism" (Stanislaus 2004, 238-239). In the present scenario, the Hindutva forces make untiring efforts to impose their cultural monistic perspectives into education, while the secular and *dalitbahujan* forces oppose strongly the efforts of advocates of cultural monism. The persistent resistance from many groups in Tamil Nadu against NEET (National Eligibility Entrance

Test) is a telling example of a continued protest against thrusting cultural monism through the back door.

Degrading Conditions of the Dalits

Even after seventy years of Independence of India, social and economic equality of Indian citizens appear to be a distant dream. Caste system is still ubiquitous and powerful in rural India with its inhuman practices. The Indian mind is still incapable of accepting all humans as equal by birth, sharing inalienable divine dignity, and honouring them as children of God. The Dalits are treated even today very badly in different ways. They become easy victims in any conflict and their houses are burnt, their women subjected to inhuman treatments and are gang-raped. The CBCI Policy of Dalit Empowerment in the Catholic Church in India (CBCI 2016, 11) states: "Every 18 minutes a crime is committed against a Dalit. Every day, 3 Dalit women are raped, 2 Dalits are murdered, 11 are beaten, and 2 Dalit houses are burnt. Official Police Statistics of 2012 observes that in the last five years, every week, 13 Dalits are murdered, 6 are kidnapped or abducted, and 5 Dalit houses or possessions are burnt."

In the name of protecting the holy cows, Dalits who skin dead cows are brutally beaten up and killed, and those who eat beef are treated as inferior humans, anti-nationals and criminals (Stanislaus 2004, 239). Amnesty International Report 2017 released on February 22 states: "At least 10 Muslim men were lynched and many injured by vigilante cow protection groups, many of which seemed to operate with the support" of the pseudo-nationalist forces. It further adds that India "secured 42nd place in the 2017 Global Democracy Index, 10 places below its 2016 ranking".

Many Dalits, who embraced Christianity for a breeze of liberty - among other things - from the clutches of inhuman caste system, stand betrayed today, because caste discriminations are rampant even within Christianity. In such a disheartening situation, many of the Dalit children are neither able to get admission in good schools, nor able to complete their schooling. Consequently, a high percentage of them become dropouts and end up as child labourers (Stanislaus 2004, 239-240). On the socio-cultural sphere, the Christians of

Dalit origin are discriminated in many ways, but the Constitutional framework in India refuses to acknowledge this life-numbing reality of discrimination and stubbornly continues to deprive them of what their neighbours in the same street are guaranteed for, namely, reservations of seats in educational institutions and opportunities for employment.

Displacement of the Indigenous People

The forces of globalization affect very much the tribal people in different parts of India. Their land, the source of their livelihood, is taken over for modern developments or for the sake of multinationals. Consequently, they are increasingly uprooted socially and culturally. The Amnesty International Report 2017 has highlighted that India's indigenous communities continue to suffer displacement because of industrial projects. It adds that more than 6500 crimes were committed against indigenous people in 2016 and their communities continue to face displacement as the government acquired land for projects such as mining. It also mentions that Sardar Dam in Gujarat had displaced some 40,000 families without paying adequate reparation. Indigenous people's "religions, cultures and languages are not given proper respect and representation. Their traditional ways of living, relating, organizing, health care, etc., are considered inferior, and the homogenizing structures are imposed on them. Uprooted from their land and traditional ways of living, they are now largely displaced in the cities without proper jobs and security. This has also engendered strong tribal assertions, assuming violent proportions, especially in the Northeast" (Stanislaus 2004, 240). The displacement of indigenous people adversely affects the education of their children and leaves them with a bleak future.

Discrimination against Women

The patriarchal domination continues to control women in India from womb to tomb. Even today in Indian society, the male is celebrated and gloried but the females face insurmountable disabilities and humiliations and are treated as inferiors. Religions venerate the female at the symbolic level, but favour patriarchal domination and violence (Stanislaus 2004, 241). Although the Population Census of 2011 shows an upward trend in sex ratio, from 933 in 2001 to 940 females to that of 1000, it is still alarmingly low. Domestic violence against women and sexual exploitation in work places continue to hit the headlines. According to the 2011 Census, the female illiteracy (34.54%) is far more than that of male illiteracy (17.86%). Thanks to the untiring efforts of social reformers and the emphasis on girls' education in the last few decades, there are women movements in India today demanding their rightful place as co-humans and partners in the project of building a humane society. Education is one of the fundamental steps to empower women.

Degradation of Eco-system

Humans enslaved by the modern technocratic paradigm perceive the Mother earth as a source for raw materials for quick profits. Human greed has no sky and their unrestrained exploitation and destruction of the natural rare resources and the disproportionate use of chemical fertilizers and pesticides pollute our earth and its environment. "The air we breathe, the water we drink, the food we eat, the sunlight by which we see and space in which we move, are all tampered with. Earth is dangerously deformed and becoming increasingly unfit for the sustenance and continuance of life" (Stanislaus 2004, 241-242). Pope Francis in his Encyclical *Laudato Si, On Care for our Common Home* (2015) pleaded humans to be stewards of God's creation, because the earth we live in belongs to all and to our future generations. Our vocation is to care for and share the fruits of the earth with all. Our education has to prepare the future generation to meet this urgent challenge with new sensitivities and responsibilities.

Commercialization of Education

Education is a state responsibility but most states have failed miserably to shoulder this responsibility. Education in India has come to be identified with commercialization and competition. Many private organizations and rich individuals have started investing in education as a business enterprise. But in reality, "in the name of providing service, they have segregated education once again to the rich and the affluent" (Charles 2017, 13).

Education has become more a competitive business. Education faces commercialization and competition. Consequently, there is a pressure for good results rather than value orientation. "With a mushrooming of many agencies, governmental and non-governmental, portraying themselves as educational providers, education and educational facilities are being made more accessible to people in all corners. With connectivity, infrastructure, and dissemination of knowledge, it has become an extremely lucrative business enterprise" (Fernandes 2017, 51). One wonders whether Christian education is becoming a prey to such market driven commercial forces!

Christian Education in the Web of Social Trends

The state and central governments, on the one hand, appreciate the educational services provided by Christianity, but on the other, their attitudes betray their suspicion towards the Christian educational institutions (Charles 2017, 13). "There is greater interference and control exercised by the government in matters of admission and appointment of teachers. The autonomy and creativity of Catholic education is hindered by the high handedness of government and education departments". Thus it is a challenge to remain with our Christian identity in the context of narrow-nationalism (Michael 2017, 7).

II

Christianity - a Trend Setter: A Historical Note

Beginnings of Modern Education

The traditional system of education in India, *Gurukulam,* was like an extended family and can be viewed as "the incipient stage for a formal system of education" and it was different from *'Parishads'* which referred to the gatherings of learned men. *Takshashila*, now in Pakistan and Nalanda in Bihar were famous eminent centres of learning in 7 BC and during the Gupta dynasty respectively. In the 16th century the Mughals established *Madrasas* (Muslim educational institutions) in Arabic medium in places like Agra, Delhi and Lahore.

The East India Company Act of 1813 set the beginnings of modern education in India and Macaulay's Minutes of Education of 1853 decided in favour of an education imparted through the English language. Macaulay wanted the English educated persons "to serve as interpreters between the Government and the masses, and who, by refining the vernaculars, would supply the means of wide-spread dissemination of Western learning" (Madathiparambil 1993, 25).

Church and Education in India: Before Independence

Even before the arrival of the British, the Portuguese started – St. Francis Xavier arrived in Goa 1542 - a few elementary schools for the education of new converts and established a seminary called The College of St. Paul in Goa for the training of priests. However, a firm foundation for the modern educational system was laid under the British rule which geared the whole system towards providing clerks and other machinery to assist the British rule. Other missionary schools were established soon in other parts of India: at Bassein (Vasai) in 1546, in Cochin in 1549, at Punnaicayil in Tamil Nadu in 1567, and in Madurai in 1595. In Pondicherry a School of High Tamil was started at Ellacurichi during the eighteenth century. During the British rule, Christian educational work spread in an organized way. Macaulay's Minutes gave a new turn to Christian educational work and paved the way for a great intellectual revolution in India (Palackapilly 2004, 84).

From 1835 till the end of the century, a number of institutions of higher learning were started [St. Xavier's College, Kolkata (1835), Madras Christian College (1839), St. Joseph's College at Trichy (1844) and St. John's College at Agra (1858), and were affiliated to the first universities - The Universities of Calcutta, Bombay and Madras -established in 1857.

Christianity's Involvement in Education: After Independence

When India attained independence in 1947, the literacy rate was only 14% and nearly 33.3% of the children were going to primary schools. Thus the educational system was quantitatively inadequate and was challenged by the great regional, gender and caste variations. The involvement of the Church in education was great and the

Christian institutions continued to be esteemed high for their academic standards, for the secular and open outlook and for the value-based education. In 2004, nearly 70% of all these schools were in rural areas serving the poor, especially the Dalits, *Adivasis* and other disadvantaged groups. Only 15% of Church institutions were in cities and large towns. Over 90% of the students in these institutions hail from other religious traditions than Christianity (Palackapilly 2004, 85).

Christianity's Involvement in the Past: A Trend Setter

Christian Institutions – Catholic and Protestant – of higher learning were established in different cities and towns of India during the period of the British rule. Towards the close of 19th century there were 26 Christian Colleges. In 1947, the number of colleges increased to 62 (20 were managed by the Catholic Church) out of a total of 450. In the period 1947-1957, 36 Christian colleges were founded and a half of these in Kerala. In 1960s, 55 colleges were established and 27 of them were in Kerala. In 1993, there were 7000 colleges and 193 universities but the Christian colleges were only 208 and out of these 140 were run by Catholic Church. An analytical study of the statistics on the growth of Christian institutions after independence shows that the number of Christian colleges did not increase on a pace with the national growth of colleges due to following reasons: (a). The places with more Christian population had already colleges, (b). Availability of colleges run either by the government or other private agencies in parts of India, and most importantly, (c). The enormous expenditure involved in establishing and running the colleges (Madathiparambil 1993, 26).

Christian Contribution to the Education of Women in India

A significant contribution of Christianity is the emphasis and encouragement given to education of women and the starting of schools exclusively for girls. Mrs. Basker and Mrs. Fenn, wives of missionaries in Kottayam, started the first schools for girls in 1819. However, the LMS and CMS had 1468 and 444 girls respectively in their schools already in 1857 (Madathiparmbil 1993, 27). "Christian missionaries everywhere were the first to break the shackles in which the women were bound, and set them free to know and understand the world" (Gray 1968, 456). The position of Indian women was pathetic in the past; the Hindu *Sastras* prevented the education of women. The first ever girls' school was opened by the missionaries in 1819 in Kottayam and a year later another in Alapuzha. These initiatives gathered great momentum in the years to follow and schools for girls were started in different parts of Kerala and other parts of India. The first ever girls' school by the government was started in 1850, more than three decades after the missionaries opened one (Palackapilly 2004, 87).

Education of women was unknown in the North East. The first attempts towards the education of women in the North East India were made at the beginning of the twentieth century (Palackapilly 2004, 87). In fact, the Naga parents resisted missionaries' initiatives for women education and used to argue: "You cannot teach our females; they are trained to bear burden, to bring wood and water, and to make the salt by which we make our subsistence" (Passah 1996, 446). Thanks to the efforts of the early missionaries, the female literacy rate in Mizoram, Meghalaya and Nagaland – the three states where Christians are the majority – is significantly higher than it is in all the other states of India, except Kerala and Goa.

Social workers and Hindu leaders rightly acknowledge the missionary service to the education of Indian women. Dr. Muthulakshmi Reddy, a freedom fighter and former Deputy Chairperson of the Madras Legislative Council observed: "I honestly believe that the missionaries have done more for women's education in this country than the government itself. The women of this country have been laced under a deep debt of gratitude to the several missionary agencies for their valuable contribution to the educational uplift of Indian women" (Gray 1968, 446).

Christian Contribution to the Education of the Indigenous Peoples of India

Christianity has immensely contributed to the education of the indigenous people - the *Adivasis* - of India, particularly in the regions of Chotanagpur and the North East India.

Education in Chotanagpur Region

Fr. Constant Lievens and his companions were convinced at the very start of their work in Chotanagpur area that every form of development begins with and is based on education. Consequently, they opened many schools in villages and towns. Oscar Severin, a great missionary bishop and educationist, made it a principle that in any new area a school must be built first, and only after that a church could be built (Tirkey 2000).

As Christian missioners expected, education brought about a transformation in *Advasi* societies, broadened their outlook and also changed their behavior patterns. Education enabled them to strengthen their *Adivasi* identity and selfhood. "In their new identity, the Adivasis crossed the social boundary of their own collective *Adivasi* community remaining part of it while becoming, at the same time, a part of the larger community of Christians, both tribal and non-tribal, in India and the world at large" (Palackapilly 2004, 90).

Education in North East India

From the beginning of the 19th century various Christian Churches played a significant role in providing formal education in North East India. St. Edmund's College and St. Anthony's College were among the first centres of higher education among the indigenous people, and contributed "in great measure to the formation of the intelligentsia of the region and paved the way for the establishment of universities in the region" (Palackapilly 2004, 91).

Opening Schools to the Marginalized

One of the significant contributions of Christianity is in the field of primary and elementary school education, particularly in the rural and remote areas. These schools admitted the children of deprived sections of the society, and they served as a means of social integration and social change. It is pertinent here to recall the words of Nelson Mandela, "Education is the most powerful weapon to change the world".

Church's Involvement in Technical and Vocational Education

There were no schools for learning technical or industrial skills before 19th century. The credit goes to Christian Churches for introducing technical and vocational training in India. The first of the technical schools was opened in Alapuzha (Kerala) in 1842, followed by others in other parts of Kerala and the country.

American Baptist missionaries who reached the North East in mid-19th century were of the view that industrial training was the need of the hour. One of the missionaries Rev. M.C. Mason was keen on opening industrial training among the Garos. In 1877 an Industrial department was opened to the already existing school in Goalpura (Palackapilly 2004, 86).

The Catholic missionaries who came to the North East in 1890 felt the need to provide basic education as well as training in agricultural and various handicrafts. In 1901, the Administrator Apostolic of Assam formulated a plan for establishing a trade school in Shillong (Palamattathil 1996, 406). The Salvatorian Brothers instructed the young Khasi boys in carpentry and shoemaking. In 1911, the government of Assam wanted the Catholic Mission to take over the government agricultural farm at Umlyngka. The Salvatorian Sisters too made a valuable contribution by opening a school for training girls in various schools. In 1922 the Salesians of Don Bosco arrived in North East and restarted the Trade School at Shillong and it came to be known as Don Bosco Technical School. It has done immense good in the technical and vocational training of the youth of the seven Northern States. A similar school was started at Maligaon in Guwahati. Other Christian religious congregation for men and women also joined in providing professional and vocation training of the tribal youth in this region (Palackapilly 2004, 85-87).

Christianity in Higher Education

Collegiate education based on the western pattern was introduced by the Christian missionaries at the Serampore College, West Bengal, in 1818. It was much before the Macaulay's Minutes of 1835 and the Hardinge Resolution of 1844 which prescribed English as a necessary qualification for joining in Government service. The Catholics' venture into higher education began in 1835 with the founding of St. Xavier's College in Calcutta (Mitra 2000, 112). At the close of the nineteenth century, the number of Christian colleges was 26, and in 1947, the Christian Colleges numbered to 62 out of 450. In 2000 there were 250 Christian colleges out of the 11,089 colleges in the country. Of these the Catholic colleges were 175. Almost 50% of these Colleges were for women and 17% for men and the rest (33%) were for both. George Palackapilly observes:

> Catholic colleges form an integral part of the Indian system of higher education. They are highly esteemed for their academic excellence, co-curricular activities and the all-round formation they give. In fact, in recent times, we notice in these colleges a new awakening to the demands of social justice and human rights. Admission policies are modified to bring in more of the underprivileged into the college and programmes of social awareness are organized to create in the students greater concern for the poor and exploited (2004, 88-89).

Christian colleges continue to function as agents of social change. They are continually challenged to face more than ever before the challenge of excellence and improve significantly the quality without compromising their commitment for social justice.

III

A Renewed Understanding of Education and Its Implications

Prior to the Second Vatican Council, 'education" was considered merely as a meritorious spiritual act of mercy. But in recent times it is understood as an essential dimension of Christian mission. It is interpreted in the backdrop of Christ's mission, which is a liberating (Lk 4:18ff) and humanizing one, inviting everyone to experience the dignity and joy of being and becoming children of God. The New Testament presents Jesus as "Teacher", who showed preferential concern and love to those who were pushed to the fringes of society, victimized by various oppressive and exploitative structures. Jesus was a friend of the poor and the outcaste. He healed them and allowed them to experience the joy and love of his Father and their dignity as children of God. His approach was person-centred, all inclusive, dialogical, and growth oriented and life-giving, Jesus in his person and ministry as a Teacher continues to inspire us to imbibe his vision and make his mission of giving life and life in abundance (Jn 10:10) our own.

Education for the Holistic Transformation of the Person

Every child, male/female, is made - as the Christian tradition teaches - in the image and likeness of God. The purpose of education is to make this a tangible and lived reality for everyone. The precepts of modern education enables the takers to respect the value of the multiple intelligence present in every one and help us to see them anew. It is the task of the educator to help each child discover his/her God-given uniqueness and multiple giftedness in a language and with a methodology that suit his/her needs (Stanislaus 2004, 247). Pope John Paul II in *Redemptor Hominis* (1980) No. 14, spoke of human person as "the primary route that the Church must travel in fulfilling her mission: he is the primary and fundamental way for the Church, the way traced out by Christ himself". Therefore, an irreplaceable aspect of the Church's task is her involvement in the field of education and "the investment of human and material resources in the school becomes a prophetic voice for the church."

Pope Francis spoke of the purpose of education on 9 February 2017: "The school and the university have full meaning only in relation to the formation of the person. In this process of human growth, all educators are called to collaborate with their professionalism and with the wealth of humanity they bear, to help the young to be builders of a more fraternal and peaceful world." He added, "Catholic educational institutes are called first to put into practice the grammar of dialogue which educates in encounter and in the appreciation of cultural and religious diversities. ... In a more specific sense, schools and universities are called to teach a method of intellectual dialogue aimed at the search for truth". He concluded the talk affirming that the educational institutions do continue to "serve growth in humanity, dialogue and hope."

The contemporary society "craves for the development of just the mind through academics," but an effective education system has "to emphasize the development of emotional intelligence and spiritual intelligence… to offer a holistic education formal or non-formal, that educates prejudiced minds and heal wounded hearts". Educational strategies from pre-primary school to university level are to be prepared to equip students to think critically and become self-learners. Both formal and non-formal education should develop "an integrated curriculum into which are woven, strategies for teaching especially emotional, social and spiritual intelligence" (Stanislaus 2004, 247). Christian higher education underscores the following as its characteristic dimensions: "all-round education of the whole human person; an emphasis on the lived values of integrity, truth and justice; a preferential option for the poor and marginalized of the Indian society, with efforts towards inclusive education; the quest for excellence and the continuing response to human need, with new initiatives even in the remotest areas of the country" (Mascarenhas 2017, 40).

Holistic development calls for refocusing our attention on the essentials of education and redesigning the curriculum. Education should aim at a passing over "from competition to collaboration, exploitation to replenishment, religion to spirituality and then only will we have peace of mind and healthy relationships". The educational process should "facilitate students to discover power in the wings and strength in their roots and build a civilization of love going beyond the boundaries of caste, creed and nationality" (George 2017, 30).

A large number of Professional Training Institutions have made the Christian presence clearly visible. Further, the establishment of the Christian universities in the country has offered new possibilities of offering quality and standard higher education on Indian shores. In fact, in the last 30 years the Christian Autonomous colleges did enjoy a limited freedom along these lines (Mascarenhas 2017, 40).

Education for Civics and Citizenship

There is a tremendous sense of irresponsibility and a lack of civic sense in our society today, for example, spitting in public places, disobeying traffic rules, destroying public properties, not paying taxes, not exercising one's franchise, etc.

Education should inculcate in the minds of the young love of the country and a sense of duty. They should be motivated to care for the poor, the sick, and those who are on the margins socially and economically. Since our country is multi-religious, education should help the young to recognize and respect the uniqueness and richness of every religion. This could be inculcated in the minds of the young in many ways. An effective educational system would help our students to grow in secular and democratic orientations, and to face social problems rationally and sensitively rather than in a sectarian way. The Christian Educational institutions - schools and colleges – could find ways and means to admit more students from the underprivileged sections of the society. This would possibly offer "an excellent opportunity of creating future citizens who live, work, play, share and receive mutual gifts in that educational climate. It is an ideal setting to help remove prejudices and negative attitudes between the rich and poor" (Stanislaus 2004, 247-248).

Education for Empowerment of Dalits

Dalits have been indoctrinated for hundreds of years to feel and believe that they are lesser persons or even less than animals. "It is the liberative task of education to breathe new life into and unbind a people whose self-image and self-identity has been deadened and trivialized. They need an education, formal and informal that reveals to them their inner potential for growth....Creating new memories in them helps to create a new identity as well. They need to rediscover the beauty and uniqueness of their culture" (Stanislaus 2004, 249-250). Empowering the Dalits through education would include also the ability to transcend the culture of silence which has trained them to be victims for so long, and to awaken in them an appreciation of the positive foundational experiences of their culture.

Education for Empowerment of Indigenous People

The indigenous people, who form 8% of India's population, are often culturally and socially exploited on the altar of globalization.

Therefore, education should help the indigenous people to counter the impact of globalization and to reaffirm their own indigenous identity. "To understand and appreciate their culture supplementary school textbooks on tribal history, customs, folk tales on tribal heroes should be introduced. To a certain level education should be imparted in tribal language" (Stanislaus 2004, 250). Continued and sustained efforts to document all resources that would reaffirm their identity, knowledge on various aspects like herbal medicine and indigenous art could be a great help to promote the cultural mosaic of India.

The most significant impact of Christianity in rural areas was on the human person. The Christian educational services have given them self-respect and identity.

> The education imparted, especially the values given and the respect with which it was given, empowered both the Dalit and the tribal to move away from a hand to mouth existence on the fringes of society. They were able to move away from a situation in which their services were beneficial to society, but where they were never thanked or respected, where they were exploited in every way for labour, sex, even for land; where they were bonded labourers in every sense, of their landlords and other upper caste people in the villages. (Noronha 2017, 68-69).

Education for Empowerment of Women

The struggles around the globe for women's emancipation have acclaimed the significant role of education in achieving gender equality. Unfortunately, India still continues to be a land of patriarchy. Continued special emphasis should be given to women education, because when a woman is educated, a generation is educated. Education should empower women to breakthrough structural injustice, to develop a healthy self-image, competencies of assertiveness, decision making and independent thinking (Stanislaus 2004, 250-251).

Education for Eco-sensitivity

Education should incorporate strategies for the children to befriend nature and realize that our lives and future, our lives and caring the Mother earth are intrinsically interconnected, and make them aware how selfish and vested interests of a few displace millions of people on our planet and leave them homeless. Education for ecological preservation and promotion is to bring about a change in attitudes and mindsets to take care of the natural treasures of our earth and to recognize that human life of the present and future generations is intrinsically interwoven with that of Mother Earth. Consequently, environmental studies should form an integral part of the curriculum. Programmes and projects that create awareness and lead the students to action towards saving the earth are to be encouraged. "We truly need an education of eco-sensitivity that helps us learn from the book of nature a rediscovery of our God given true self-worth and our need to co-exist in harmony and peace with the cosmos" (Stanislaus 2004, 250-251). The higher education institutions in India should "promote environmental consciousness and promote green technology and sustainable development.... must help everyone evolve an eco-spirituality which alone sustain the universe" (George 2017, 34).

Promotion of Value Education

India has witnessed in the recent past huge scams and corruption in the corridors of powers and in the temples of knowledge. Our everyday experiences from the violation of traffic rules to violations of humans, especially the women and children, indicate how our society is fast becoming a monster of egoism and indifference. In every aspect of civil life, India is confronted with deteriorating moral standards affecting the social fabric of the country and its people. Therefore, the need of the hour is value education. The Second Vatican Council document, *Gaudium et Spes,* No. 2 states: "the general goals of Christian education are described as that of developing a mature sense of responsibility, authentic freedom, positive and prudent sex education, participation in social life, useful skills, involvement in community organizations and willingness to act for the common good".

Various education commission and committees in the past decades have duly emphasized the importance of value education. For instance, The Radhakrishnan Commission (1948), The Secondary Education Commission (1959) and The Kothari Commission (1966) highlighted the need for moral education in all the educational institutions. The National Policy on Education (1986) stated: "The growing concern over the erosion of essential values and an increasing cynicism in society has brought into focus the need for readjustments in the curriculum of social and moral values". The Programme of Action (NPE 1992) suggested "value education as an integral part of the school curriculum" (George 2017, 26-27).

The Second Vatican Council document *Gravissimum educationis, No. 4* describes what a school ought to be in the following way:

> Among the various organs of education the school is of outstanding importance. In nurturing the intellectual faculties which is its special mission, it develops a capacity for sound judgment and introduces the pupils to the cultural heritage bequeathed to them by former generations. It fosters a sense of value and prepares them for professional life. By providing for friendly contacts between pupils of different characters and background it encourages mutual understanding.

The UNESCO International Commission on Education for the Twenty-first century headed by Jaques Delors, identified "learning to be" and "learning to live together" as two important pillars of education. "Learning to be" focuses on the development of the inner capacity of a person that will prepare him or her to meet social and political responsibilities. "Learning to live together" implies creation of a harmonious life by transcending sectarian loyalties and differences. The educational institutions in India must translate this dream into action to build a better nation (George 2017, 27). Swami Vivekananda said: "What we are today is the result of what we valued yesterday. What we will be tomorrow will be the result of what we value today".

"The Right of Children to Free and Compulsory Education Act, 2009" asserted the fundamental right of every child for education. This Act must be welcomed without reservation by all and must be implemented in letter and spirit.

Christian Higher Education to be Trend Setters

Thanks to the untiring efforts and generous dedication of women and men serving in Christian institutions in India. Some Christian institutions have been consistently rated among the top institutions in India, and a good number of Christian institutions have been ranked A-grade by the National Assessment and Accreditation Council, several being awarded the title, "College of Excellence" by the University Grants Commission in Delhi. Six out of the 14 colleges so awarded in January 2015 were run by Catholics. However, the following two challenges stand out: a). Achieving excellence in academic standards and in personality formation, and b). Bringing about equity and social justice in the fractured Indian reality today. "Can Christian Higher Education contribute to these two national tasks in a significant way?" (Mascarenhas 2017, 39-40). The urgent need of the hour is "the formation of creative, analytical and caring global citizens.... Features that expose students to interdisciplinary thinking, to group dynamics and soft skills, to international collaborations and to digital educational methodologies need to be incorporated." The Christian institutes of higher education can lead the way and be trend setters (Mascarenhas 2017, 41).

Excellence along with inclusion, equity and social justice are equally important goals for higher education. For instance, off-campus social involvement, a common practice in Christian Institutions, operates on the principle that, "where the heart is touched by direct action, the mind is challenged to change". Such experiences of social involvement help students to develop a commitment to a more just world. "Involvement in justice issues starts with awareness and the education of the conscience and this should begin in an academic centre of higher learning which is not insulated from real life issues." Further, a respectful understanding of other value systems and an open dialogue on world-views and religious traditions promote a healthy acceptance of the other. "Relationships built during such educational experiences serve as pattern of what is possible in civic life as citizens" (Mascarenhas 2017, 42).

Christian Higher Education has to orient and train Christian students to go for competitive examinations and join the cream of Indian bureaucracy that shapes the decision-making process in the country. Christian institutions must help students to pursue administrative services like IAS, IPS, IFS, and in administrative service in States (George 2017, 30).

Conclusion

Christian involvement in the field of education opened the horizons of knowledge to all and it had great impact in the socio-cultural aspects of Indian society. Christianity's efforts in India to provide education to all "did much for the democratization of education" and "successfully destroyed the monopoly in education enjoyed for ages by a single privileged caste, namely, the Brahmins" (Palackapilly, 2004, 96). Christianity made it possible for the downtrodden, weaker sections of the society to dream of social mobility in life. Christian Churches, following the footprints of Jesus, the Teacher, through their active involvement in the field of education made a historical contribution and a breakthrough in widening the horizon of hope for the Indian society. Let me conclude with *Laudato Si,* No. 215: "Our efforts at education will be inadequate and ineffectual unless we strive to promote a new way of thinking about human beings, life, society and our relationship with nature."

References

CBCI (2016). *Policy of Dalit Empowerment in the Catholic Church in India: An Ethical Imperative to build Inclusive Communities.* New Delhi: CBCI.

Charles, Maria (2017). "Challenges of Catholic Education in India," in *The Challenges of Catholic Education in India Perspectives.* 11-20. Janina Gomes (ed.). Bangalore: Claretian Publications.

Fernandes, Joaquim (2017). "Challenges to Catholic Education in the 21st Century – Special Reference to the Indian Scenario," in *The Challenges of Catholic Education in India Perspectives*. 51-56. Janina Gomes (ed.). Bangalore: Claretian Publications.

Flannery, Austin (1982). *The Conciliar and Post-conciliar Documents, Second Vatican Council.* Bangalore: St. Pauls Publications.

George, Davis (2017). "Catholic Higher Education in India: Exploring New Frontiers," in *The Challenges of Catholic Education in India Perspectives*. 21-38. Janina Gomes (ed.). Bangalore: Claretian Publications.

Gray, H., (1968). "The Progress of Women," in L.S.S. O'Malley (ed.). *Modern India and the West: A Study of the Interaction of their Civilizations*. Reprint. London: Oxford University Press.

Kanjirakkatt, Berny and Gabriel Vaz (eds.) (2013). *The Catholic Directory of India 2013*. Bangalore: Claretian Publications.

Madathiparambil, Geroge (1993). "Higher Education in India," in *Catholic Higher Education in Asia and the Pacific Region*.E. Mariana Setiadarma and Marc Coudron. Jakarta: *UniversitasKatolik* Indonesia Atma Jaya.

Mascarenhas, Fraser (2017). "The Challenge of Catholic Higher Education in India," in *The Challenges of Catholic Education in India Perspectives*. 39-44. Janina Gomes (ed.). Bangalore: Claretian Publications, 2017.

Michael, S.M., (2017). "Foreword," in *The Challenges of Catholic Education in India Perspectives*. 5-8. Janina Gomes (ed.). Bangalore: Claretian Publications.

Mitra, S.K., (2000). "Contribution of Christianity to Bengal," in *Indian Christian Directory*. Kottayam: Rashtradeepika.

Palackapilly, George (2004). "Christian Contribution to Education, Language and Literature," in *Christian Contribution to Nation Building: A Third Millennium Enquiry*. Selvester Ponnumuthan, Chacko Aerath and George Menachery (eds). Cochin: Documentary Committee of CBCI-KCBC National Celebration of the Jubilee of St. Thomas & St. Xavier.

Palamattathil, George (1996). "Christian Contribution to the Development of Technical and Vocational Education in North East India," in J. Puthenpurackal (ed.). *Impact of Christianity on North East India*, Shillong: Vendrame Institute.

Passah, Philomath (1996). "The Contribution of Christianity to Socio-Economic Development of North East India" in J. Puthenpurakal (ed.). *Impact of Christianity on North East India.* Shillong: Vendrame Institute.

Noronha, Marie and Pratibha Pinto (2017). "Church's Contribution to Education in Rural India," in *The Challenges of Catholic Education in India Perspectives.* 63-72. Janina Gomes (ed.). Bangalore: Claretian Publications.

Stanislaus, L., (ed.) (2004). "Conclusion on the National Consultation on Education As Mission," in *Education As Mission.* Pune: Ishvani Kendra.

Tirkey, Agapit (2000). "Cultural Identities and Education," A Paper Presented at the National Consultation on Indigenous Cultures of India at Mumbai.

Website:

"Amnesty Slams India for Increased Religion-Based Violence" – Amnesty International Report 2017. http://india.ucanews.com/news/amnesty-slams-india-for-increased-religionbased-violence/36697/daily accessed on 25 February 2017.

Pope Francis. "Catholic schools and universities in the service of the growth of humanity, dialogue and hope, 09.02.2017" in *Summary Bulletin: Holy See Press Office.* 2017/02.

4

Uniform Civil Code: An Appraisal

L. Sahayaraj

Deputy Secretary General, Tamilnadu Bishops' Council

India is a unique country in the world not only because of its rich traditions, cultures, variety of languages, dialects and race, but also because of its personal laws based on religions. Each religious community has its own system of personal laws with regard to family matters and it is an important provision of the Indian legal system. The civil personal law, under which the spouses are married, determines all matters that are applicable to them after marriage. Consequently, succession, inheritance, adoption and the custody of children are determined by the corresponding civil personal laws. While there is a criminal Code which is applicable to all people irrespective of religion, caste, tribe and domicile in the country, there is no similar civil Code when dealing with respect to marriage, divorce, adoption and succession which are governed by personal laws and there are lot of challenges and complexities in the application of the personal laws.

At the time of drafting the Constitution of India, the Fathers of the Constitution wanted to frame a Uniform Civil Code to unify and integrate the people of India. But they could not establish it due to various practical reasons and so they allowed the existing religious laws to govern the believer of every religion in matters of family life.

For more than half a century, efforts were made without success to adopt a Uniform Civil Code. Since 1950, the debate over Uniform Civil Code is going on and in fact it has often become a communal debate where Muslims and Hindus are treating it either as an exercise to flex their muscles or as a paranoid reaction to some deep-rooted fears. The voice of the Church in India is not loud in this matter and also not united, although there were some discussions here and there. The present-day BJP government seems to be more interested in bringing out the Uniform Civil Code. In 2016, it requested the Law Commission to examine the feasibility of ushering in a Uniform Civil Code. The Law Commission has sought the opinions at various levels and still it has not come out with its proposal draft of the Uniform Civil Code.

In fact, the enactment of Uniform Civil Code seems to be very difficult especially in our times. To understand the difficulty, it is essential that we examine this issue of Uniform Civil Code from legal, religious, constitutional, historical and moral grounds and also from ethical-pragmatic point of view.

Complexity of Civil Personal Laws

It is good to know what the personal laws are and how they govern the family matters in each religious community in order to understand the complexity of the personal law system in India. There is no single, specific and accurate definition for personal laws. J.D.M. Derret notes that the civil personal law is a personal system of rules applicable by any court to an individual depending on the subject determined by reference to the religion he/she professes or claims to profess or is presumed to profess.[1] The civil personal laws are applied in limited fields, that is to say, they govern only the

[1] J.D.M. Derret, *Religion, Law and State in India* (London, Faber and Faber, 1968), 39.

interpersonal relationships, or the family. They deal with the validity of marriage, the mutual rights and obligations of husband and wife, parents, children, guardians and wards, and the effect of marriage on property rights of husband and wife, divorce, annulment of marriage, though only to a limited extent, the legitimization and adoption, and inheritance by will or *ab intestat.* The civil personal laws are based on the religious texts, the interpretations of the religious texts by the followers or by the courts, mingled with the customary law which may vary according to different regions of the country.

Hindus, Muslims, Christians, Zoroastrians and Parsees, as well as Sikhs and Buddhists who, for legal purposes, are treated as Hindus, have their own personal laws. Thus, there are five main groups of civil personal laws governing the family matters in India, with reference to religions. The Hindu personal law governs all Hindus, Buddhists, Jains and Sikhs.[2] The Muslim personal law governs the Muslims,[3] the Christian personal law, the Christians,[4] the Parsee personal law, the Parsees[5] and the Jewish personal law, the Jews. Thus, every citizen in India has his / her own personal laws with regard to his / her social relationships and family.

The personal laws of each religious community are not homogeneous and there are several personal laws for different groups of the same religious community, basing on their origin and customs of the places in which they live. For example, for the Christian community, the diversity in inheritance laws is greatly intensified by making domicile a criterion for determining the application of

---

[2] The personal civil laws amended in various times and applicable to Hindus are the following: *The Hindu Marriage Act, 1955, The Hindu Adoptions and Maintenance Act, 1956, The Hindu Minority and Guardianship Act, 1956, The Hindu Succession Act, 1956.* These laws were amended several times.

[3] The personal civil laws of the Muslims are: *The Dissolution of Muslim Marriages Act 1939, Muslim Personal Law Application Act, 1937* and *Bihar & West Bengal Mohamedan registration of Marriages Act, 1876, Muslim Women (Protection of Rights on Divorce) Act, 1986.*

[4] The personal laws applicable to the Christians in India are: *The Christian Marriage Act, 1872, The Indian Succession Act, 1925, The Special Marriage Act, 1954; The Indian Divorce Amendment Act, 2001.*

[5] *The Parsee Marriage and Divorce Act, 1988* applies to the Parsees.

laws. Christians in the State of Kerala are governed by two different Acts: those domiciled in Cochin are subject to the application of the Cochin Christian Succession Act, 1921 while the Travancore Christians are governed by the Travancore Christian Succession Act, 1916. However, the Travancore Christians following the *Marumakka Avakashi* system, Roman Catholics of Latin rite[6] and the Protestant Christians living in the five taluks, i.e., Karunagapally, Quilon, Chirayinkil, Trivandrum and Neyyattinkara, have their separate customary laws. Similarly, the European Christians, Anglo Indians, Parangi communities of Cochin and the Tamil Christians of Chittur taluk of Cochin are governed by their distinct customary laws. Further, Christians in the State of Goa and the Union Territories of Daman and Diu are governed by the Portuguese Civil Code 1867 while those in Pondicherry adhere to any of the following laws: (i) Customary Hindu Law, (ii) The Indian Succession Act 1925, and the (iii) The French Civil Code 1804. Indian Christians who are not subject to any of the above customary or statutory laws are governed by the general scheme of inheritance laid down under the Indian Succession Act, 1925.

The civil personal laws of other religious communities can be applied to the Christians because of their birth or origin.[7] For example, the question, 'which personal law is applied to the children, born of a marriage between a Hindu and a Christian' was discussed already in 1894 by the Madras High Court.[8] It decided that the child born to a Hindu father and a Christian mother is a Hindu, because a child in India must be presumed to have his father's religion and his corresponding social and civil status. In the case of *Commissioner of Wealth Tax Madras vs R. Sridharan*, the Supreme Court has held, after considering various textbooks like Hindu law and usage by Mayne and Mulla's Principles of Hindu law (14th edition) that son of a Hindu father will be a Hindu irrespective of the religion of the

---

[6] *Abdurahiman vs. Joseph*, AIR, 1952, TC, 176.

[7] E. D. Devadasan, *Handbook on Christian Law* (Madras: DSI Publications, 1988), 13-14.

[8] ILR, 18, MAD, 1894, 230.

mother.[9] Therefore, the Courts have affirmed that the civil personal law of the father is the civil personal law of his children in matters of inter-religious marriage.

In the case of *Nepen Bzala vs. Sitakanta,* the question was which civil personal law should be considered for the devolution of property of a deceased? The Calcutta High Court decided that it was the civil personal law of the deceased and not of the beneficiaries or heirs.[10] In this case, a Hindu converted himself to Christianity and died leaving a Christian widow and a Hindu brother and sister. The court decided that the distribution should be made according to Section 33 of the Indian Succession Act 1925, and thus the Court allowed the Christian widow to take half and the Hindu brother and Hindu sister to take half equally (even though they were Hindus). Thus, the civil personal law of Hindus or Muslims can be applicable to Christians in some cases.

The Civil personal laws are more complex when one converts to another religion. For example, if a Hindu converts to Christianity, he/she cannot inherit any more from his / her parents; he/she risks breaking his / her family relationship and cannot adopt, etc. It is certainly against the right to freedom of religion and to human dignity. Also, the system of personal civil law does not assure equality between the citizens belonging to various religious communities. For example monogamy is imposed on the Hindus and not on the Muslims. It is discrimination between the citizens.[11]

Article 44: Directive for Uniform Civil Code

Realizing all these difficulties, the framers of the Constitution wrote their dream of bringing whole of India under a Uniform Civil Code in article 44 of the Constitution and thus expected to put an end to

---

[9] *Commissioner of Wealth Tax Madras vs R. Sridharan,* 1976, SUPPL SCR, 478.

[10] 15, Calcutta, Weekly Notes, 158.

[11] In my book, "Religious Conversion in a multi-religious context – An outlook on civil and canon laws", I have elaborated the complexity of the system of civil personal law especially in the field of conversion. See, Sahayaraj LOURDUSAMY, *Religious Conversion in a Multi-religious Context – An Outlook on Civil and Canon Laws* (New Delhi: Media House, 2011), 319.

a hodgepodge of personal civil laws. According to them, the primary purpose of the Uniform Civil Code was to govern uniformly all family matters and to assure unity of the nation and equality of all citizens.

Article 44 of the Constitution reads as: 'The State shall endeavour to secure for the citizens a Uniform Civil Code throughout the territory of India.' It is very important to note that the implementation of the article 44 seems to be difficult, because this article is placed in the section of the directive principles, and so the Government is not obliged to execute it at once by means of law or Constitutional amendment. By its moderate language, this article expresses rather a hope than a mandate.

During the debate in the Constituent Assembly, Dr. B. R. Ambedkar, while supporting the need to frame a Uniform Civil Code, expressed the hope that its application might be purely voluntary. However, he demonstrated his will to reform the Indian society by recommending the adoption of a Uniform Civil Code. He had then opposed the delegates who wished to immortalize the personal laws:

> I personally do not understand why religion should be given this vast, expansive jurisdiction so as to cover the whole of life and to prevent the legislature from encroaching upon that field. After all, what are we having this liberty for? We are having this liberty in order to reform our social system, which is full of inequalities, discriminations and other things which conflict with our fundamental rights.[12]

This recommendation was to remain a dead letter, notably because the minorities, to begin with, the Muslims took a hard line on their personal law. Not only the Muslims, even many Congress members and also Hindu leaders opposed a reform of Hindu practices concerning inheritance, marriage, divorce and adoption and thus the adoption of Uniform Civil Code was put aside. It is to be noted that

---

[12] Cf. Zafar Ahmad, *Personal Laws and Constitution of India: A Study in Contemporary Perspective with Special Reference to Dr. B.R. Ambedkar* (unpublished, 1992).

at the time of drafting the Constitution, the Christian community did not oppose vehemently the proposal for the Uniform Civil Code.

Supreme Court of India on Uniform Civil Code

More than ever, the Supreme Court of India has been insisting on the adoption of the Uniform Civil Code in the recent decades. It feels that it is the need of the hour to establish a Uniform Civil Code to govern personal matters of all citizens irrespective of religion and custom. The Supreme Court considers that such Code is the cornerstone of secularism, since it would not only help end discrimination against women on religious grounds but also strengthen the secular fabric of the country and promote unity; moreover, most of the personal laws which are old and religious in origin will be replaced.

In the case of *Mohammed Ahmad Khan vs. Shah Bano Begum,*[13] the Supreme Court ruled in favour of Shah Bano, who had moved the Supreme Court seeking maintenance under section 125 of the Code of Criminal Procedure after her husband divorced her. The Supreme Court opined that a Uniform Civil Code would help in the realization of the national integration by removing laws resulting from incompatible ideologies. It has also indicated that it is the responsibility of the Government to assure this Uniform Civil Code.[14]

In 1995, in the case of *Sarla Muggal vs. Union of India*, the Supreme Court had observed:

> Pandit Jawaharlal Nehru, while defending the introduction of the Hindu Code Bill instead of a Uniform Civil Code, in the Parliament in 1954, said 'I do not think that at the present moment the time is ripe in India for me to push it through'. It appears that even 41 years thereafter, the Rulers of the day are not in a mood to retrieve Article 44 from the cold storage where it is lying since 1949. The

---

[13] *Mohammed Ahmad Khan vs. Shah Bano Begum, AIR,* 1985, SC, 945.

[14] But this intervention of the Court provoked the deep opposition of the Islamic community, and *The Muslim Women (Right to Protection on divorce) Act, 1986* was promulgated in order to stop the Muslim divorced woman to get the benefit of the section 125 of the Criminal Procedure Code 1974.

> reasons are too obvious to be stated. The utmost that has been done is to codify the Hindu law in the form of the Hindu Marriage Act, 1955, the Hindu Succession Act, 1956, the Hindu Minority and Guardianship Act, 1956, and the Hindu Adoptions and Maintenance Act, 1956 which have replaced the traditional Hindu law based on different schools of thought and scriptural laws into one unified Code. When more than 80 percent of the citizens have already been brought under the codified personal law, there is no justification whatsoever to keep in abeyance, any more, the introduction of Uniform Civil Code for all citizens.[15]

In 2003, in the case of *John Vallamattom vs. Union of India*, John Vallamattom, a catholic priest, disputed section 118 of the Indian Succession Act, 1925 which stipulates that one cannot bequeath his/her possessions by charity outside the family, for example to an orphanage, if the will was not registered twelve months before his/her death. He argued that this is a discriminatory section against the Christians, and it is not present in the personal laws of Hindus and Muslims. The Supreme Court judged this as an anti-constitutional section. It also observed that "it is a matter of regret that Article 44 of the Constitution has not been given effect to. Parliament is still to step in for framing a common civil code in the country."[16]

In 2015, the Supreme Court said that there was a total confusion due to various personal laws and it sought to know whether the Government was willing to implement a Uniform Civil Code. It observed: "What happened to it? Why don't you (the Government) frame and implement it?" However, later the Supreme Court declined to direct the Parliament to bring a Uniform Civil Code and allowed a Public Interest Litigation filed in this regard to be withdrawn.

---

[15] *Sarla Muggal vs. Union of India, AIR*, 1995, SC, 153.

[16] *John Vallamattom vs. Union of India, AIR*, 2003, SC, 2902.

Oppositions to the Uniform Civil Code

If we look at the debates of the Constituent Assembly, the turn of events regarding the proposal of Uniform Civil Code is highly ironical. It was Congress leaders like Nehru and Ambedkar, woman's rights groups and Left parties who were originally trying to push the Uniform Civil Code, but the Hindu parties like Hindu Mahasaba and even some Congress leaders were not ready to accept it. Now, when the Hindu parties are ready to accept the Uniform Civil Code, others are reluctant to welcome it.

Today as ever, the Muslim community opposes strongly to the secularization of its personal law and to the Uniform Civil Code. For them, resolving the family conflicts is the task of the Ulemas. All India Muslim Law Convention of 1972 declares categorically that the Muslims will not tolerate that the legislator touches the slightest of their principles, since their personal law is an inseparable element of their religion.[17]

A comparative study of the personal laws of Hindus, Muslims and Christians will reveal that the sheer diversity of these laws, coupled with the dogmatic zeal with which they are adhered to, cannot permit uniformity of any sort. In fact, some of the provisions of Muslim personal law are already modern. Since 1930s, it has enshrined individual rights to property, unlike Hindu law, in which the family's natural condition is assumed to be "joint". In the decades of 1930s and 1940s, contrary to later opinions about Muslim law being backward, it was Hindu laws that were considered "backward" and needing to be brought into the modern world of individual property rights.

Again, Muslim marriage understood as a contract, protects better in case of divorce than the Hindu marriage taken as a sacrament. *Mehr*, in Muslim personal law, paid by the husband's family to the wife upon marriage, is the exclusive property of the wife and it is hers upon divorce, offering her a protection which Hindu women do not have.

---

[17] Mahmood, "An Indian Civil Code and Islamic Law," in *Religion in Modern India*, ed. Bodley (New Delhi: Manohar, 1981), 73.

It is to be remembered here that the personal laws of each religion is also mingled with the customary law. Thus, to make all the personal laws in the family matters uniform to the satisfaction of all the religious communities is a Herculean task and seems that it could be imposed only by force.

A survey conducted by the Bharatiya Muslim Mahila Andolan found that more than 90 percent of Muslim women in India want a ban on "triple talaq" and polygamy in Muslim personal law.[18] That is, the demand is made within the framework of codifying Muslim Personal law and not in favour of a Uniform Civil Code. The reasons are: there is no clarity on what a Uniform Civil Code would look like, and the demand comes from clearly Hindutva quarters for whom both women and minorities are expendable. They are afraid that the Hindu Law which has inequalities will be imposed upon them under the garb of Uniform Civil Code.

When the Law Commission called for a national survey in 2016, All India Muslim Personal Board (AIMPLB) was not ready to debate on the code and even rejected the law panel's survey, terming it an 'affront' to their personal laws. It had even accused the Law Commission of behaving like an agent of the BJP Government, arguing that the proposed Uniform Civil Code, promised by the BJP in its poll manifesto ahead of the 2014 general elections, is a threat to the country's pluralism and diversity.

---

[18] This survey was released in New Delhi on 12 June 2017. Around 91.7% or 4,320 women of 4710 women surveyed have opposed polygamy, saying that a Muslim man should not be allowed to have another wife during the subsistence of the first marriage. An unprecedented report was also published which carries case studies of 117 Muslim women who have been victims of "triple talaq". The case studies were gathered from Maharashtra, Rajasthan, Madhya Pradesh, Tamil Nadu, Odisha, West Bengal and Karnataka. The reports shows essentially that **92.1% Muslim women want this biased system of verbal triple *talaq* to stop. Cf. Zakia SOMAN & Dr. Noorjehan SAFIA NIAZ,** *Talaq Talaq Talaq – Muslim Women Call for a Ban on an UnIslamic Practice* (Mumbai: BMMA Publications, 2015), 35.

Position of the Catholic Church in India on Uniform Civil Code

By the end of the 20th century, secular law had substituted Canon law of the Church in many aspects of public life. Hence, the Church has to depend on secular organisations, financial models, and juridical structures to accomplish its global mission in all spheres of activities - spiritual, financial and other temporal matters. The Catholic Church has accepted secular law in certain areas in order to be in tune with the emerging trends and necessities of the modern world. The Canon law urges the observance of civil law inasmuch as it is not contrary to the Divine law: "When the law of the Church remits some issue to the civil law, the latter is to be observed with the same effects in canon law, insofar as it is not contrary to divine law, and provided it is not otherwise stipulated in canon law."[19]

Thus, where it applies, the civil laws need to be observed with the same diligence as Canon law. However, all matters cannot be left to civil law entirely, for example when its prescriptions are contrary to Divine law, or if Canon law has made other alternate provisions.

With this provision in Canon law, we can say that the Catholic Church in India welcomes the Uniform Civil Code but with certain conditions and reservations. It supports the Uniform Civil Code on the condition that the legislation must confirm the 'spirit and mandate' of the Constitution. A secular India is what the founding fathers promised when they formulated the Constitution and that has to be guaranteed in the Uniform Civil Code. The rights to religious freedom, guaranteed by the Indian Constitution have also to be ascertained by the Uniform Civil Code and the new legislation should not impose rules, dictated and influenced by the majority religious community.

The Church in India is fully aware that it has to lose some of the privileges and has to make a great sacrifice, if Uniform Civil Code is enacted. The Constitution guarantees the cultural rights and minority rights to the religious communities like Christianity. If the Uniform Civil Code is enacted, then the Christian community would lose its cultural rights and the cultural diversity of the country

[19] Canon 22 of the Code of Canon law of the Catholic Church.

protected by the Constitution would disappear. For example, the Naga minority community in Nagaland fears that the implementation of Uniform Civil Code would bring about clear trouble for the culture and dignity of the Naga people, since their personal and social life are quite distinct from the rest of people in the country.

In fact, the Christian community in India has already made a sacrifice at the time of drafting the Constitution. Rev. Fr. Jerome D' Souza, who was a member of the Constituent Assembly as the representative of the Christian community, was firm in giving up the special seats for the Christians in the legislatures. His reasoning was:

> When these fundamental rights were made justiciable, that is when any violation of them by individuals or governments could be challenged in a court of law, the Christians felt that the safeguard of preserving minority rights by resorting special seats for them in the legislatures on the basis of their population, was no longer necessary, and that in the interests of national integration it was best to merge with and become part of the general electorate… But apart from this question of Christian candidates, the common electorate will bring the Christian citizens into close contact with their fellow citizens and other communities and specially with the members of the legislatures, be they Hindu or Muslim, whom they will have helped to get elected. Christians can certainly ask of them to see to it that justice is done to them and their rights safeguarded. Such co-operation will foster communal harmony and will promote the political homogeneity of the country. It will secure for us a large group of sincere friends who will understand our ideals and in case of need, defend our rights.[20]

Whenever the proposal for Uniform Civil Code comes up, the Christian community always welcomes it, but at the same time, it demands the Government to adopt it with precaution, after a

[20] Rev. *Jerome D'Souza* (Member for Madras), speaking on 25 May 1949, CAD, Vol. VII, 308.

complete study of the situation of the minority communities and in a serene atmosphere. In addition, it seeks an assurance that minority communities who are constantly being attacked in various areas in the country will be safe.[21] It also wants the Government to amend first the old and irrelevant personal laws and to remove injustice and indiscrimination on the basis of religion and custom.[22] For example, according to various religious personal laws, inheritance, marriages, etc., are male dominated. The subtext of all the personal laws, regardless of religion, is that women are not equal to men. They, therefore, discriminate against women in marriage, inheritance and guardianship of children. After seven decades of independence also women are battling for equality. Individual women from different communities have been challenging the constitutional validity of the discriminatory aspects of the personal laws in courts. Their main concern is the threat of forced marriage, murderous attacks in cases of inter-caste, inter-class and inter-religious marriages and property disputes even while they have to deal with issues like adultery, bigamy, polygamy, divorce, custody of child/children, property and incest in their marital homes.

On 7th October 2016, the Law Commission of India made an appeal regarding the comprehensive exercise of the revision of family laws with reference to Article 44 of the Indian Constitution. It had asked for responses from citizens, religious groups, social groups, minority groups, etc., to respond to the appeal. The National Council of Churches in India (NCCI) and the Catholic Bishops Conference of India (CBCI) had a brainstorming session on the Uniform Civil Code on 16th November 2016. They expressed their desire for any serious discussion on the Uniform Civil Code, but did not want to respond to the questionnaire, sent by the Law Commission of India. In their letter to the Chairperson of the Law Commission of India, they emphasized the following points:

---

[21] Akshaya Mukul, "Christian Body Welcomes SC's Civil Code Suggeation", in *The Times of India,* 24th July 2003.

[22] Royen D'Souza, "CBCI Welcomes Supreme Court's Civil Code Suggestion," in *The Times of India*, 24th July 2003.

"1. The Constitution of India recognizes and protects the religious and cultural diversity of India and this should be the guiding principle while taking up any initiative that seeks to reform the personal laws of religious and cultural communities.
2. Though the appeal by the Law Commission states that '...the norms of no one class, group or community, dominate the tone and tenor of family law reforms...' the accompanying questionnaire does not reflect this sentiment.
3. Issues related to the religious practices of a certain community should be discussed with that particular community and cannot be subject of a general questionnaire of the type which demands 'yes and no' answers since a large number of the respondents may not understand the theological, religious and cultural ethos of that particular community.
4. We strongly uphold the need for just laws that recognize the due dignity of and respect for women and we support any move that will ensure this. Such issues should be addressed while amending the personal laws of the respective different communities; we however question the wisdom of imposing a Uniform Civil Code on all communities on the excuse of rendering justice to women."[23]

The CBCI's stand is that the unity of India should be impeccably safeguarded. All discussions on the Uniform Civil Code must be done taking into account the diversity and freedom ensured by the Constitution and without hurting sentiments of various religious groups.

However, the Tamil Nadu Bishops' Council (TNBC) has taken a strong stance against the Uniform Civil Code. In its response to Law Commission, it stated that national integration can be accomplished only in the context of pluralism and Indian Constitutional pluralism also provides for legal pluralism:

---

[23] http://ncci1914.com/2016/11/24/response-ncci-cbci-proposed-uniform-civil-code/

> India is not only pluralistic in religion, but also in culture, language, traditions, etc. Indian democracy is a celebration of pluralism, underscoring the principle of unity in diversity. National integration has been ensured more by celebrating this pluralism and its holistic interconnection between law and religion rather than enforcing blind uniformity. India cannot be compared with any other European, Asian, African or American Nation-States. There is a very little cultural diversity or pluralism in these countries. But India is a sub-continent and a common wealth of communities with different cultures and traditions. We firmly believe that the Constitution strikes a balance between uniformity and diversity.[24]

In fact, there are several provisions in the Constitution which are transitory, such as the number of years of provision for reservation of seats for representation in the Parliament and the Legislative Assemblies (Article 334), the time frame when Hindi will substitute English as the lingua franca for official purposes (Article 343), and the special status to Jammu and Kashmir (Article 370). The withdrawal of special status to Kashmir in the present atmosphere will be an invitation to anarchy; reserved constituencies are absolutely essential for several more years to assure adequate political space for the Scheduled Castes / Scheduled Tribes; Hindi has still very little currency in the Southern States. Thus, enactment of Uniform Civil Code also can be postponed until inequality, discrimination, gender injustice, etc., are removed in the existing personal laws of each religious community.

It is true that the status of women is not good in the personal laws of all the religious communities as there are so many bigotry practices in our society. Women have to countenance to all these impediments. Even though the Hindu law has been codified, certain discriminatory provisions still exist even today: women's right to adoption, women's right to dwelling house, property succession of male and female intestates, widow's property rights, maintenance for

---

[24] TNBC's Response to Law Commission, 2016 (unpublished).

women, etc., are to be ascertained. Similarly there is gender injustice in Muslim personal laws too.

As regards the Christian community, certain provisions of the personal laws are to be amended. For example, the Christian spouses have to wait for a period of two years after their separation and before filing a petition for consented divorce and whereas one year is sufficient for the spouses of other religions. This discrimination can be amended in the Indian divorce amendment Act, 2001.

But, in practice, almost all the communities vehemently oppose any, however small it may be, interference with their personal laws. Hence, whenever the reforms are brought about in personal laws, it should be accepted by the Community as part of their lives and should be ready to give up the meaningless age-old traditions and norms solidified among them through generations. On the part of the Government, it is necessary that what laws it would want to absolve, it would have to justify that those laws violate basic human rights and thus need to be abolished for proper governance. Another practical difficulty we witness is that the Government is reluctant of bringing about the amendments in the age-old personal laws, because of the fear of political antagonism. Sometimes, the Government is reluctant to take action on its own initiative, in order to please the community leaders. Unless the demand for reforms comes within the community, the Government does not come forward to make the amendments. Proper motivation and awareness have to be given to the people of all communities, both by the Government and the community leaders, in order to have laws which assure freedom and equality among the citizens.

As the community matures, its personal law can be amended to become more progressive. We have to take up reforms in each personal law through independent initiatives, and we will have created laws that are uniform over a period of time. For example, the opposition to a private Bill for uniform adoption law was thrown out by loud protests in Parliament some years ago. The apprehension of the Muslim community was that concepts alien to its socio-religious practices will march one after another if change in legislation is permitted in one field. It was a prospect of suffering forced indignity that was the cause for the opposition. The opposition by Christians was no less vociferous. When adoption was made possible through the Juvenile Justice Act, the Bombay and Madras High Courts adopted dynamic interpretations to hold that adoption under the Act will be applicable to Christians as well. Soon enough the Supreme Court ruled that Muslims could also adopt under the Act. All the communities accepted it without any protest.

Thus, the Government can slowly achieve by seamless transition through secular laws. It must remember that the dynamics of social transformation through the instrument of law from diverse civil code to uniformity shall be gradual and cannot happen in a day.

Conclusion

If we look at only the legal side, we may conclude that it is easy to bring out the Uniform Civil Code in India, but if we look at the social, ethical and pragmatic sides, then we can understand the difficulty as well as the non-necessity of bringing out the Uniform Civil Code at present. As long as the personal law for each community is amended to the values of the Constitution and does not infringe on the rights of other communities, we should embrace our differences.

There was an effort from within the Muslim community to change their personal law with the abolition of the triple *talaq* by a Supreme Court appeal. Under normal circumstances, this would have been welcomed by most of the Muslim community with only a few taking the side of the conservative clerics. But the present political situation makes it more difficult, because it was painted as "an act of others imposing their will on Muslims" rather than the internal reform which it was.

The Indian government also recognizes that it is very difficult to adopt a Uniform Civil Code in the present context and it cannot set up a time limit to frame the Uniform Civil Code. Its immediate concern then would be to continue to examine the personal civil laws of all the religious communities and to amend them if any of their dispositions are against the human dignity. It can continue to dialogue with legal experts and leaders of all religious communities to modify their personal civil laws to assert equality, indiscrimination, justice to each citizen of the country and thus paving the way to adopt a Uniform Civil Code when the opportune time comes.

The Church in India has been involving actively in the discussions on the Uniform Civil Code. In a major step towards building consensus around the proposed Uniform Civil Code, Mar Gregorios College of Law from Thiruvananthapuram, patronised by the Catholic Bishops' Conference of India (CBCI) has launched a competition in which law students across the country have been asked to research the subject. They have been asked to produce a draft incorporating the views of different communities by including constitutional values of secularism. It is the mind of the Church that only if a draft is in public domain, then the people can understand what Uniform Civil Code is about and whether it is acceptable or not. Thus the Church listens to its people and discusses with them before raising its voice to the Government and handles this issue more prudently, without giving place to mere sentiments.

Bibliography

AHMAD Zafar. *Personal Laws and Constitution of India: A Study in Contemporary Perspective with Special Reference to Dr. B.R. Ambedkar* (unpublished, 1992).

AMALADOSS, Michael. *Making Harmony: Living in a Pluralist World.* Delhi: IDCR & ISPCK, 2003.

ANANTHAKRISHNA AYYAR, L. K. *Anthropology of the Syrian Christian*. Ernakulam-Cochin: Government Press, 1926.

APPASAMY, A. J. *Law Applicable to Christians*. Madras: The Christian Literature Society for India, 1928.

CHANDRA, Bipen. *Communalism in Modern India*. New Delhi: Vikas Publishing House, 1989.

__________ *Essays on Indian Nationalism*. New Delhi: Har-Anand Publications, 1993.

CHAUDHARI, R. L. *The Concept of Secularism in Indian Constitution*. New Delhi: Concept Publishing House, 1987.

CHAVAN, Sheshrao. *The Makers of Indian Constitution: Myth and Reality*. New Delhi: Oxford University Press, 1992.

DERRET, J. D. M. *Religion, Law and the State in India*. New York: The Free Press, 1968.

DEVADASAN, E. D. *Christian Law in India: Law Applicable to Christians in India*. Madras: DSI Publications, 1974.

DEVADASAN, E. D. *Handbook on Christian Law*. Madras: DSI Publications, 1988.

GAJENDRAGADKAR, P. B. *Secularism and the Constitution of India*. Bombay: Bombay University Press, 1971.

GHOUSE, M. *Secularism, Society and Law in India*. New Delhi: Vikas Publishing House, 1973.

GOPAL, R. *India: Its People and their Secular State*. New Delhi: Criterion Publications, 1987.

http://ncci1914.com/2016/11/24/response-ncci-cbci-proposed-uniform-civil-code/

KASHYAP, Anirban. *Communalism and Constitution*. New Delhi : Lancer Books, 1988.

KEITH, Arthur Berriedale. *A Constitutional History of India (1600-1935)*. Allahabad: Central Book Dept., 1961.

LARSON, Gerald James, ed. *Religion and Personal Law in Secular India: A Call to Judgment*. Bloomington, USA: Indiana University Press, 2001.

LOURDUSAMY, Sahayaraj. *Religious Conversion in a Multi-religious Context – An Outlook on Civil and Canon Laws*. (New Delhi: Media House, 2011).

Mahmood. "An Indian Civil Code and Islamic Law." In *Religion in Modern India*, edited by D. Baird ROBERT. New Delhi: Manohar, 1981.

MASSEY, James. *Minorities and Religious Freedom in a Democracy*. Delhi: Manohar, 2003.

PANTHANMACKEL, George, ed. *The Constitution of India: A Philosophical Review*. New Delhi: Media House, 2003.

PINTO, William E. *Law of Marriage and Matrimonial Reliefs for Christians in India - A Juridical Evaluation of Canon Law and Civil Law*. Bangalore: Theological Publications of India, 2000.

SALDANHA, Jerome, A. *Civil-Ecclesiastical Law Applicable to Christians in British India*. Trichy: The Catholic Truth Society of India, 1935.

THOMAS, A. V. *Christians in Secular India*. New York: Dickinson University Press, 1974.

PART II

PUBLIC THEOLOGICAL EXPLORATIONS

5

Indian Christianity: Public Theological Explorations

Archbishop Prakash Mallavarapu
Archdiocese of Visakhapatnam

"Public Theology" is a theological discipline that opens up unlimited possibilities for exploration for the benefit of the one who is theologizing and for the benefit of the students of theology, and for the benefit of the society at large. God talk is what defines or describes theology. Who can or what can put limits to this God Talk, or faith seeking understanding? Who can qualify or disqualify someone who wants to do this God-talk? God and Human being, and the ever evolving dynamics of life, all the three, have something of a "Mystery" about them. In the words of Gabriel Marcel, the existential philosopher of the last century, mystery can only be explored. All the above three realities have something like in-exhaustible depth or extension as it were but not fully manifested as yet. Public theology, as it is beginning to be recognized, is a branch of theology on its own right. Therefore, I intend to do a little exploration – its nature, relevance, importance and its benefit for today's humanity.

Religions, Spirituality and Morality

Any religion or for that matter every religion and every secular or a-theistic philosophy implicitly keeps proposing a particular "spirituality" and "morality," thereby proposing a belief system, theocentric or otherwise, a way of life, and a way to behave or conduct oneself, grounded on a particular manner of understanding of realities with the intra-relatedness as well as the inter-relatedness between the given realities. It is in and through the spirituality and morality it proposes that a particular religious tradition relates itself to or with the private and public spheres of life of a given society or community. The meaningfulness and relevance of a particular system of beliefs for the individuals and communities, I believe, would depend upon what it has to offer to people in their day-to-day journey of life. At least it is necessary that there is a convincing persuasion on the part of the proponents of the religious teachings as to why they think that what they are putting forward before the individuals and societies need be accepted or adhered. I think, spirituality and morality transcend the dichotomy of private and public spheres of life. How can the private sphere of life be truly possible without being simultaneously involved and affected by what is and what keeps happening in the public arena of life, unless one is all alone in an island or as an island? We should see here that there can only be a distinction and not a separation of the private from the public. If one stubbornly argues for separating the two, he or she will have to live in contradictions, trying to be like an alien in one's own country. Religion is a private affair but this private life lived in the public sphere of life, affected and challenged in myriad ways.

Religion and Public Sphere

Religions should have something to say to the public sphere of life as it is lived and practiced in the real world of public life. If so, the "locus operandi" for the 'public theology' is not "private" vis-a-vis public life. The legitimate "locus operandi" for theology, including public theology, is religion that affects public life and is also affected by what happens in the "public sphere of life." This logic is valid in so far as religion is for the human beings and religious teachings are for, supposedly, giving certain direction and guidance to human beings to think and to act. God, or some may prefer to call it the "Ultimate Reality," is connected to human life with all its complexities, the socio-economic, politico-cultural, religious and ethical, and so many other aspects as well. And theology, faith seeking understanding, has a mission at hand, namely, to do the God-talk so as to help the society /community to make sense of the "public sphere" and facilitate to see the reality in the light of faith; here in our case, it is doing theology in the light of the Christian faith. While the fundamentals of the orthodoxy are affirmed and upheld critiquing the events and trends, persons and powers that affect the "public" sphere of life is the duty of those of us who think that they have a special call to theologize. In truth, there is no area or aspect of life that cannot be or should not be left un-interpreted by the hermeneutic keys provided by a particular religion. But, there is a catch here: The hermeneutic key is not to be used as a tool only for defending the status quo of orthodoxy or orthopraxis but to uphold the human dignity and honour, to defend the basic rights and privileges due to the human person, and above all, to uphold fundamentals of ethics and morality in the public sphere of life. Dehumanizing processes and dynamics and the consequences thereof are and should be the concerns. Otherwise, orthodoxy and orthopraxis can be in a state of being at home with the dehumanizing situations as if one has become deaf, dumb and blind. What can be the truth, if one has nothing to say or do about the issues in the public sphere of life or one does not want to say anything due to fears, apprehensions, and insecurities?

Presence, Absence, and Relevance

Public theological discourse is about theology being present or absent, and being relevant to the existential reality in a practical way or even in a pragmatic way. It is David Tracy, one of the leading proponents of public theology in North-America, who said about three different audiences of public theology: the academy, the church, and public realm – the wider society. Max Stackhouse, another known theologian of North-America, identifies different "publics" of public theology: 'religious' public, the 'academic' public, 'political' public, the 'economic' public and 'legal' public. Perhaps one can go on adding to the list, like 'the subaltern' public, the 'migrant' public, etc.[1] Theology cannot be therefore considered as an exercise or a discipline that is confined to purely religious concerns or issues of a faith community or religion. Public theology is, in the words of William Storrer, "a collaborative exercise in theological reflection on public issues which is prompted by disruptive social experiences that call for thoughtful and faithful response."[2] Therefore, the call that is being placed before us is to see how a Christian or the Church wants to be present to the wider reality of public life and the issues or areas that the 'public' is concerned or is 'grappling with,' and the issues that are affecting life. Engaging in theologizing should not only be limited to or concerned with interpretation, explanation and justification of the tenets of the orthodox faith of the Church or of a given religion but to critique the public life from the standpoint of the Christian Scriptures, Doctrine and Tradition. Theological discourse on public issues is the door way to enter and be present there having something to say. Deliberate silence, either out of fear or out of indifference, would lead to a state of being spectators who have nothing to say! Theology that is alienated or disconnected from the public sphere of the socio-economic, political and cultural, etc., will have to face the danger of losing its relevance and importance. Theology as a systematic exercise should move in the direction of becoming an applied science as well! If not, the "public" will also be disinterested in theology and theologians! So much about the presence or absence and relevance of theology, public theology at that!!

India and Public Theology

In India engaging in public theology is not only desirable but also necessary at this point of time in history. In the first week of January this year I happened to pick up the 'Year-end Special' edition of the magazine, "Outlook," carrying rather an interesting and instigating

---

[1] Gerard Manion, "A Brief Genealogy of Public Theology, or, Doing theology when it Seems Nobody is Listening," https://books.fbk.eu/media/pubblicazioni/allegati/Mannion_121-152.pdf accessed on 09 January 2019.

[2] Ibid., 123.

title on the cover page: "Is God Harmful to Human beings?"[3] There are more than sixteen articles written by well known personalities, modern gurus, university professors, social analysts, journalists, and representatives of religions. There are some interesting interviews with popular religious personalities like the Kerala based 'Mata Amritanandamayi.' God, religion, politics, violence, casteism, peace, etc., were the subjects dealt with, all of them seen as connected with religion. The underlying concern, however, is about issues connected to life in the society and how religion seems to play or was manipulated for a negative role! I begin to see how something of the public theology is present in all those articles. See, for instance, the first few lines of the editorial written by Rajesh Ramachandran:

> Visuals and voices of violence from across the globe have one thing in common—mindless, soulless murder in the name of God and religion. God, we are sadly reminded day after day, cannot be love. In all these videos God means death. Hindutva is trying to achieve what Christianity and Islam had done over the millennia. All the incidents of grave violence—bomb attacks, mass murders, wars or even individuals trying to drive a car into a crowd—are being done in the name of Loving, Caring, Merciful, Father, Mother, Son or Formless God.[4]

This is the scenario and this is the frustration prevalent today in the public arena about what is happening. Christian Theologians and thinkers should read the signs of the times in this way. We should feel impelled and compelled to get involved with the conviction that we have a mission and we have something to offer now to the public sphere of life. And "doing public theology" is one door or one opportunity that is open before us. We do have a theological language, sufficiently sophisticated and intelligible, and we have different methodologies for the theology "ad intra!" So much is also being written, we know. I believe, public theology invites us to think

---

[3] *Outlook*, dt. 22 December 2017.

[4] Rajesh Ramachandran, "The Good God," *Outlook*, December 22, 2017.

another language for the theological discourse for the reality "ad extra" to the Church.

Public Theology and Religious Traditions in India

Public theology has, we know, a "sitz-im-leben" and this holds good for all religious traditions. I see public theology happening in the mission of Dalai Lama, in Christian and Buddhist circles, in theologies of subaltern perspectives, and in liberation theologies of many hues. These prevailing public theologies can keep providing models or perspectives that can help to do further explorations. Indian Christian Public Theology should contribute to the "public sphere of life by addressing the social, economic, cultural, ethnic, and political issues. Orthodoxy will not suffer in this process from any serious disadvantage; instead, it perhaps gives the necessary foundational principles to go into the arena of public life and address the issues that are affecting the society. The message of salvation and liberation in Jesus Christ should keep urging us to read and respond to the signs of the times manifest in the public domain!

Public Theology of "Laudato Si"

I hope everyone who has read through or heard of the earnest appeal of Pope Francis in his Encyclical, "Laudato Si," can find evidence and inspiration of public theology of the Church. Today more than ever, climate change is the main concern before the whole humanity. It is a challenge to all the nations of the world and it is one of the immediate concerns of the "public." As the head of the Catholic Church and drawing resources from the Scriptures, the Holy Bible, and inspiration from the fourteenth century saint, Francis of Assisi, the Pope takes the Christians and people of all religions and cultures across the world through a path of serious reflection, appealing to all the men and women of good will to consider and commit themselves to taking of our planet earth, our common home. "It is my hope," he says, "that this Encyclical Letter, which is now added to the body of the Church's Social teaching, can help us to acknowledge the appeal, immensity and urgency of the challenge we face."[5] He invites the

[5] *Laudato Si*, no. 15.

whole world to see this concern for the earth in a disposition of contemplation: "Rather than a problem to be solved, the world is a joyful mystery to be contemplated with gladness and praise."[6] Pope Francis' concern represents the concern of the Church but a concern of the whole humanity. The discourse in *Laudao Si* puts forward a very convincing message to the Christian Community and to the entire humanity. We all should see yet another initiative of doing "public theology" and this should inspire and lead the theologians and other professionals in the Christian communities to indulge in doing public theology. Let us reflect on 'other similar public concerns' affecting either the whole humanity or some disadvantaged sections in the society. In the evolving and changing scenario in our country at present resorting to public theology will enable us to fulfil the mission we and our Church are called for.

Conclusion

To conclude my brief reflection, let me say this: As members of the Christian Community, what should we be taking care? As theologians what should we be preoccupied with when the reality before us is telling something about taking forward the Mission of Christ? Are the issues that are disturbing and destructive forces affecting the beauty of the "public life" disturb us and prompt us to think and act? To handle every issue and every disorder, it is true, is impossible but that "nothing is possible cannot be true! So, let us explore the possibilities and we are sure to find some!

[6] *Laudato Si*, no. 12.

6

Public Theology: Concept, History and Relevance for India

P. T. Mathew
Professor – Emeritus, Vidyajyoti College for Theology, New Delhi

Introduction

The concept of *public theology* has gained salience in theological reflections in recent times, and it is fast emerging as a promising field within the discipline of theology. A growing volume of literature on it is readily available. The term still has no consensual meaning, and continues to be debated. It was introduced by Martin Marty in his writings in 1974 in the North American context. It gained currency because, as Max Stackhouse puts it, "it seemed to capture one wide and deep, but widely neglected, strand of the classical theological tradition."[1] The immediate precursors of public theology are: the social gospel movement in North America, the civil rights

[1] Scott R. Paeth et al., eds., *Shaping Public Theology: Selections from the Writings of Max L. Stackhouse* (Grand Rapids, Michigan: William B. Eerdmans), 2014, 195.

movement spearheaded by Martin Luther King Jr., the Catholic social encyclicals, and forms of liberation theology. A feature that characterizes public theology is that it is not confined to specific confessional identities, and is ecumenical in approach. Therefore, it is necessary to situate public theology within the long theological tradition of the Church through centuries. The aim of this paper is to trace the major milestones in its evolution of the idea, starting with the initial proclamation of Christian faith. Public theology is particularly relevant to relatively stable democratic societies since it proposes a constructive agenda. The pluralistic and democratic society which we have in India seems to offer a fertile ground to explore the possibilities of public theology.

Apologetics: Early Christian Attempts to Step Out

A salient meaning of public theology can be traced back to the historical context of the emergence of Christian theology through apologetics. The dictionary meaning of apologetics is 'reasoned defence'. An apologist is a person who defends something by argument. The term has emerged in the Christian tradition, and so apologetics generally refers to the defence by argument of Christian belief and the Christian way of life against critics and opponents. Christian writers of the second and third centuries who made a reasoned defence of their faith before people outside the Church are generally called 'apologists'. Well-known among them are Aristides, Justin Martyr, Athenagoras, Tatian, Theophilus and Tertullian. They confronted the Jewish opposition, on the one hand, and the Gentile rulers and their philosophies, on the other. They refuted false allegations against them using the vocabulary and philosophical categories of the opponents themselves. The aim was to prove the intelligibility and superiority of the Christian faith. The language of the apologists was no more that of religious proclamation but one of appeal to a wider public.

Walter Kasper writes succinctly about the contributions of the first Christian apologists, as:

> Justin and Clement of Alexandria defended against Jews and Pagans the continuity and the pedagogical purpose of

the salvific action of God, while Irenaeus upheld the unity of creation and covenant against Gnosis. Origen used the doctrine of the Logos to depict history as a unified whole. Eusebius and Orosius had a theology of the empire based on the *Pax Romana*, while Augustine stressed the ambivalence of political power in his *De Civitate Dei*.[2]

The first apology of Justin Martyr is a beautiful illustration of the passionate argumentation of the apologists.[3] He writes to the Emperor, his sons, and 'to the sacred Senate, with the whole People of the Romans': "I, Justin, the son of Priscus and grandson of Bacchius, natives of Flavia Neapolis in Palestine, present this address and petition in behalf of those of all nations who are unjustly hated and wantonly abused, myself being one of them."[4] He refutes the allegation that Christians profess atheism and practise immorality, and appeals to Greek philosophers like Socrates and Plato in support of his defence. He even summarizes the teachings of the Bible and of Christ, and presents the cross as the greatest symbol. "Are these not reasonable and true?" -he asks in conclusion.

What is significant in these early Christian apologists is that they dared to step out of the internal Church domain and made efforts to engage the 'Gentile' world outside in order to defend the Christian doctrine. They used philosophical categories drawn from Platonic ideas. Scholars point out that these apologists helped theology to free itself from the framework of early Biblicism. Merely quoting from the Bible does not generate theology; Scripture has to be brought to interact with the wider world and its questions and challenges. It was in such a process that foundational Christian doctrines like the doctrine of the Triune God evolved. The story of creation took

---

[2] Walter Kasper, "Theology of History", in *Sacramentum Mundi*, Vol. III, (Karl Rahner, ed., London: Burns and Oates, 1969), 44.

[3] Justin Martyr (c.100-c165) was a philosopher who became a Christian in c.130, and taught Christianity first in Ephesus and later in Rome. His first apology (c.155) was addressed to the Emperor Antonius Pius, and his sons, and the second apology (c.161) was addressed to the Senate. Justin and some disciples were denounced for their Christian faith and beheaded in c. 165).

[4] http://www.newadvent.org/fathers/0126.htm, accessed on 22.07.2017

the form of cosmology; Logos from Platonism became a handy tool in shaping a Christology. In short, the apologists provided the basic images and concepts for future theologians to build on.

Traditionally the rational basis of Christian apologetics is located in 1Pet 3:15: "Always be ready to make your defence to anyone who demands from you an account of the hope that is in you; yet do it with gentleness and reverence." Central to the discussion is the phrase "make a defence" (*apologia* which is translated as apologetics). Apologetics is an activity that makes a rational defence of the Christian faith. Historically, apologetics gave importance to rational arguments thus making faith appear mainly as an intellectual activity. The 'hope' aspect that Peter speaks of often got sidelined, especially since the period of persecution came to an end; but the term 'apologetics' continued to be used in theological discourse, though with modified meanings.

Every period of Christian history has had an apologetic stream active in contextual forms. The high points of apologetic theology are *Contra Celsum* (against Celsus) of Origen in the third century, and *Summa Contra Gentiles* of Thomas Aquinas in the thirteenth century. In the *Summa Contra Gentiles,* Aquinas confronted Averroism offering a comprehensive exposition of Christian doctrines using Aristotelian categories. The Reformation and the consequent counter-reformation were centred on divergent approaches to the faith tradition by Christian groups; the result was *polemic apologetics* which was mostly church apologetics. Argument from authority gained ground. Theology was kept away from the wider world outside. In the 17th century, theology had to face religious scepticism and a rationalist challenge of the truth of the Christian faith. The emerging scientific worldview forced theology to stay focussed on showing the scientific credibility of the Christian faith, and that continued till the 20th century. The Cartesian philosophy and its scientific method of exploring truth facilitated the emergence of a 'rationalist apologetics'. Defence of the Scripture, its supernatural character and historical reliability became major concerns. Here too the concerns and struggles of the world outside did not figure prominently.[5]

---

[5] For an overview of the history of apologetics, see "A brief history of apologetics", Ch 3 in *Faith Has its Reasons*, by Kenneth Boa and Robert Bowman,

The emergence of *Political Theology* in the 1960s, spearheaded by theologians like Jürgen Moltmann and Johann Baptist Metz, enabled theology again to interact with the socio-political reality of human existence in a new light.[6] The post-World War II context of Germany became ideal ground to critically live the eschatological message of Christianity in present-day society. Its identity as *theology with its face towards the world* had its influence on the Latin American Liberation Theology. A discernible change in Catholic theology occurred with the Second Vatican Council, 1962-65. The Council underscored the *human in the world* since human persons exist in the temporal order confronting it and being confronted by it.[7] The novelty of its approach to atheism is illustrative of the new approach to engage the world in a spirit of dialogue.[8] However, gradually, the term 'apologetics' seems to have become unpopular mainly due to the pejorative connotations it carried. Besides, the advent of postmodernism has made apologetics irrelevant, some argue. Both rationalist apologetics as well as rationalist critics of religion assume an ideal of rational knowledge, which is being shaken by postmodernism. Today the concerns of apologetic theology have come to be treated under the umbrella term 'fundamental theology'. No theology can remain merely church-centred since the faith of individuals gets constantly challenged by a secular and pluralistic milieu demanding to show the intelligibility and credibility of the Christian doctrine. Theological account of the faith is increasingly assuming a dialogic form.[9] This openness to dialogue is taking the

---

2009. https://bible.org/series/faith-has-its-reasons. accessed 23.07.2017.

[6] See Jürgen Moltmann, *The Crucified God: The Cross as the Foundation and Criticism of Christian Theology* (London: SCM, 1973), and Johann Baptist Metz, *Faith in History and Society: Toward a Practical Fundamental Theology* (Crossroad Publ. Co., 2007 (1977).

[7] This is most evident in Vatican II, *Gaudium et Spes*, the Pastoral Constitution on Church in the Modern World.

[8] See, for example, Vatican II, *Gaudium et Spes*, nos. 19-21.

[9] The title of a recent article is insightful; it reads: "From Apologia to Dialogic Theologizing", by Victor Ezigbo, in *Journal of Ecumenical Studies* Vol. 50, No 3 (January 1, 2015).

discipline of theology to new realms, and 'public theology' is one logical outcome of that process.

Emergence of Public Theology

The notion of *public theology*, as already noted, is of recent origin, and lacks a homogeneous understanding. Public theology (or public theologies, as some prefer to say) is not another branch of theology to appear on the theological horizon; rather it is an attempt to awaken a dormant dimension of theology that has always been there. Theology for long remained largely insulated from public life and its struggles. The near absence of theology and theologians from public debates on issues of importance is a matter of concern. Theology needs to wake up from this slumber. The emerging field of public theology indicates that theology is slowly waking up from slumber and assuming the public role it is destined to play. Though public theology became popular only in the 1970s, the term was present earlier in the works of Jürgen Moltmann and others. It gained currency through the writings of men like Martin E Marty, David Tracy, Duncan Forrester, Ronald Thiemann, Max L. Stackhouse, Sebastian Kim, and others; 'the term is as much a symbol as a concept' - Stackhouse writes. Public theology is not a finished product, but a theological perspective in the making. It is a new sensibility and a responsibility theology needs to grow in awareness of.

Two tendencies may be observed in the evolution of any discipline. One would insist on keeping the discipline tightly guarded and confined to its practitioners free from contamination by the lay public or issues of everyday life. It busies itself with categories and terminologies specific to it, offering its findings to an unquestioning consumer public. The other would take the discipline to the open forum for interaction with other disciplines and persuasions; it would stay in touch with the burning issues and live concerns of the day, participating in public debates, contributing its mite, and getting challenged in return. True, the second tendency can cause discomfort and at times threaten the very existence of the discipline, yet this step is inevitable for any discipline to grow and stay relevant. Theology is not immune to the above dynamics. The nature of issues selected, and the manner of engagement in public discussions and debates will determine the quality of any discipline.

Authors make a careful distinction between *theology of public life* and *public theology*. The former focuses on Christian believers' engagement in contemporary public life from the perspective of Christian faith. It motivates the faithful to engage in the affairs of the world; it is a discourse within the Church about the world. Many Social Encyclicals and the new opening made by Vatican II are good examples of it. *Public theology*, on the other hand, involves interaction and encounter between faith and the world. It enters into dialogue with the public sphere and its concerns. It engages in public discourse using a language that is comprehensible to those from other disciplines and faith traditions.[10] It is important to note this necessary shift in our standpoint.

Clarifying the meaning of 'public'

As public theology is gradually unfolding in the Indian context too, we need to clarify what this *public* means for theology. Recent global developments of thought systems have provided the term with a rich variety of meanings in diverse contexts. Public square, public sphere, public space – these have become part of contemporary discourses. *Public space* is a notion being used by a wide range of disciplines - from architecture to information technology. The social sciences have begun to use it to indicate a dimension of social space in understanding the structure and dynamics of human societies. The social categories of public and private are related to the notion of social space, and have a long history in social theory. The ancient Greeks made the distinction between the public world of politics and the private world of family and economic relations. Modern thinkers like Hannah Arendt and Jürgen Habermas helped in exploring the concept in depth, and various models of it are being applied

[10] See Charles Mathewes, *A Theology of Public Life* (Cambridge: Cambridge Univ. Press, 2007). See also Felix Wilfred, "Asian Public Theology" in *Harvesting from the Asian Soil: Towards an Asian Theology*, ed. Vimal Tirimanna (Bangalore: Asian Trading Corporation, 2011), 139.

worldwide in cultural studies, subaltern studies, feminist studies, and Dalit studies.[11]

Hannah Arendt presents public space in relation to the practice of citizenship, and hence it becomes basically a political concept. Public space is nothing but public political space which enables individuals to fashion a world for free political discourse and action. Here citizens meet one another, exchange their opinions and debate their differences, and search for collective solution to their problems. Arendt dwells much on the notion of *polis* in the ancient Greece where one who was not permitted to enter the public space was considered a slave or barbarian. She stresses the connection between political action, i.e., active engagement in public space, and the exercise of effective political agency which makes them 'participants in government'. The concern for public space is the concern for justice and participation, and involves struggle against all forms of marginalization and discrimination. The struggle becomes a laboratory to learn the art of networking with diverse people and groups instead of choosing to act on one's own. It calls for commitment to plurality that respects the identity and resourcefulness of every person and every social segment.

The typology of the *three publics of theology* that David Tracy, American theologian, presents is insightful. Who does theology address is the critical question here. Tracy observes that theological discourse primarily addresses any of the three distinct but related social realities, which he calls 'publics': the *wider society*, the *academy*, and the *church*.[12] He is discussing it in a Euro-American context; still the frame can be useful for critically situating theological pursuit in India. Presently much theological energy is spent on intra-ecclesial issues, and the academic public is limited mostly to the less threatening group of seminary professors. Let us take a look at the journals/periodicals displayed in any Christian library. The number of theological publications emerging from India is not insignificant.

---

[11] See Hannah Arendt, *The Human Condition* (Chicago: University of Chicago Press, 1998 (1958); J. Habermas, *The Structural Transformation of the Public Sphere* (Cambridge: MIIT Press, 1989).

[12] See David Tracy, *The Analogical Imagination – Christian Theology and the Culture of Pluralism* (New York: The Crossroad Publishing Co., 1991), chapter 1.

The number of articles our theologians produce also is massive. But who do they address? What is the impact? K.C. Abraham makes a perceptive observation. "Although our theologians write on public issues, their writings seldom reach an audience outside the boundary of the Churches. It has a public character, but 'consumers' are largely Church people – at best students in the theological colleges. How to break this isolation?"[13] Public theology may indicate the direction for an answer.

Public debates - whether on the open stage or in the print/visual media or other civil society forums - have a role in shaping public opinion and public policy. It is necessary to equip theology, and theologians, to take up this role with competence and with confidence. *Capital punishment* is a hotly debated issue in contemporary India, both in the academy and in the mass media. Its advocates as well as its adversaries put forward seemingly strong arguments that leave the less informed masses confused. Christian theological voice remains conspicuous by its absence in these debates. Is not Christian theology rich in its vision of human life and its dignity? It has the wisdom of centuries of systematic reflection on matters of life and death, and on the culture of death in its various avatars – murders, wars, terrorism, and judicial killings. It is unfortunate that this wisdom fails to enrich public discourse and state policy. Similar is the case with the ongoing debate on development in our country. Are we to keep the Christian theories of authentic development as our best kept secret?

Theology's Public Character and Mission

The biggest hurdle public theology faces is the *mantra* that religion is a very personal and private matter. The mantra is repeated by both conservative religionists and rationalist secularists, though with different goals in mind. Both argue for keeping religion out of politics relying on a faulty interpretation of the same Bible text, "give back to Caesar what belongs to Caesar - and to God what belongs to God" (Mk.12:17). Following the same logic theology gets confined

---

[13] K. C. Abraham, "Asian Public Theology: Its Social Location", in *Theology to Go Public*, ed. by Felix Wilfred (Delhi: ISPCK, 2013), 17.

to the private realm with no role in public secular life of a society. The logic of this argument needs closer scrutiny.

Scholars indicate different factors that contributed to the above argument of privatised religion and theology, the ideology of secularism being the foremost. The ideology of secularism was the logical child of the European Enlightenment. *Laicite*, the French articulation of it, and *the wall of separation between church and state* as envisioned in the American Constitution are key points of reference. Secularism, as a rational and scientific worldview, constructs a public sphere where religion and theology have no place. This view implies that religion is incompatible with the modern scientific worldview, and with secularism, its by-product. The logical conclusion is that religion and matters religious must be abolished from the public sphere. The secularisation thesis of modern Sociology holds that religious beliefs, practices and institutions tend to lose social significance as societies get modernised. Religion can survive only as a private set of beliefs or feelings, it argues.[14] Secularism in India, however, is more accommodative of religion as it is built on the principles of equal respect for all religions and non-discrimination based on religion while maintaining the separation of the religious and the secular. Yet the Western, rational meaning of secularism has dominated India's public consciousness. Secularist intellectuals in India argue for relegating and confining religion to the private sphere, on the assumption that religion is, and continues to be, at the root of much conflict and bloodshed in the country. Such a context naturally inhibits theologians from entering the 'secular' public space. This inhibition needs to be overcome.

A careful inquiry would show that religion and theology can never be purely private or personal. Scholars help us to unearth the meaning of the scriptural injunction on giving to Caesar and giving to God.[15] The verse is not meant to legitimise the dualistic separation of religion and politics as Jesus is deeply rooted in the prophetic tradition of Israel which disapproved such separation. Yet it affirms that loyalty to God is a different and higher category than loyalty to

---

[14] See Peter Berger, *The Sacred Canopy* (New York: Doubleday, 1967), ch. 5.

[15] See Mk.12:17; cf. Mt.22:21 and Lk 20:24.

Caesar. "The pronouncement is not a nuanced treatise on church-state relations or on the civil duties of the Christian. Rather, it is an aphorism that teases the mind to remember that one's duty to God exceeds all other duties."[16] J. D. G. Dunn writes more emphatically:

> Jesus' reply makes it clear that in his view the antithesis was false: political and divine authority need not necessarily conflict. The payment of tax is a legitimate obligation within the network of human relationships. As such it did not conflict with the higher and all-embracing authority of God.... To pose Caesar and God as mutually exclusive authorities is to make all human relationships antithetical to divine authority.... Jesus did not sanction such an either-or.[17]

De-privatization of the Christian message was on the agenda of *political theology* which emerged in the 1960s in Europe. It argued that the Good News was addressed not only to individuals but to society as a whole. It challenged a purely private understanding of sin and conversion, and tried to recover their social dimension, thus paving the way for the notion of 'structural sin' that was further refined by Latin American liberation theology.[18] Yet public theology cannot be equated with political theology. Stackhouse, in an attempt to distinguish both these, writes that 'public theology tends to adopt a social theory of politics', while 'political theology inclines to have a political view of society.'[19] Public theology, in short, is not a finished product, but a theological process that is in the making.

---

[16] *The New Interpreters Bible*, Vol. IX, (Nashville: Abingdon Press, 1995), 384-87.

[17] J.D.G. Dunn, "Caesar", in *The New International Dictionary of New Testament Theology*, Vol. I, ed. Colin Brown (Michigan: Regency Reference Library, 1971), 270.

[18] Gregory Baum, "Structures of Sin", in *The Logic of Solidarity*, ed. Gregory Baum and Robert Ellsberg (New York: Orbis, 1989), 110 ff.

[19] In Scott R. Paeth et al., eds., *Shaping Public Theology: Selections from the Writings of Max L. Stackhouse*, (Grand Rapids, Michigan: William B. Eerdmans), 2014, 198.

Public Theology in the Indian Context: Some Pointers

The Indian context that is relatively democratic and pluralist in character provides a unique opportunity for reflecting on the meaning and potential of public theology. Its democratic institutions are sufficiently strong to provide avenues of participation and dissent. The rich diversity of cultures, religions and worldviews is a rare arena for multiple encounters that can nourish not only theology but also the common mission. However, since theology is still caught up with the academy and the church community, much effort is needed to prepare the ground for engaging in public theology. Given below are some pointers:

Refocusing the Audience that Theology Addresses

Theology needs to reorient itself in terms of its *public* – less of church and academy, and more of society, if we use Tracy's framework. Presently much theological energy is spent on intra-ecclesial issues, and the academic public is confined to some theological centres. Theological writings too follow a pattern that rarely enters the public space. The nature of issues selected, and the manner of discussion and debate on them determine the quality of any theology in terms of its participation in the public space. Recent efforts to situate theological training and research within the framework of secular universities are certainly in the right direction. Theology gets an opportunity to interact with other disciplines, to be challenged by them and to challenge them in return. But that too is not adequate for public theology as the university itself is only a wider academy.

Refocusing the audience implies a broadening of the space where theology operates. Here I refer to the three distinct dimensions of space that Hannah Arendt speaks of, viz., the private, the public and the social.[20] Christian thinking in general reveals a tendency to restrict its concern to the private and the social, ignoring the public/political. Biblical metaphors often receive a personal or social interpretation thus disfiguring the very metaphor, while a public/political way of looking at them may shift the meaning to the public space. Jesus lived in an age when leprosy remained a dreaded disease,

[20] See Hannah Arendt, *The Human Condition*, 28.

and such patients were cast out on the margins of society. Jesus touches and heals such a person and asks him to go and show himself to the priest for certification (Lk.17:14). Jesus is directing him to present his self in the public space; it is not merely an act of healing, but putting an end to his societal exclusion. Similar is the case with the woman caught in adultery and was brought to Jesus, silenced and helpless. Jesus in turn silences the accusers, allows the woman to speak up, and helps her regain her personhood (Jn.8:10-11). It is easy to get into the trap of reducing the public/political to the personal and the religious, and any public theology has to be wary of this trap.[21]

Setting New Goals: Oriented to Public Policy

We have already noticed that public theology has special significance in democratic societies in that it utilizes the opportunity to contribute to the building up of the wider polity. To succeed in that it has to move over to *apologetics ad extra,* as Johannes-Baptist Metz distinguishes it from *apologetics ad intra.*[22] The near absence of theological contributions in the public sphere of open debates and discussion forums is a painful reality. Often we witness a Christian approach that is 'reactionary', protesting or opposing programmes and policies based on deductive logic. In a parliamentary form of democracy, policies and legislative measures are finalized after debates and discussions on various platforms. Ignorance of the political processes and intervention strategies keeps theologians and church personnel out of the public sphere. Policies are always made

[21] The Kairos Document that took shape in the South African context in mid 1980s speaks of three theologies: state theology, Church theology and prophetic theology. The goal of state theology is to justify the status quo, thus often blessing a system of injustice. Church theology is characterized by a refusal to engage deeply in the signs of the times and a neutrality in conflict situations. It upholds a spirituality that is devoid of social engagement. Prophetic theology discerns the signs of the present time and foresees the future, and brings a message of hope to a suffering people. See *Kairos Document*, nos 2-4.

[22] Johannes-Baptist Metz makes a valid distinction between *apologetics ad extra* and *apologetics ad intra*, depending on whether the audience it addresses is within or outside the Church. See his "Apologetics in General", in *Sacramentum Mundi*, Vol I, Karl Rahner, ed. (London: Burns and Oates, 1968), 68.

in response to situations that arise at a particular time and place, and depend largely on public opinion. In order to influence public policy it is necessary to influence public opinion, which today is being shaped largely by the print and visual media, and more recently the social media. In a democratic society no theology can stay away from its responsibility to contribute to the formulation of public policies.

The litmus test of public theology is in its ability to influence public policy in line with its theological vision of the human society and of planet earth. It is possible only when it engages in dialogue with academicians and activists, Christians and other religionists, politicians and atheists. It presupposes some competence in dialoguing with other disciplines in a language that they understand. It recognizes the all-encompassing role of politics in coordinating and regulating other segments including religion in the creation of a just social order, and so accepts it as a key dialogue partner. The resources of theology and biblical studies are thus made available to the public debates in an attempt to generate positive energy.

The annual seminars and publications of the Indian Theological Association (ITA) offers hope since these indicate a deep awareness of the public sphere and its concerns in the choice of topics for its annual seminars.[23] But the impact of the ITA statements, if at all, is still limited to the academy, the small group of theologians and theology students, and rarely reaches policy makers. Changing theology's mind-set and equipping its practitioners for public engagement remains a challenging task ahead. Perhaps the creation of public opinion among theologians and church personnel is the first step. To expect an insignificant group of theologians to influence the public policies of a vast nation may appear foolhardy. But chapter 13 of the book of Daniel provides a new paradigm. A young lad named Daniel shouted out with a loud voice, "I want no part in shedding this woman's blood!" (Dan 13:46). That cry was powerful enough to bring the judges back to the court and reverse the judgement of the elders based on false evidence against Susanna. "Thus innocent

[23] Jacob Parapally has compiled the annual statements of the ITA; see *Theologizing in the Indian Context: Statements of the Indian Theological Association*, ed. by Jacob Parappally (Bengaluru: Asian Trading Corporation, 2017).

blood was spared that day" (Dan 13:62). A new approach to the delivery of justice, indeed!

Exploring Appropriate Methods

What distinguishes public theology is the fact that it is indispensably dialogical. The dialogic approach accepts other traditions and knowledge systems as dialogue partners in a joint search for theological insights. Admitting that all theologies are fragmentary and provisional, and that the span of God's action in the world is beyond the grasp of any one's reading, public theology welcomes other readings as enriching; openness to mutual learning and mutual critiquing remains crucial to this dialogic model.[24] Public theology can never be done in isolation. It has to engage in an ongoing conversation with disciplines, religions, ideologies and life issues. Academic disciplines and religious traditions become dialogue partners in a conscious attempt to tap the positive energy to nourish public life and to ensure the well-being of humanity, nay, the whole planet earth. To engage in such a theology is obviously a risky affair as theology gets exposed; whether theology is prepared to take this risk is a question we need to ask.

Clarifying the method and the approach in doing public theology, Butelli writes:

> Public theology then is much more about conceiving new methodologies, tasks, ways, modes, styles, different places in the public sphere, and different "publics" to relate to.... public theology can contribute to our theological reflection specifically on this point - not by creating a new theological or biblical hermeneutic, nor suggesting new systematic contents to the theological debate, but by finding ways through which liberation theology could be done in a different society with quite different

[24] See Victor Ezigbo, "Imagining Mutual Christian Theological Identity: From Apologia to Dialogic Theology", published in *Journal of Ecumenical Studies*, Vol. 50, no 3 (January 1, 2015), 455-57.

> challenges.... It is the praxis that must define what the challenges are that theology must face.[25]

Theology going public to the secular world of conflicting worldviews would demand of it a new theological language and grammar that can resonate with the secular world and its concerns. Traditional theological vocabulary, language and idiom may have to be revamped, and it must begin with the very framework of theological training and its methodology. It demands new competencies in theologians and trainers. More imaginative steps are required to make such a dream a reality.

Another feature of the method of public theology is that it involves social learning, not merely social teaching. Church documents during the past half a century (since Vatican II in the case of the Catholic tradition) contain valuable insights on the relationship between faith and the world around, though often these remain unexplored. *Deus Caritas Est,* the 2005 encyclical of pope Benedict XVI, for example, discusses 'the just ordering of society and the State' and affirms the role of the Church to "form consciences in political life and to stimulate greater insight into the authentic requirements of justice as well as greater readiness to act accordingly."[26] These are certainly valuable principles from the social teaching of the Church. What is missing is a spirit of dialogical encounter. Public theology envisages a church that engages others in the public sphere, and is willing to confront and be confronted. Social teaching and social learning must go hand in hand. Otherwise theology will remain 'theology of public life' rather than 'public theology'.

Content of Public Theology is Ever Evolving

Traditionally theology remained preoccupied with its content, with the correctness of its doctrine. Aberrations were frowned upon, if not condemned. The hermeneutical turn shifted the focus to the method and its significance. Public theology builds on this foundation, and

---

[25] Filipe Gustavo Koch Butelli, "Public Theology as Theology on Kairos: The South African Kairos Document as a Model of Public Theology", in *Journal of Theology for Southern Africa 143* (July 2012), 102.

[26] *Deus Caritas Est,* no. 28.

any talk of content must be subject to this approach. Felix Wilfred, while discussing the Asian context, mentions four crucial areas as subject matter of Asian Public Theology: (i) defence of freedom against state despotism of various kinds and grades, (ii) defence of the poor from the tyranny of the market, (iii) creation of harmonious and non-exclusive communities, and (iv) protecting the environment.[27] These areas are to be approached necessarily from inter-religious and subaltern perspectives which remain the distinguishing marks of Indian public space. These may be valid at the present moment of our history, but new themes may emerge tomorrow. Public theology has to stay alert to the changing concerns of every age.

In the Indian context public theology has to take the margins seriously. How do people on the margins negotiate their faith life in the midst of various struggles for survival, for dignity and against discrimination? Concerns of caste-victims, indigenous people, fisher people and women have to find a prominent place in theology if it goes public. Confrontation of conflicting ideologies and worldviews takes place sharply on the margins, and hence it will ever remain a creative site of public theology. The marginalized people find religion not merely a refuge in times of distress, as noted by Marx, but also as an instrument in their engagement in the public space. Margins are relatively free from the rigid control of structures and dogmas to explore new avenues of public theology. Struggles and issues are perceived not in religious or caste terms but as basic human issues, and that offers space for wider encounter.

Better Interface with the Field of Communication

During a recent visit to an international book exhibition I was stunned by the total absence of any stall of Christian /theological literature. That too in a city with a good Christian presence and many Christian publishing houses! The exhibition ground hosted daily sessions of scholarly discussion, literary debates, and book releases. "Where is the Christian voice?" I couldn't help asking. Free distribution of Bible and Christian literature is no substitute for active participation in public forums and active engagement in dynamic communication.

[27] See Felix Wilfred, *Asian Public Theology – Critical Concerns in Challenging Times* (New Delhi: ISPCK, 2010).

The term 'preacher' for priests and pastors is a misnomer. Communication technology has moved far beyond mere preaching. Priests in general remain conditioned by a culture of verbal communication, whether from the pulpit or at the retreat centre, with an assured captive audience. Theologians are at best good teachers and occasionally writers. The dialogical mode of communication and engagement with multiple disciplines and viewpoints still remain an alien territory. Familiarity with the dynamic character of contemporary modes of communication is a must to engage in public theology. 'Theology of communication' is slowly gaining ground in recent times. The world of the print and visual media and of the social media involves aggressive encounter of ideas and viewpoints. The outcome is a more enlightened understanding of human situations and problems which no discipline can deal with in isolation. Church personnel and theologians in particular, need to be better equipped with tools of communication with adequate theoretical knowledge. Not only our mind-set but also our theology syllabus needs to be reset accordingly.

Conclusion

Public theology is not just another fashionable jargon in the theological enterprise, but is a new realization of the nature and mission of theology in the changing times. It is a wake-up call to all who are engaged in theology, and it is still in the making. What is discussed in this paper is only a broad framework along with some pointers. On the last page of his autography Gandhiji wrote: "To see the universal and all-pervading Spirit of Truth face to face one must be able to love the meanest of creation as oneself. And a man who aspires after that cannot afford to keep out of any field of life. That is why my devotion to Truth has drawn me into the field of politics; and I can say without the slightest hesitation and yet in all humility, that those who say that religion has nothing to do with politics do not know what religion means."[28] The spirit of what Gandhi said about religion applies equally to theology. Do we not find in Gandhi one model of public theology at work?

---

[28] M.K Gandhi, *An Autobiography, or The Story of My Experiments with Truth* (Ahmedabad: Navjivan, 1927), 283

Bibliography

Abraham, K. C. "Asian Public Theology: Its Social Location." In *Theology to Go Public*, edited by Felix Wilfred, 15-27. Delhi: ISPCK, 2013.

Arendt, Hannah. *The Human Condition*. Chicago: University of Chicago Press, 1998 (1958).

Baum, Gregory. "Structures of Sin," In *The Logic of Solidarity*, edited by Gregory Baum and Robert Ellsberg, 110ff. New York: Orbis, 1989.

Benedict XVI, Pope. *Deus Caritas Est*. Encyclical, Vatican: 2005.

Berger, Peter. *The Sacred Canopy*. New York: Doubleday, 1967.

Boa, Kenneth and Robert Bowman. "A brief history of apologetics." In *Faith Has its Reasons*. 2009. https://bible.org/series/faith-has-its-reasons, accessed 23.07.2017.

Butelli, Filipe Gustavo Koch. "Public Theology as Theology on Kairos: The South African Kairos Document as a Model of Public Theology." In *Journal of Theology for Southern Africa 143,* 90-106. (July 2012).

Ezigbo, Victor. "Imagining Mutual Christian Theological Identity: From Apologia to Dialogic Theology." In *Journal of Ecumenical Studies*, 452-472. Vol. 50, no 3 (January 1, 2015).

Flannery, Austin, ed. *Vatican Council II, The Conciliar and Post-Conciliar Documents*. Bombay: St Paul's, 1995.

Gandhi, M.K. *An Autobiography, or The Story of My Experiments with Truth*. Ahmedabad: Navjivan, 1927.

Habermas, J. *The Structural Transformation of the Public Sphere*. Cambridge: MIIT Press, 1989.

Justin Martyr – *First Apology*, http://www.newadvent.org/fathers/0126.htm, accessed 22.07.2017

Kairos Document. Challenge to the church A Theological Comment on the Political Crisis in South Africa.https://kairossouthernafrica.wordpress.com/2011/05/08/the-south-africa-kairos-document-1985/accessed 24.07.2017.

Kasper, Walter. "Theology of History." In *Sacramentum Mundi*, Vol. III, edited by Karl Rahner. London: Burns and Oates, 1969.

Mathewes, Charles. *A Theology of Public Life*. Cambridge: Cambridge Univ. Press, 2007.

Metz, Johann Baptist. *Faith in History and Society: Toward a Practical Fundamental Theology*. Crossroad Publ. Co., 2007 (1977).

Metz, Johannes-Baptist. "Apologetics in General." In *Sacramentum Mundi*, Vol. I, edited by Karl Rahner. London: Burns and Oates, 1968.

Moltmann, Jürgen. *The Crucified God: The Cross as the Foundation and Criticism of Christian Theology*. London: SCM, 1973.

Paeth, Scott R. et al., eds. *Shaping Public Theology: Selections from the Writings of Max L. Stackhouse.* Grand Rapids, Michigan: William B. Eerdmans, 2014.

Parapally, Jacob, ed. *Theologizing in the Indian Context: Statements of the Indian Theological Association*. Bengaluru: Asian Trading Corporation, 2017.

Tirimanna, Vimal, ed. *Harvesting from the Asian Soil: Towards an Asian Theology*. Bangalore: Asian Trading Corporation, 2011.

Tracy, David. *The Analogical Imagination – Christian Theology and the Culture of Pluralism*. New York: The Crossroad Publishing Co., 1991.

Wilfred, Felix. *Asian Public Theology – Critical Concerns in Challenging Times*. New Delhi: ISPCK, 2010.

7

Christianity and Democracy in India

Moses Manohar
Director, ICSA, Chennai

Politics, the Forbidden Fruit!

India, as a Constitutional Nation was born on 26th January, 1950. On that day, "India that is Bharat" became a 'Union of States' (Art.1 of the Constitution). The Preamble of the Constitution makes a loud promise of justice, liberty and equality for all, and fraternity among all the citizens. But we increasingly see the dichotomy between the Constitution which stands on Equality and Rule of Law and the culture which believes in inequality by birth, social hierarchy and ritual ranking based on purity and pollution. The Constitution recognizes Indians as citizens, and guarantees Fundamental Rights to them. Yet we see a multitude of Indians who have no guarantee for their life and dignity. Oppressions based on caste, gender and poverty could not be tackled satisfactorily by the Indian democracy. At times, we wonder whether India is a 'Union of States' or still a 'Union of castes'. Yet, we are not without hope! Our democracy can deliver, if citizens begin to play their role as the 'guardians' of democracy.

The main reason for the prevailing injustice and disparity is that majority of Indians do not know what is politics. There is an ignorance which promotes fear or cynicism about politics. The reason is that Indians were denied the right to politics for thousands of years. The right to politics includes the right to learn, know, discuss, debate, articulate, speak, express, decide, choose, contest and hold public office. Those rights were reserved only for Brahmin males and to some extent to Kshatriya men. Others were denied this right,[1] and so the Indian mind was not trained in political thinking.

Invention of the Greek State

On the contrary, the popular study of politics began in the West over two thousand five hundred years ago. The Greeks were pioneers who discovered that in nature, there is a cosmos, order.[2] Having been fascinated by this cosmos, they wanted to have one such order to civilize their lives. Thus, they invented the State which they thought of as the visible sign of the invisible cosmos. Plato believed that provision of distributive justice was the duty of the State. He invented the idea of 'Rule of Law' because he disqualified both gods and men from being rulers. Law became the ruler. He produced a team of dedicated persons to lead the State, whom he called 'Philosopher-Kings'. One who sought wisdom alone could be a guardian of the State. Aristotle emphasized the importance of virtue in the State and ordered the functioning of the State as per a written constitution. Prestigious educational institutions were dedicated to impart political education to citizens. Plato started the Academy in Athens in 356 BC in which Aristotle was a student. Later Aristotle started his own school and named it Lyceum in 334 BC. Romans admired patriotism and valor. They considered it an honor to earn their freedom, and defend their State as free-men. The word 'politics' originated from the Greeks as

---

[11] For an elaborate discussion Cf. Moses Manohar, *Rights Based Politics, The Role of the Indian Constitution*, (Chennai: ICSA-Books, 2014), 22-28.

[2] In a limited sense the Greek cosmos could be compared with the principle of *Rta* expounded by the Vedic seers. *Rta* was understood as a sustaining principle that stood for the order of the Universe. But while the discovery of cosmos led to the patenting of the State in Greece, the principle of *Rta* was reduced into *Yajna*, *dharma* and *karma*, before it was lost completely.

the art of providing order and stability to the city, i.e. the 'polis'. The Greco-Roman world created the ideas of rule of law, justice, liberty, public order, knowledge, virtue, personal dignity, and so on. The West inherited the political vocabulary of the Greeks – policy, police, politics – and the civic vocabulary of the Romans – civility, citizen, civilization.[3] Unfortunately, India never had such a splendid variety of ideas in the field of politics.

The Gospel of Jesus

With the arrival of Jesus in history, political thinking saw a great change. Jesus universalized what the Greeks and the Romans developed. Love, knowledge and justice became universally applicable for all. The Platonic State excluded the slaves, artisans and women. But Jesus included the poor, sinners, aliens, women, sick, lame, and the slaves and called them blessed. Love became more powerful than the Platonic knowledge and Aristotelian virtue. He preached to the multitude and made knowledge available to the public, free of cost. He spoke from the mountains, seashore, boats, temple gates, and the public square. He upheld the value of every single person. He practiced sharing of food, touched the lame and the lepers, and healed the sick even in the evenings. Thus he rejected the laws of purity and pollution. He sternly proclaimed that what you eat doesn't pollute but what comes out of one's heart, like anger, desire, violence etc., do pollute. Through the parable of the Good Samaritan, he convinced that people of different ethnic groups are not enemies but relatives.

Jesus introduced God as a relative, a caring father. He demonstrated that the godly kingdom can be established not by purse and weapons but by love and sharing of food. He spoke of a kingdom without a king but a father, without a battle field but a table, without rank and file but with children. He taught that the world could become a paradise if we repent, love and share. The Greeks believed in the 'Rule of Law' but Jesus preferred the Rule of Grace. For those who exercised power over others by appointing themselves

---

[3] Cf. Kenneth Minogue, *Politics* (New York: Oxford University Press, 1995), 20.

as the sole possessors and interpreters of 'God's Law', Jesus said that the Sabbath was made for the people and not otherwise.

Jesus defined power as pastoral while the Romans understood it as imperial. The aim of power is not to conquer but to serve. In the context of a Shepherd and Sheep, Jesus explained power and leadership. The Shepherd is the one who risks his life for the safety of the Sheep. Thus, the leader is the one who serves the people and even dies for them. Jesus considered human life very important. He said that the purpose of his life was that every human must have abundant life. Even when he was unjustly arrested, humiliated and crucified, he pronounced forgiveness and prayed for his tormenters. Violence and revenge were replaced with forgiveness and grace. By his resurrection, Jesus demonstrated that the power of an unjust State cannot quell the cause of truth and love. In the interest of keeping the State from falling apart, Plato vehemently opposed change. He taught that 'change is evil and rest is divine'.[4] Similarly Aristotle did not allow even children to play a new game as he feared it would lead to change.[5] But, change was the core message of Jesus. In the context of claiming perfection of the State or the empire by the Greeks and the Romans, Jesus categorically said that no one was perfect except the father in heaven. So he urged the people to change and grow in perfection. Jesus taught equality not in terms of strength, knowledge and valor. For him, people were equal because they shared the image of God the father. Thus the Gospel of Jesus brought many new ideas into politics like new wine. It was so fresh and radical that it could burst out the old social order.

Christianity

The followers of Jesus, called Christians, internalized the teachings of Jesus and developed new political ethics. They called their assembly the Church which became an order that could remove cultural and ritual differences. It made the Greeks, the Jews, the

---

[4] K. R. Popper, *The Open Society and its Enemies*, Vol. I, (London: Routledge, 1945), 37.

[5] Moses Manohar, *A New Political Paradigm for India* (New Delhi: Promilla & Co., 2009), 56.

Gentiles and all as part of one body and the fellow heirs of God's grace. Thus, the Church became a mystery (Eph. 3). According to Frederik Engels, "by rejecting all national religions and ceremonies and addressing itself to all peoples without distinction, Christianity became the first possible world religion.... Christianity struck a chord that was bound to echo in countless hearts."[6] By caring for the weak and the vulnerable, the Church presented a political model. It replaced the absolute States with Welfare States. Kings were replaced by ministers or public servants and absolute kings were changed into constitutional monarchs. By collecting and sending aid to the famine affected people in Jerusalem, the Church became the first international aid organization. By loving, sharing, caring, forgiving and interceding for the public, Christianity set a new model in political governance. Christianity took history very serious because they knew that God loved this world and Jesus went around doing good, died and resurrected. Thus the world is not just created and given but it is where God is active. History is a testimony of God's act of salvation through Jesus.

The Gospel of Jesus and the practice of the Christians in the Jewish-Greek-Roman setting contributed a civilization which developed many concepts. When the Church lost its vigor in feudalism, Reformation and counter-Reformation theologians led to the new understanding of the value of individual life, liberty and the importance of labor. This led to the new definition of sovereignty. The State became the final authority to interpret law and thus the idea of secularism was born. Politics became a contract, the nation became a common wealth belonging to all the members and the State became a product of the contract that exists for the benefit of the citizens. The importance of the individual above cultures, institutions and belief systems was upheld. It promoted trade, commerce, technological inventions, modern industry, scientific understanding of life and global community.

---

[6] Mark & Engels, *On Religion* (Moscow: Progress Publishers, 1975), 177-178.

Christianity in India

The Christian message was brought to India in A.D. 52 by St. Thomas, a disciple of Jesus. It is believed that before he attained martyrdom in Mylapore, Chennai, St. Thomas established seven churches in Kerala.[7] But Christianity came with a liberative message only in the 16th Century. However, the Reformation and Counter-Reformation events in Europe altered the focus of Christianity. More than spreading the liberative message of Jesus, attention was drawn towards establishing Church denominations. This was done quite often with a sense of rivalry. Indian Christianity became an extension of the European ecclesiastical divide. Consequently, Jesus became a casualty.

Later when European countries started trade expeditions to India, it resulted in the establishment of colonies. Christian missionaries came along with traders and colonial officials. They were touched by the plight of the people who suffered caste oppression, gender discrimination and poverty. So, they started charity work. Thus, Indians came to hear about Jesus through the charity work. Schools, colleges, hospitals, vocational training institutes, rehabilitation homes, translation and printing works, etc., came into being.

Finally, the colonial association of Indian Christianity limited her ability to study and discuss politics. Any discourse about politics by Christians could be easily construed as pro-colonialism during pre-Independence days and as anti-nationalism in post-Independent India.

Of late, the label of 'minority' is being thrust upon the Christians by the right wing political ideologies. This creates insecurity among Christians to engage in politics. Political education, discussion on democracy, law, rights to equality, liberty and property could not be undertaken seriously by the Church in India.

---

[7] C. B. Firth, *An Introduction to Indian Church History* (New Delhi: ISPCK, 2017), 14.

Indian Theological Explorations

Indian Christian theology got developed within the constraints described above. In addition to that, our theologians were fascinated if not bewildered by the rich variety of Hindu philosophy and mythology. Indian Christian theologians by and large portrayed Jesus as a Sadhu in the least or an Avatar at the most. The gospel of Jesus was studied in the light of Advaita and other philosophical systems. No doubt they created many wonderful interpretations and both Christianity and Hinduism became richer by their efforts. This was safe and well appreciated because the exhortations did not touch power and politics that could alter the destiny of the people. Jesus, an exemplary teacher of politics was missing in the discourse. Thus, the inability of Indian Christianity to overcome denominational differences, the historical association of Christianity with colonialism and the minority consciousness of Christians in India have proved as limiting factors. Consequently, we are not able to present the Jesus the transformer.

This deficit was expected to be addressed when 'Liberation Theology' entered the portals of India, during the last quarter of the 20th century. With the overdose of Marxism, our liberation theologians waited for the formation of working class, proletariat revolution, expropriation of private property, withering away of the State and the establishment of a Socialist Society. Jesus was presented not as a Sadhu but as a revolutionary and a friend of the oppressed. However, with the inability of Marxism to address the question of caste oppression and with the collapse of Soviet model, Liberation Theology lost its steam. It is important to note that Marxism and Liberation Theology made a negative impact. Marxism depicted the State as an enemy of people. Consequently, Liberation Theology discouraged the people to creatively engage the State, the Election process, study of the Constitution, study of the Budget allocation, Government spending, functioning of Government departments, relating with Panchayat, State and Union Government representatives, etc. Democracy was disclaimed as a bourgeoisie exercise and only revolution was considered the alternative. Therefore, it has become necessary to create a theology which helps people to relate with the

Government through democratic means. Later, Dalit Theology emerged but it quickly faded away due to its sectarian overtones.

Democracy in India

Democracy as a political system was introduced in India by the British. The Indian sub-continent was ruled by nearly 600 princes. According to Jawaharlal Nehru, majority of them were sinks of reaction and incompetence and unrestrained autocratic power.[8] Indians did not know about the Magna Carta, Renaissance, Reformation, Industrial Revolution, French Revolution, American Declaration of Independence and the Bill of Rights. The caste system gave social stability with slaves and bonded labor. Social mobility was ruthlessly arrested by the caste regime. The British introduced the rule of law, bureaucracy with command and control and a responsible Government in the areas which were directly under their rule. Liberal education in English was made available. Indians, irrespective of caste differences, were recruited to the military and civil services. Indian leaders got the opportunity to go to England and study liberal arts, science and law. The ideas of Life, Liberty and Equality were part of their academic exercise.

The Christian missionaries also contributed their mite by opening schools, orphanages and colleges for men and women, cutting across caste and creed. They were seriously challenging the caste and gender based injustices. The activities of the Church immensely contributed towards social awakening, human dignity, self-respect and social mobility, which are the preconditions for a democratic society. However, the Church did not teach political systems, constitutions, law making, public administration, taxation, property rights, laws related to civil, criminal and penal procedures and the administration of Justice. Therefore, the Christian education on democracy has been negligible during pre-Independence days. After Independence as already mentioned, the minority consciousness prevents the Christian community to give political education.

---

[8] Sir Maurice Gayer and A. Appadorai, *Speeches and Documents on the Indian Constitution*, Vol. I & II (London: Oxford University Press, 1957), 759.

Political Theology

Indian democracy needs substance. This necessitates a systematic study of political concepts. In this context, can Indian Christianity develop a political theology? The task of political theology is to study politics, simplify the fundamentals and educate the public. Political education should be an ecclesiastical and theological commitment. The purpose of political theology is to enable the poor to be proud citizens and to be the guardians of Indian democracy. The citizens must be enabled to make the State to translate political concepts into legal rights. For example, 'Life' is both a theological and political concept, but in a democratic polity, life is a right. The Indian Constitution Article 21 makes the right to life a Fundamental Right. The Supreme Court interpreted the idea of life to cover livelihood. Thus, the State made laws to ensure food security and rural employment as a matter of rights. This should be exactly the aim of political theology. Thus, connecting theology and law is the core of political theology. Political principles must be translated into legal rights.

Definition of Politics

The word politics could be quite misleading in India, where there is so much of distortion. But politics in a democratic context could mean only three things. They are life, liberty and property. Politics has no role except to protect and promote the citizen's right to life, liberty and property. Democracy must uphold the right of citizens to life. But life will be meaningless without liberty which includes freedom, dignity, etc. And, life and liberty will be meaningless without property. So, the role of the State is to help citizens to work, earn, own and enjoy property. In India, the caste system restricts the right to take up a work of one's choice. Similarly, the value of life also differs on the basis of caste and gender. An illiterate person cannot exercise liberty. Majority of our people are landless. They neither own any property nor are assured of any gainful employment. This means that we are not qualified to be called a democratic nation.

Further, political theories which support these values must be studied. Indian political systems, decision making processes, the

Indian Constitution, Indian Governmental system, electoral politics, and the idea of citizenship must be studied. The offices, such as that of the Prime Minister, Chief Ministers, Ministers, MPs, MLAs, Panchayat presidents must be studied. The institutions of oversight and restraint such as the Parliament, the Presidency, Controller and Auditor General (CAG), CBI, Lok Pal, and Judiciary must be monitored.[9] All these efforts will train the poor citizens in self-government.

Both Liberation Theology and Dalit Theology could not contribute much with regard to political theology because theology remained as theology without translating into legal rights. The importance of this link could be seen within the Biblical narrative itself. For example, YHWH made a contract or covenant with Abraham (Genesis 12) and when the Israelites suffered under bondage in Egypt, YHWH remembered the covenant (Exodus 2:24). Similarly, democratic polity is a covenant /contract between the citizens and the State. The State has to honor the conditions of the contract. Later YHWH liberated the Israelites and settled them in the promised land. He did not just leave them there, but gave them the Torah, the Law. Torah gave the legal force to protect the weak and punish the violators. Similarly, the teachings of Jesus got an institutional framework in the founding of the Church. The Church became the embodiment and the agent of the Gospel of Jesus. Thus, political theology must not only create principles and postulates but must suggest political means to translate them into legal entitlements and rights.

Conclusion

Democracy as a political system is interesting because it holds the citizen as the hero. The quality of democracy changes in consonance with the quality of the citizens. Enlightened citizens can make an enlightened democracy. Democracy can be feeble and in peril, because it believes that everyone is equal. Continued education is necessary to break the divisions and move towards real equality.

---

[9] Devesh Kapur et al, *Public Institutions in India* (New Delhi: Oxford, 2005), 25.

Modern democracy comes with a package. It has citizens, voting right, elections, right to civil disobedience, public opinion, national constitutions, international laws, and so on. Citizen is a legal construct. He / She is a product of law and at the same time is vested with the power to amend or make laws. In a democracy, law can be more lethal than a gun. Every election could be a qualified revolution (Alwin Toffler). India has a democracy only in its form and not in its substance. A substantial democracy requires enlightened citizens; citizen making is a national challenge and it is very much a challenge to Indian Christianity.

Let me conclude with an advise of Jacque Rousseau, who says, "[L]ove of a country cannot subsist without freedom, nor freedom without virtue, nor virtue without citizens. If you create citizens you have gained everything, but otherwise all you will have is wretched slaves, beginning with the leaders of the State."[10]

Bibliography

Agur, C. M. *Church History of Travancore*. Madras: SPS Press, 1903.

Altekar, A.S. *State and Government in Ancient India.* Delhi: Motilal Banarsidass, 1949.

Austin, Granville. *The Indian Constitution: Cornerstone of a Nation.* Oxford: Oxford University Press, 1972.

Baird, Robert D. et al, eds. *Religion and Law on Independent India.* Delhi: Manohar Publishers, 2005.

Bhargava, Rajeev, ed. *Politics and Ethics of the Indian Constitution.* Delhi: Oxford University Press, 2009.

Crick, Bernard. *Essays on Citizenship*. London: Continuum, 2000.

Dean, Mitchell. *Governmentality – Power and Rule in Modern Society.* London: Sage Publications, 1999.

Foucault, Michael. *Religion and Culture.* Selected and Edited by Jeremy R. Carrette. UK: Manchester University Press, UK, 1999.

[10] Jean-Jacques Rousseau, *Discourse on Political Economy and Social Contract*, Tr. Christopher Betts, (New York: Oxford University Publications, 1994), 22.

Hampton, Jean. *Political Philosophy, University of Arizona*. Delhi: Oxford University Press, 1998.

Jones, Kenneth W. *The New Cambridge History of India*. Cambridge: Orient Longman, 1989.

Kaviraj, Sudipta. *The Enchantment of Democracy and India*. Ranikhet: Permanaet Black, 2011.

Lakoff, Sanford. *Democracy – History, Theory, Practice*. USA: Westview Press, 1996.

Lipson, Leslie. *The Great Issues of Politics*. Delhi: Prentice – Hall of India Ltd., 1996.

Menon, Vepal Pangunni. *The Story of the Integration of Indian States*. Bangalore: Indian Council for World Affairs, 1955.

Nelson, Brian R. *Western Political Thought*. Delhi: Pearson Education Ltd., 2004.

Pylee, M. V. *India's Constitution*. Delhi: Chand & Co. 1994.

Rousseau, Jean-Jacques. *The Social Contract*. New York: Oxford University Press, 1993.

Sher, Syed Osman. *The Culture of Tolerance*. Delhi: Originals, 2001.

Shapiro, Ian. *The Moral Foundations of Politics*. Delhi: Akbar Books, 2004.

Srinivas, M. V. *India: Social Structure*. Delhi: Hindustan Publishing Corporation, 1986.

Sundar, Shanthakumari. *Values and Influence of Religion in Public Administration*. Delhi: Sage Publications, 2011.

Thomas, Geoffrey. *Introduction to Political Philosophy*. London: Gerald Duckworth & Co., 2000.

Vivekananda, Swami. *The Complete Works of Swami Vivekanada*, Vol. III. Calcutta: Advaita Ashrama Edition VIII, 1960, XIII Reprint 1984.

Vora, Rajendra et al, eds. *Indian Democracy*. New Delhi: Sage Publications, 2004.

Wayper, C.L. *Political Thought*. Madras: B. I. Publications, 1974.

8

Being Authentically Plural in the Contemporary World: Challenges and Prospects

Varghese Manimala
Rector, Vianney College, Janampet, Vijayarai, Eluru, Andhra Pradesh

"Soon I shall see God, it is inevitable. One day everyone must see God. I am a simple man a solitary monk travelling through this world with a leaky umbrella"
- Mao Tse Tung

"I left [Europe] as a Christian, found myself a Hindu, returned as a Buddhist,
without ceasing to be a Christian"
- Raimon Panikkar

Introduction

Permit me to begin with my experience at the World Parliament of Religions at Melbourne, Australia, in 2009. A few fundamentalist

Christians were standing outside with a big banner: "All those who go into this Parliament will go to hell." We were nearly 7,000 representatives from 220 religions from various parts of the world experiencing peace and harmony, and mutually participating in ceremonies, colloquia, meditation sessions, etc. There was not a single police man to control us, and during the whole week we experienced such richness of pluralism and dialogue, and we left the Parliament with contentment for having been together for a week. The final general session was graced by Dalai Lama, and there were only two 'religious' leaders on the stage – besides Dalai Lama there was a great woman, the leader of the Indigenous Religions of Australia. Similarly, in 2004 during the World Parliament of Religions in Barcelona, in which too I had the great privilege of being a participant, deriving a lot of happiness I could also be a witness to the wonderful and generous activity of our Sikh brethren. There were nearly 8,000 delegates from various parts of the world; and our Sikh brethren under the leadership of their elders from Birmingham organized a beautiful *langar* (Sikh custom of offering food to the devotees who come especially to the Gurudwara) for all those who would like to have a light vegetarian lunch were served for the whole week. They put up three big *pandals* on the beach of the Mediterranean, and these Sikh brethren themselves served food to all those who came in. Seeing their good action of serving food, people from various countries and religions joined them in serving. Whenever these people appeared on the stage for some performance there was such thunderous clapping, acknowledging their wonderful hospitality. Taking a cue from these experiences, I would like to reflect a little on how to be authentically plural, and in the present Indian and world context what approaches we have to adopt to build up 'public theology' based on commitment and availability in a true dialogical attitude.

Pluralism – the Needed basic Theological Position Today

Pluralism as a religious attitude is not that easy as we may think, because it calls for giving up many of our time-honoured traditions, customs, and convictions. Before speaking of Pluralism as a needed attitude, Raimon Panikkar speaks of four other positions that need to be taken into consideration.

Exclusivism

A believing member of a religion in one way or another considers his/her own religion to be true, and one cannot be blamed for that. The claim to truth has a certain built-in claim to exclusivity; the principle of contradiction will automatically be applied here. If a certain human tradition claims to offer a universal context for truth, anything contrary to that 'universal truth' will have to be declared false. This attitude has certain amount of heroism in it. You consecrate your life and dedicate your entire existence to something that is really worthy of being called a human cause, to something that claims to be not just partial and imperfect truth, but a universal and even absolute truth. To be sure, an absolute God or Value has to be the final guarantee for such an attitude so that you do not follow it because of personal whims or because you have uncritically raised your point of view to an absolute value. It is God's right you defend when asserting your religion as 'absolute religion.' This does not imply an outright condemnation of the beliefs of all other human beings who have not received the 'grace' of your calling. You may consider this call a burden and duty (to carry vicariously the responsibility for the whole world) more than a privilege and a gift. But this attitude presents its difficulties: first, it carries with it the obvious danger of intolerance, hubris, and contempt for others. It further bears the intrinsic weakness of assuming an almost purely logical conception of truth and the uncritical attitude of an epistemological naiveté. Truth is many-faceted, and even if you assume that God speaks an exclusive language, everything depends on your understanding of it so that you may never really know whether your interpretation is the *only* right one. We need also to admit that God 'speaks' to others, and both partners relying on God's authority will always need the human mediation so that ultimately God's authority depends on Human interpretation (of the divine revelation). As a matter of fact although there are many de facto remnants of an exclusivistic attitude today, it is hardly defended de jure. It would be the height of hypocrisy to condemn others and justify oneself.[1]

Inclusivism

In the contemporary world one can hardly fail to discover positive and true values – even of the highest order – outside one's own tradition. Traditional religions are forced to face this challenge. "Splendid isolation" is no longer possible. The most plausible condition for the claim to truth of one's own tradition is to affirm at the same time that it includes at different levels all that there is of truth wherever it exists. The inclusive attitude will tend to reinterpret things in such a way as to make them not only palatable but also assimilable. Hence, when a contradiction arises, it will make the necessary distinctions between different planes so as to be able to overcome that contradiction. It will tend to become a kind of universalism of an existential or formal nature rather than of essential content. This attitude has certain quality of magnanimity and grandeur in it. While you follow your own path, you need not condemn the other. You can even enter into communion with all other ways of life, and if you happen to have the real experience of inclusivity, you may be at peace not only with yourself, but with all other human and divine ways as well. But this attitude also entails some difficulties. First, it also presents the danger of hubris because it is only you who have the privilege of an all-embracing vision and tolerant attitude, you who allot to the others the place they must take in the universe. You give the impression of being tolerant, but that is not the case with others who challenge your right to be on top. Further, it has the intrinsic difficulties of an almost alogical conception of truth and a built-in inner contradiction when the attitude is spelled out in theory and praxis. With this approach there can be the risk of truth being purely relative. In such a position there is always a superiority expressed, even if one may not state it openly. Still there are many such tendencies

---

[1] Cf. Raimon Panikkar, *Intrareligious Dialogue,* Revised Edition (New York: Paulist Press, 1999), 5-6.

in several religious traditions that consider themselves all-inclusive; in other cases, perhaps, the claim of pluralism has overtaken them.[2]

Parallelism

If one becomes aware that the religion being followed is far from being perfect and yet it represents a symbol of the right path, and also a similar conviction seems to be the case for others, if you can neither dismiss the religious claim of the other nor assimilate it completely into your tradition, a plausible alternative is to assume that all are different creeds, which, in spite of meanderings and crossings, actually can run parallel, to meet only in the ultimate, in the *eschaton*, at the very end of the human pilgrimage. Religions would then be parallel paths and our most urgent concern would be not to interfere with others, neither to convert nor borrow from them, but to deepen our own respective traditions; be a better Christian, a better Hindu, a better Muslim, etc. Perhaps, this attitude has some positive advantages like tolerance, respect for others, being non-judgmental, and so on. Yet, this position is also not free from difficulties; first of all, it forgets the fact that human traditions have grown through mutual influences, and even through conflicts. Besides, it assumes that every human religious tradition has in itself all the elements for further growth and development, in a word it assumes the self-sufficiency of all the traditions, and denies the need for mutual influence and learning. Mere parallelism eschews the real issues. It will not favour dialogue.[3]

Interpenetration

We come to realize that however we may claim to be independent, we become aware and sensitive to the religiousness of the other; that we are mutually being influenced whether we like it or not. We come to the realization that our neighbour's religion not only offers challenges, but may even enrich our own. We begin to accept that the other religion may complement mine, that it may supplement some of my beliefs, provided that my religiousness remains an

---

[2] Cf. Ibid., 6-7.

[3] Cf. Ibid., 7-8.

undivided whole. Thus, we can find Marxists accepting Christian ideas, Christians subscribing to Hindu tenets, and Muslims accepting Buddhist views, etc., and all the while remaining Marxists, Christians and Muslims. But there is still more; it appears as if we are today all intertwined and that without these particular religious links my own religion would be incomprehensible for me and even impossible. Religions as if constitute a 'horizon' against which I grasp my own religion and convictions. Religions cannot exist in isolation but over against each other, whether we like it or not, that is the givenness of the situation. There is a mutual interpenetration without the loss of proper peculiarities of each religion. The most important values this attitude inspires are tolerance, broadmindedness, and mutual confidence. As no religion is foreign to my own, I may encounter the religion of the other in our own religious tradition, in some way accepting the fact we need one another mutually complementing and correcting things. This attitude too is accompanied by its own dangers. First of all, one has to ask if this type of thinking is not a little wishful. Although we may hold that creative hermeneutics justifies this position, but still the question remains whether all religions are imbued with such advanced form of hermeneutics. Besides, there can be a certain amount of choice involved in making a selective use of main tenets of traditions while neglecting others. Still, this attitude may offer perspectives which others lack. It can contribute to the spiritual growth of partners, especially through a mutual enrichment within a synthesis. Being an open process, the values of other traditions are not merely juxtaposed to those of our tradition but truly assimilated and integrated into our beliefs and our being.[4]

Pluralism

This is a polysemic word and not a super-system, which gives a complete answer to the vexed problem of religious pluralism. The attitude of pluralism[5] keeps the attitude of intrareligious and

---

[4] Cf. ibid. 9-10.

[5] Panikkar gives a lot of stress to Religious Pluralism as it is at the core of one's being, and, hence, he discusses it in many of his works. In his book *Invisible*

interreligious dialogue permanently open. If dialogue has to survive, there needs to be this attitude of pluralism. Pluralism stands between unrelated plurality and monolithic unity. It takes the experiences of our ancestors very seriously; being intelligent they were able to assimilate the different belief systems, and could live together in harmony and understanding. A certain evolutionist thinking, making us believe that we are at the top of the spiritual insights of the human race and all the others are "undeveloped" smacks of modern hubris and ignorant naiveté. Pluralism is inclined to overcome the monopoly of the mental power over everything. Perhaps, the more realistic basis on which to ground human conviviality is not rational knowledge but loving awareness.[6]

Pluralism needs to be understood in a proper perspective, and for this, first we shall approach it from a 'negative' point of view, and then move to the positive. The pluralism that we discuss is not a political pluralism or technological one or any other normal plural experience we deal with, but religious pluralism. Pluralism means neither plurality, nor multiplicity, nor a reduction of multiplicity for unity's sake. It is not a mere acknowledgment of the plurality of religions, and then awaiting for the day when such plurality will cease to exist and unity will reign. Pluralism does not regard unity as an indispensable ideal, even if variations within this unity were to be acceptable. Pluralism accepts the irreconcilable aspects of religions or world myths without being blind to possible common aspects. It is not the eschatological expectation that in the end everything will come to unity by itself. Pluralism does not contend that truth is singular, nor even that there are many truths. If truth were only singular, we could not accept the positive tolerance of a pluralistic attitude and would have to assume that pluralism allows error. If there were many truths, that would land us in plain contradictions.

Harmony: *Essays on Contemplation and Responsibility,* edited by Harry James Cargas (Minneapolis: Fortress Press, 1995), he allots two chapters (almost 50 pages) for a rather detailed description of this issue. As time and space will not let us go into all the details we shall try to summarize pointing out to the important concerns regarding this problem.

[6] Cf. Panikkar, *Intrareligious Dialogue,* 10-11.

Pluralism does not admit of a universal system. The incommensurability of ultimate systems cannot be overcome by the *logos*. This incommensurability is not a pesky evil but a primordial revelation of reality's nature. Pluralism makes us aware of our contingency, our limitations, and it shows us that reality cannot be fully comprehended; the reason is nothing else than that reality cannot be reduced to mere intelligibility. Hence, when we look at pluralism from a positive perspective it is a symbol; it is an attitude of cosmic trust, which permits a polar and tension-filled coexistence of ultimate human convictions, cosmologies and religions. It does not deny the rights of the logos, as for example the principle of contradiction. We need to remember that pluralism belongs to the level of mythos as well, not as an object of thinking but as the horizon that ultimately makes thinking possible. Thus pluralism is not a mere theoretical one but it is grounded in the nature of Man and Reality.[7]

We need to constantly bear in mind that pluralism belongs to the sphere of the *mythos*. A Christian pluralistic attitude must be willing to be excommunicated by non-pluralistic viewpoint without seeking to revenge in judging the other as non-Christian. Pluralism undermines the arguments for a power struggle. A Christian pluralistic attitude should cling to Christian tenets when facing other religions without forgetting the limitation and contingency of the particular subject that is formulating them. We can point out and even oppose individual wrong conceptions, but we need not brand them as absolute evils; we should keep in mind the limitations of one's own power of judgment. A pluralistic Christian will not confess many saviors; that would be a non-pluralistic assertion, since the faith experience of savior is unique for each believer and cannot be multiplied. A pluralistic Christology will begin by saying that the mystery of Christ cannot be reduced to a quantitative understanding. While believing that the mystery of Christ is of far-reaching significance, I cannot possibly say that it is only important

---

[7] Cf. Raimon Panikkar, *A Dwelling Place of Wisdom*, translated by Annemarie S. Kidder (Westminster: Westminster John Knox Press, 1993), 146-147. For a detailed description and study of pluralism from different perspectives see Panikkar, *Invisible Harmony*, 57ff.

to my own personal salvation, my own church, or my church's doctrinal tradition. I or my congregation cannot monopolize this mystery. Similarly impudent is the presumption that all savior figures of religious history are in reality the Christian Christ only with different names.[8]

From the aforesaid principles follow certain conclusions as: While we should not ignore or neglect the past, but respect the traditional understandings, yet we need to subject them to appropriate interpretation. Pure exegetical or hermeneutical interpretation of tradition is not enough; we should always consider the possibility of a new Christian consciousness. The most important change in Christian self-understanding relates both to the text and context. For example, a reflection on the "Christian economy of salvation" cannot ignore the existence – and challenge – of world religions. We should understand that the new context is not simply a new territory added to the old; it is not the same territory viewed in a new light. The new context not only introduces many new elements that were previously non-existent; it also transforms the old context. Still, we should not forget that new context is limited and concrete as much as the old. Going further, we should not identify the christic principle with *Christianity* as a religion, and much less with *Christendom* as a civilization. There is no single way of viewing Christ because no single view can embrace the reality of Christ. Religions may be incommensurable, apart from a few common traits, because every religion is unique. Every religion represents the whole of human experience in a concrete way. We have to bear in mind that every religion expresses a concrete form of humanness; but this does not exclude a possible divine influence on the *humanum;* neither does it exclude a possible religious aberration. When religions come face to face, they can enrich but also destroy each other. If Christians have the capacity to liberate themselves from their religion - Christianity, this applies to other religions as well, then there is the possibility of a transcendence which will take the followers of such religions to a higher level. Besides, Christians may discover in the christic principle the key to unity, to understanding and love for all humankind, and

---

[8] Cf. Panikkar, *Dwelling Place of Wisdom*, 146-150.

to the whole of the cosmos, thus leading to a communion with the whole of reality. The Christian starting point is the kenotic experience of Christ, which involves the acceptance of, and openness to, the Spirit.[9]

We have tried to identify how the principle of pluralism would work in the Christian theological perspective. As is evident, for a proper interreligious dialogue there is no other way than to recognize the need of, and the inevitability of acknowledging pluralism as a necessity. If we are grounded in pluralism, certain convictions will dawn upon us, as we see in the statement of the "World Conference of Religions for Peace," held in Kyoto, Japan; some of the salient points are:

> When we were together to deal with the overriding theme of peace, we discovered that the things which unite us are more important than the things which separate us. We found that we have in common:
>
> - a conviction of the fundamental unity of the human family, of the equality and dignity of all men and women;
> - a feeling of sacrosanctness of the individual and his conscience;
> - a feeling of the value of the human community;
> - a realization that might is not the same as right, that human power cannot be self-sufficient and is not absolute;
> - the faith, love, sympathy, selflessness have in the end, greater power than hatred, hostility and self-interest;
> - deep hope in the ultimate victory of good will.[10]

With an attitude of pluralism one is able to see possibilities of challenges to new life in every person, situations; and even our enemies can become sources of change for us as Walter Wink points out:

---

[9] Cf. Ibid. 150-152.

[10] See Hans Küng, *Theology for the Third Millennium: An Ecumenical View* (New York: Doubleday, 1988), 243. Also Varghese Manimala, *Toward Mutual Fecundation and Fulfillment of Religions: An Invitation to Transcendence and Dialogue with a Cosmotheandric Vision* (Delhi: Media House & ISPCK, 2009), 465.

> [This] the gift our enemy may be able to bring us: to see aspects of ourselves that we cannot discover any other way than through our enemies. Our friends seldom tell us these things, they are our friends precisely because they are able to overlook or ignore this part of us. The enemy is thus not merely a hurdle to be leaped on the way to God. The enemy can be the way to God. We cannot come to terms with our shadow except through our enemies, for we have almost no other access to those unacceptable parts of ourselves that need redeeming except through the mirror our enemies hold up to us. This then is another, more intimate reason for loving our enemies. ... we may not be whole people without them.[11]

Search for Fulfillment in the Context of Pluralism

Today religions have come to realize in a deeper sense the fact of religious pluralism, and they cannot wish it away, but have to live with it. Pluralism is, perhaps, one of the upshots of globalization. The religious life of mankind, as W. C. Smith has noted, from now on, if it is to be lived at all, will be lived in the context of religious pluralism.[12] Not only religions have to live in a historical context and be aware of their givens but need to offer hope to the modern man, only then can they be relevant. History is experienced as meaningless when the horizon of hope and purposes is dark and obscure. On the other hand, the horizon of human hope and purpose become dim and uncertain if the history experienced and caused by human beings can no longer be related to it. Human beings are beings of hope, hoping for a better future, transcending the present conditions, and expecting to gain liberation beyond the historical tragedies and sufferings. We need to distinguish between the 'historical future'

---

[11]Walter Wink, *Engaging the Powers: Discernment and Resistance in a World of Domination* (Minneapolis: Fortress Press, 1992), 273. See also. Manimala, *Toward Mutual Fecundation and Fulfillment of Religions,* 465.

[12] Cf. Chris Arthur, *Religious Pluralism: A Metaphorical Approach* (Aurora, Colorado: The Davies Group Publishers, 2000), 29, 113. See also Manimala, *Toward Mutual Fecundation and Fulfillment of Religions*, 485.

and the 'eschatological future.' There is an alignment towards the synchronization of different historical times or tenses; different human histories fuse into a single history because, through growing interdependencies and growing conflicts, either 'a single humanity' will come into being as the object of a common history, or the hostile groups will all perish together in the one, single catastrophe. The 'present future' is aligned towards the synchronization of human historical time with the rhythms of natural time – the rhythms of the ecosystem of the earth, and bio-rhythms of the human body. Either human history and the history of nature will arrive at a coordinated harmony, or human history will find its irrevocable end in ecological death.[13]

Religions are on search for fulfillment because as long as they are on earth, they stand in need of completion. Hence, whether it is acknowledged or not, no religion is in its final phase and need to seek its fulfillment with openness towards other religions and the whole of reality. Being in history, religions have a historical role and also are conditioned by history, and if meaningfully they play the role, they can contribute positively towards the history of the world. Religions have to realize that solitary seeking of fulfillment is a non-viability; the main reason being that they are not self-sufficient. We cannot dream of an absolute religion on earth with all perfections, and as long as we journey through this world, we need others for our own realization. Mutual fecundation, on which a lot of stress has been laid by many serious theologians like Raimon Panikkar, John Hick, Harvey Cox, Tissa Balasurya, etc., is the only way (*mārga*) for the fulfillment of any religion however advanced its claims be. Without a basic openness to other religions and other ideologies no religion can claim to achieve its own fulfillment today.

Religions need to realize one important fact that they can in no way claim absolute rights; that they together with the whole of humanity are on a pilgrimage in hope and mutual trust. Today we

[13] Cf. Jürgen Moltmann, "The Interlaced Times of History: Some Necessary Differentiations and Limitations of History as Concept," in Hans Küng and David Tracy (eds.), *Paradigm Change in Theology: A Symposium for the Future,* trans. Margaret Kohl (New York: Crossroad, 1989), 321-323. See also Manimala, *Toward Mutual Fecundation and Fulfilment of Religions*, 486.

need to apply a new hermeneutics for understanding reality and culture, as both are mutually complementary. Panikkar has indicated that the intercultural and interreligious are inseparable in matter of theology and theological hermeneutics. We need to be enriched not only by our culture and religion but also by other cultures, religions and ideologies. Just as Panikkar places himself in the middle of the Christian, Hindu, and Buddhist approaches to understand the mystery of the cosmos, and evolve a theology that has a triple dimension, all of us need to be challenged to desert the towers that we have built for ourselves, and occupied and fortified them with our customs and traditions. The life situations in which we live must help us to open our eyes and meet the reality that stares at us. As Aloysius Pieris has pointed out, there are two prevalent realities that are so much a part of the life and experience of the masses of Asian people: Asia's abject poverty and its deep religiosity. If these do not form part and parcel of any theology, that theology is an exercise in the ivory tower, and it does not address the reality and is not rooted in the *Sitz im Leben*, and therefore also a futile exercise. The salvation or fulfillment of religions is not taking place in an imaginary world, but in the real world where God is active. Hence, a theology that has to be relevant needs to have a 'baptism by immersion,' as Pieris suggests. It is only this 'double baptism' in 'the Jordan of Asian religion and Calvary of Asian poverty' that the 'church in Asia' can become the 'church of Asia.'[14] In order to come to this level there is the urgent need of cooperation and trust among religions; and this can be developed only through recognition of equality of religions. The isolation of religions in which we have been continuing to exist for centuries has to become past history if religions will have to survive meaningfully. If this does not happen, religions and churches have to meet with the

[14] Cf. Wesley Ariarajah, "Intercultural Hermeneutics – A Promise for the Future?" in *Voices from the Third World* (Vol. xxIx No. 1, June 2006), 99. Also the reader could profitably consult the books of Aloysius Pieris for getting a good idea of the 'relevant theology' that he was trying to build up. His books *An Asian Theology of Liberation, Love Meets Wisdom,* etc., give a glimpse of his radical theological position. Cf. also Manimala, *Toward Mutual Fecundation and Fulfillment of Religions*, 488-489.

inevitable doom which they bring upon themselves and there is no use of cursing the modern situation.

Pitfalls that Need to be Avoided

If we are serious about the approach mentioned above there is the need for a cautious approach and certain pitfalls need to be foreseen and avoided for minimum success.

Domination

When we keenly observe, there is so much of religious acrimony and urges of domination which many religions harbour. Such an attitude of domination results from the claim of some religions to uniqueness and as the sole mediators of salvation that will automatically invite other religions to isolate themselves and also make claims to uniqueness and self-sufficiency. In general, monotheistic religions did make claims to supremacy and looked upon other religions with disdain. Domination also leads to intolerance, which is as old as humanity, and no one can claim to be free of this and throw stones at others. One of the reasons for intolerance is absolutization of human realities, especially the ideologies and religions. Another reason for intolerance is the idea or the pretension of possessing the truth exclusively. This can be dangerous for the living together of various religions and ideologies. Still another source of intolerance is the idea of "the chosen people." If I am chosen, the other *ipso facto* is not; and I pass for a king or prince, and the rest of the majority are simply people of little worth. Such a pretension of being chosen is very much part and parcel of Israelite culture and this by auto-reference has to be inherited by the Christians too. Similarly is the superiority of race, culture or development. Self-esteem is good and legitimate if corresponding to a good value system, but if it is beyond respectable limits and disesteems others as clowns, it trespasses the boundary.[15]

---

[15] Cf. Manimala, *Toward Mutual Fecundation and Fulfillment of Religions*, 494-497.

Dogmatism and Ritualism

One of the defects into which creedal religions can fall is dogmatism. Dogmatism suppresses the true spirit, and makes religion subservient to law and tradition. Denominational religions have been known for their dogmatic attitudes so much so a great scholar like T. R. V. Murti protested against such attitudes in these terms: "Denominational religions with their dogmas [tend] to create vested interests and to breed corruption. They stifle freedom, they coerce conformity, they promote religious conflicts."[16] Any ideology, when it becomes dogmatic, loses its true spirit, tries to become oppressive of its adherents, and sees others as enemies who are to be brought into subjection even by forceful means. Christianity in general is accused of being very dogmatic, so also are other monotheistic religions like Islam and Judaism. There should be an effort made to go beyond dogmatism and reach the 'depth' level of religion. Today's world yearns for such an authentic approach. Dogmatism can only constrain people, and in such a situation there will be a tendency to break away from churches and traditions.

Just as dogmatism is something undesirable, similarly ritualism is also an evil that can make religion lifeless and meaningless especially for the present generation. Ritualism destroys the true spirit of religion and makes it more a superstition. It was this ritualism that prophets attacked, and we find that persons like Buddha and Jesus revolted against the ritualistic religion. Ritualism sucks the life-blood of religion and makes it more of a magic leaving the faithful with no other option but to go through rituals as a process. Rituals may be necessary for they are in some way expressing the inner spirit of man, but when legalism and drudgery enter into rituals they lose their relevance. Similarly occasions will call for liturgies to be properly adapted. What is important is not the type of vestments or vessels that are used, but with what spirit and meaning the liturgy is celebrated. There is a beautiful incident shown in the movie *Oscar Romero* (the life-story of Archbishop Oscar Romero). When he visits a church occupied by the army he is refused entry into the church, and his

[16] Cf. T. R. V. Murti, *The Central Philosophy of Buddhism* (London: Allen and Unwin, 1955), 340.

cassock and clothes beneath are torn to pieces, and he is left almost half naked. Then an old lady approaches him with a turkey towel and covers him; and then he utters these beautiful words: "This is the time to begin the Holy Eucharist: In the name of the Father, and the Son and the Holy Spirit. …" How touching the scene is! But there have been certain cities in India with churches packed with the faithful on Maundy Thursday and liturgy is celebrated with police protection! What a travesty of the enactment of the memorial of the cenacle! Is it not better that the Eucharist be not celebrated in such a situation? The Eucharist which Christ intended to be celebrated is a communion of hearts and not a ritual to be repeated without having any relevance to the community. Without communion among the participants of the Eucharist there is no communion with Christ. It is the communion with Christ that is the basis of the Christian community, and a divided community can never claim to belong to Christ who offered his life for the sake of the community. Here is where the leaders should have the courage to call for true conversion, but sad to say our leaders have failed us miserably![17]

Unilateralism

Many religions fall into the trap of unilateralism, stressing the fact that their religions are the only true ones and the rest are looked down upon with suspicion. In a unilateral approach a crypto-missionary will-to-power is still operative. In the present context such an intention for sheep stealing is highly detestable; for no forced conversion is true conversion. Even in settling controversies one has to avoid the unilateral approach, and search for possible common grounds. There is an either/or mentality that is very much at the root of present human malaise, and religions which deal with ultimate problems are especially sensitive to this kind of exclusivism which condemns the other. Giving up unilateralism we should draw upon the strengths of all the traditions of humankind in order to surmount the impasse. A sane and humane attitude will prompt us to admit that no religion or ideology, culture or tradition can

---

[17] Cf. Manimala, *Toward Mutual Fecundation and Fulfillment of Religions*, 502-504.

reasonably claim to exhaust the universal human experience or even the manifestation of the Sacred. We know that with the attitude of unilateralism, dialogue turns to be monologue; and in the course of time dialogue and ecumenism cease to be. When such an attitude is coupled with domination, there results what we have seen in past history: crusades, holy wars, inquisitions, colonialism, imperialism, and all sorts of oppressions. Even now this continues in the form of excommunications, anathemas, *fatwas*, etc. In the name of religion we can declare to kill people, and yet we will be at the same time claiming to be in union with God who is kind, merciful and just. Those in authority cannot brook any opposition, and they make use of all means at their disposal to alienate and ostracize and destroy people by even maligning them. Only through sincere and honest criticism can we overcome problems and failures of ours, because none of us, however holy or intelligent, is free from human incongruencies and weaknesses. Our idiosyncrasies, both individual and communitarian, continue to accompany us. What is important is that instead of justifying them we should have the courage and humility to acknowledge them, and enter into common endeavours with other religious groups and ideologies to overcome them as far as possible. Let us remember that our frailties accompany us, willy-nilly.[18]

Values to be Nurtured and Enhanced

Democracy and Reverential Attitude

Today if Christianity, or for that matter any religion, has to fulfill its mission there should be a paradigm shift. One of the important values that religions will have to promote is democracy or a reverential attitude for others. Democracy calls for a commitment to the weak and oppressed (Dalits). There should be a concerted effort to build up an egalitarian society. The fostering of a democratic ethos respectful of diversity of cultures and commitment is an important task. Democracy has to be redefined and understood as protection of minorities, the oppressed and weak, not a despotic rule by the

[18] Cf. Ibid. 504-506

majority.[19] As is well-known, established religions and churches are very tardy in implementing democracy in administration. Even today what is seen in the structure of the Church is that of a pyramid; authority is very much centralized, and there isn't the willingness to practice the principle of subsidiarity (*subsidiarité*). Vatican II, for example in the case of the Catholic Church, had given ample directions for democratizing the administration of the Church, but hardly any diocese, not even the papal administration, implemented the norms.[20] First and foremost what is to be emphasized in the Church or a movement is the aspect of "communion." Unless we remain faithful to this ideal there is always the tendency to dominate and to turn authority into an autocracy. If democracy has to be practiced in an enduring manner in any organization three important dimensions are to be maintained: ***participation, pluralism*** and ***tolerance of dissidence.*** A sense of collegiality has to prevail if democracy has to survive in a church or a religious sect. It is good to remember that the exercise of power is best done in getting the cooperation and good will of all involved rather than a caucus. This will call for respect and a reverential attitude for all persons especially from the part of those who are in authority.[21]

Promotion of Human Rights

After the horrors of World War II, the United Nations adopted the Universal Declaration of Human Rights; and by this it was declared to the world community that there were universal standards of human treatment. Many consider this event the beginning of a new era making human rights as the philosophy, language, and

---

[19] Cf. Kajsa Ahlstrand, "Toward a Paradigm Shift in Christian Mission: South Asia and North Europe," in the book *Theology and the Religions: A Dialogue*, edited by Viggo Mortensen (Grand Rapids, Michigan: Eerdmans Publishing Company, 2003), 166-168.

[20] It is good to recall what Pope Francis spoke about the Vatican Curia when he shortlisted 15 sins of the Curia; what a great analysis it was!. The reader could profitably consult *Concilium* 243 (Oct. 1992). The whole issue is discussing on the Taboo of Democratization in the Church.

[21] Cf. Manimala, *Toward Mutual Fecundation and Fulfillment of Religions*, 508-509.

politics of our time. Despite the wide agreement, there is still a lot of disagreement regarding the implementation of the same, and we know the violation of human rights go unabated. Human Rights is a twentieth century name for what has been traditionally known as natural rights or rights of 'man'. Although much has been said and written about them, they still remain purely an ideal in many countries of the world, and, surprisingly, many countries have not yet signed the charter of Human Rights.[22] In recent years there is a great interest evinced by many agencies in Human Rights issue, and the Catholic Church has a set of documents which stress on Human Rights. Pope John XXIII, through his encyclicals especially *Pacem in Terris,* made a fervent appeal to all the nations to respect and practice Human Rights. Various other documents like *Mater et Magistra, Gaudium et Spes, Populorum Progressio, Octagesimo Adveniens, Justice in the World, Evangelii Nuntiandi, Redemptor Hominis, Dives in Misericordia*, etc., and quite recently Pope Francis' encyclicals especially *Laudato Si*, make fervent appeals to the protection and practice of Human Rights. These rights are meaningful because of the dignity of the human person. Regarding this a few words from *Gaudium et Spes* may be in place:

> At the same time, however, there is a growing awareness of the exalted dignity proper to the human person, since he stands above all things, and his rights and duties are universal and inviolable. Therefore there must be made available to all men everything necessary for leading a life truly human, such as food, clothing, and shelter, the right to choose a state of life freely and found a family; the right to education, to employment, a good reputation, to respect, to appropriate information, to activity in accord with the right norm of one's own conscience, to protection of privacy, and rightful freedom in matters religious too.[23]

---

[22] It is good to note that these rights have been beautifully summed up in our Constitution under title "Fundamental Rights."

[23] GS, 26. 1.

The ideals mentioned in Human Rights have been beautifully summed up in these words; but when we look at the contemporary society, how far are we from these ideals, which we have proclaimed for ourselves? One of the important tasks of religions and ideologies is to strive together for the implementation of Human Rights.

Peace-building

As the contemporary world is torn asunder by wars and conflicts, if religions and ideologies are to be authentic, an all-out effort should be made for peace-building. In the past, religions have been associated with many conflicts; hence, today many people of good intentions, especially the youth, question whether religions are on the way to peace or conflict. Thus religions themselves are responsible for modern atheism. The primary task is to begin by asking pardon for our past failures, as some of the recent Popes have done, and give up the self-righteous hubris and intolerance. We need to acknowledge the fact that there are "fundamentalist" extremists within contemporary religious communities, and some of them are so powerful that they can easily have a good following. Religious peace-building involves a range of activities performed by religious actors and institutions for the purpose of resolving and transforming deadly conflict, with the goal of building social relations and political institutions characterized by an ethos of tolerance and nonviolence. There is an urgency laid upon religions and ideologies to come out of their self-imposed isolation and in a concerted manner to work for peace-building.[24]

Mutual Participation and Assistance in Humanitarian Concerns

One of the important values of various religious traditions and ideologies is promotion of mutual participation both in religious and social activities that contribute to the building up of the community. As mentioned earlier, no religion is perfect, and we depend upon one another for religious as well as social activities. One of the ways

[24] Cf. Manimala, *Toward Mutual Fecundation and Fulfillment of Religions*, pp. 522-527.

religions and ideologies can communicate a great value to their followers is by mutually assisting one another, and by calling for promoting such assistance in all the fields that are not opposed to justice, peace and harmony. In natural and social calamities, our hearts should burn with compassion for others, and should feel their struggles as our own and rush with whatever help needed for them so that in the company of compassionate people their hurt emotions and loss of dear ones will be compensated to some extent.[25] It is the common humanity that we all share, which should prompt us to come forward with all resources at our disposal. Religions or churches that hinder their followers from doing this have to be denounced by all people of good will. When religions engage in true dialogical praxis it must include in some way praxis for liberation and well-being.[26]

Dialogue and Sharing

Today for religions to attain their goal there is the necessity to enter into dialogue in its various aspects and also practice sharing in a spirit of hospitality. Dialogue coming to the level of praxis could be thought of in cooperation about concerns, such as poverty, discrimination, injustice, conflicts, militarism, environmental degradation, etc. Then there is the daily dialogue (dialogue of life) between neighbors of diverse faiths; this is the actual living of dialogue. Various types of dialogue belong to different contexts; they are expressions of different concerns and cannot be easily compared; but they may all lead to experiences and insights that are relevant for other levels

[25] We can recall the recent Ockhi cyclone which affected both Kerala and Tamil Nadu. The Churches, in association with other religions and agencies, could have organized the relief works so that we give a better witness to peace and harmony. I recount some of my personal experiences, as in 1971, the Spirit impelled me to go and work for East Pakistan (present Bangladesh) refugees, I felt that I could not resist it; similarly when a few cyclones struck the coasts of Andhra Pradesh we organized relief work by staying with the victims and cooperating with the government. There should an inner compulsion to engage in such social activities which will help us to transcend our religious boundaries.

[26] Cf. Manimala, *Toward Mutual Fecundation and Fulfillment of Religions,* pp. 528-530.

of dialogue.[27] Dialogue could be seen also in a different light. For those persons who assume that the human reason is competent to lead individuals into an understanding of truth, the activity called 'dialectic' or 'debate,' when transmuted into dialogical terms may be characterized as 'discursive dialogue.' It involves meeting, listening and discussion on the level of mutual competent intellectual inquiry. Sympathy and respect for the other person's position are absolutely essential; so, too, accurate knowledge of one's own religious tradition and scrupulous honesty in expressing its content. But going beyond this, we know that doctrines divide; humanity unites. In its simplest form this is the conviction that underlies the greater part of the activity that is today called interreligious dialogue. The 'I-Thou' relationship is all-important; what is said or done is less so. Here it is good to recall the beautiful distinction that Panikkar, the 'apostle' of interreligious dialogue, makes between "dialectical dialogue" and "dialogical dialogue." Moving beyond interreligious dialogue, we could also think of *secular dialogue*; it is that type of dialogue which concentrates entirely on the situation of man in the world. Some hold that 'desacralization' has helped in this respect. 'Secular dialogue' is more of emphasis than of exclusive concerns. Another important form of dialogue is the *interior dialogue*. Its *locus* is the mystical contemplative tradition, and its advocates are normally those trained in that tradition. Dialogue is, indeed, a practical activity, and it has to percolate into our daily life, and then religions will perceive how it is helpful for mutual fulfillment.[28] Such dialogue will call for the practice of the great virtue of hospitality. The German word used is *Gastfreiheit*[29] (literally 'freedom for guests', and it is used for hospitality); and the proper meaning of this word indicates that the host has no authority over the guests, nor to express a disinterest

---

[27] Cf. Notto R. Thelle, "Interreligious Dialogue: Theory and Experience," in the book, *Theology and the Religions: A Dialogue*, edited by Viggo Morternson (Grand Rapids, Michigan: Eerdmans Publishing Company, 2003), 130-131.

[28] Cf. Eric J. Sharpe, "The Goals of Inter-Religious Dialogue," in John Hick (ed.), *Truth and Dialogue* (London: Sheldon Press, 1974), 82-91. See also Manimala, *Toward Mutual Fecundation and Fulfillment of Religions,* 531-532.

[29] Jürgen Moltmann has a section on this in his book *Der Geist Lebens* (1991), the English translation is *Spirit of Life* (1992)

in them, but a friendly encompassing, and open interest towards 'foreign' people. The act of hospitality shows a rejection of freedom as authority and a choice of freedom as communion; it is a getting out of alienation and a call to embrace. An invitation would be more pressing, when this would involve the freedom as a common project for the future. In the language of Christian symbolism it involves an invitation to the Kingdom of God, to the eternal life, and to the recreation of all things.[30] Such a disposition will call for fellowship, availability and generosity, humility and friendship, courage and gratitude. These will strengthen us for greater commitment.

Ecology, Ecofilia and Ecosophy

As there is a tremendous awareness growing regarding the future of humankind as well as Mother Earth, we will be failing in our duty if we do not at least hint at the responsibility of religions and ideologies for protecting Nature and the flora and fauna, not only for ourselves, but for the future generations as well. Here three important terms stand out, and we shall briefly explain them. We are using three important terms in our discussion – *Ecology, Ecofilia* and *Ecosophy*. All these are based on the Greek language: the first term coined from Eco + logos (έκο-λογός) = science of the earth, Eco + filia (έκο-ψιλία) = friendship with the earth, and Eco + Sophia (έκο-σοψία) = wisdom of the earth. In the first term there is a clear cut duality expressed, namely the Earth is made an object of a subject's analysis; and hence there is a lot of imposition of the pre-suppositions of the subject on the object, and the analysis is done not with any prescribed ethics or norm but Earth as an object to be made use of. At present there may be some amount of biological ethics being brought in because of the impending danger that may overtake us. In the second term, *Ecofilia*, there is a movement from reducing the Earth to an object to a companion as if, because the term *filia* means friendship. As we can guess, friendship is possible only between beings who can acknowledge one another as inter-subjective and inter-protective. A

[30] Cf. Susanne Hennecke, "Related by Freedom: The Impact of Third World Theologians on the Thinking of Jürgen Moltmann," *Voices from the Third World* (Vol. XXVII No. 2, Dec. 2004), 136-137.

true friendship is not possible in a relationship of over-protection or domination. In friendship there is an assurance given: "I shall be there for you," and there is also a certain mutuality expressed in the notion of friendship; there cannot be a one-way friendship. Thus we find that in *ecofilia* there is a little more intimacy expressed. This leads us to the final term of our discourse – *Ecosophy*, the wisdom of the earth. Here it is not the subject who imposes a concept or a notion upon the object but the Earth itself is inviting the humans to learn from her, thus calling for an attitude of receptivity from the part of the human being. Wisdom is the result of 'enlightenment' and an attitude of humility, and it will call for commitment. Wisdom is not so much the result of analysis and research but is more of intuition, and it is more a gift rather than an attainment. Hence, one remains always grateful for this gift, and that attitude makes one more receptive. The attitude of Receptivity is very much at the core of wisdom (*Sophia*). Wisdom also indicates a willingness to share and be co-responsible. Pope Francis through his encyclical *Laudato Si* has proclaimed our responsibility and the needed commitment to protect the Earth. He says that the urgent challenge is to protect our common home, which will call for a sustainable and integral development. Let us heed to this call and become relevant people for the society.[31]

Conclusion

Our attempt in this paper has been to delineate in some measure Pluralism which has become a necessity, and in this context how to live a relevant life in the contemporary society. As we have seen the challenge before us is great, but we cannot shy away from our responsibility as committed and civilized citizens. The greatest Christian virtue is hope, and we need to believe that we can overcome the hurdles if we have the courage to transcend our religion and situations, and join hands with people of other religions and ideologies. We need to be committed people by becoming co-pilgrims with people of other faiths, realizing that we are all on

[31] Cf. Pope Francis, *Laudato Si* (Trivandrum: Carmel International Publishing House, 2015). The whole encyclical is good for a spiritual reading and retreat.

search for Truth, and since Truth is nobody's monopoly we can sincerely join hands with all people of good will. We need to have the prophetic courage to denounce the unjust structures and announce the Kingdom of God established in peace, justice and harmony. Let us heed to the challenge of Jesus, and break ourselves up for healing the brokenness of the world. The counter-culture that Jesus practiced and asked us to hold fast need to be implemented if we have to be relevant today.

Select Bibliography

Ahlstrand, Kajsa. "Toward a Paradigm Shift in Christian Mission: South Asia and North Europe." In *Theology and the Religions: A Dialogue*, edited by Viggo Mortensen, 166-168. Grand Rapids, Michigan: Eerdmans Publishing Company, 2003.

Ariarajah, Wesley. "Intercultural Hermeneutics – A Promise for the Future?" In *Voices from the Third World*, Vol. xxIx No. 1, June 2006.

Hennecke, Susanne. "Related by Freedom: The Impact of Third World Theologians on the Thinking of Jürgen Moltmann," *Voices from the Third World*, Vol. XXVII No. 2, Dec. 2004, 136-137.

Küng, Hans. *Theology for the Third Millennium: An Ecumenical View*. New York: Doubleday, 1988.

Manimala, Varghese. *Toward Mutual Fecundation and Fulfillment of Religions: An Invitation to Transcendence and Dialogue with a Cosmotheandric Vision*. Delhi: Media House & ISPCK, 2009.

Murti, T. R. V. *The Central Philosophy of Buddhism*. London: Allen and Unwin, 1955.

Panikkar, Raimon. *Intrareligious Dialogue,* Revised Edition. New York: Paulist Press, 1999.

Panikkar, Raimon. *A Dwelling Place of Wisdom*, Translated by Annemarie S. Kidder. Westminster: Westminster John Knox Press, 1993.

Sharpe, Eric J., "The Goals of Inter-Religious Dialogue." In *Truth and Dialogue*, edited by John Hick, 82-91. London: Sheldon Press, 1974.

Thelle, Notto R. "Interreligious Dialogue: Theory and Experience." In *Theology and the Religions: A Dialogue*, edited by Viggo Morternson, 130-131. Grand Rapids, Michigan: Eerdmans Publishing Company, 2003.

Wink, Walter. *Engaging the Powers: Discernment and Resistance in a World of Domination*. Minneapolis: Fortress Press, 1992.

9

Social Teachings of the Church and their Relevance for Public Theology

X.D. Selvaraj
Moral Theologian, Thoothukudi

Introduction

Reading the signs of the times and responding to them adequately in the light of the Gospel are the fundamental processes of doing theology in the Christian tradition. By so doing, different denominational Churches have come out with significant teachings, which could be revisited today in the context of the emerging public theology. The Catholic Church has a body of teachings known as the 'Catholic Social Teachings', and the Protestant Churches have theirs primarily in the teachings of the World Council of Churches. It would do well to take a look at their salient themes, so as to relate them to public theology today.

Social Teachings of the Catholic Church

Social teaching of the Catholic Church (STC) is a growing body of teachings, engaging with social concerns of humanity across space and time. Its official teaching began with Pope Leo XIII's encyclical *Rerum Novarum* – (of the workers' state) which was issued in 1891 against the background of the industrial revolution and the emergence of the working class consciousness. And, the latest teachings are of Pope Francis - *Evangelii Gaudium* (the 'Joy of the Gospel') and *Laudato Si* (Praise be to God). Let me begin with briefly pointing out to the central themes of the social teachings without going into their historical context and their details. They are:

Human Dignity, Equality and Rights

"The dignity of the human person must be honored and advanced also in the socio-economic realm along with the welfare of the state as a whole. For man is the source, the centre and the purpose of all socio-economic life."[1]

"Basic equality of all must receive increasingly greater recognition … human institutions, both private and public, must labour to minister to the dignity and purpose of man. At the same time, let them put up a stubborn fight against any form of slavery, whether social or political and safeguard the basic rights of man under every political system."[2]

"All share a true equality with regard to the dignity … common to all the faithful…."[3]

Love – Justice and Evangelization

"Christian … love implies an absolute demand for justice, namely a recognition of the dignity and rights of one's neighbour. Justice attains its inner fullness only in love."[4]

"Action on behalf of justice and participation in the transformation of the world fully appear to us as a constitutive dimension of the preaching of the gospel, or in other words, of the

---

[1] Vatican II , "Church in the Modern World (GS)" 1965, No. 63.

[2] Ibid, No. 29.

[3] Vat II, "The Church (LG)," No. 32; cf. also canon law, 208.

[4] Synod of Bishops, *Justice in the World*, 1971, No. 34.

church's mission for the redemption of human race and its liberation from every oppressive situation."[5]

Two observations are in place here: one, in today's unjust world, justice as the constitutive element of evangelization means that all works – charitable, developmental, liberative – should be oriented towards the transformation of society / world; otherwise they are not considered as evangelization. Secondly, the Bishops of India are making a path-breaking statement that in India "justice needs to be viewed as a privileged expression and an apostolic priority."[6]

The Church of the Poor and Solidarity with them

"The Church is firmly committed to this cause (of justice), for she considers it her mission, her service, a proof of the solidarity to Christ, so that she can be truly the church of the poor."[7]

"Social injustice is caused by 'structures of sin' or social sin."[8] This must be overcome by taking a stand in solidarity with the poor. The Pope calls for solidarity as the new social virtue.

"The trade unions are indeed a mouthpiece for the struggle for social justice for the just rights of the working people."[9]

"Intergenerational solidarity is not optional. But rather a basic question of justice, since the world we have received also belongs to those who will follow us."[10]

Pope Leo XIII recommends 'Christian Association' only to obtain justice. But Pope John Paul II calls for free trade union as mouthpiece for the struggle for justice. Pope Francis calls for intergenerational solidarity as obligation towards future generations.

---

[5] Ibid, No. 6.

[6] Cf. John Desrochers, *The Social Teaching of the Church in India* (Bangalore: NBCLC/CSA, 2006), 57.

[7] Pope John Paul II, *Laborem Exercens (Human Labour)*, 1981, No. 8.

[8] Pope John Paul II, *Sollicitudo Rei Socialis (Social Commitment of the Church)*, 1987, No. 36.

[9] Pope John Paul II, *Laborem Exercens*, No. 20.

[10] Pope Francis, *Laudato Si (Praise be to You)*, 2015, No. 159.

Universal Destination of Created Goods

"Attention must always be paid to the universal purpose for which created goods are meant…. If a person is in extreme necessity, he (*sic*) has the right to take from the riches of the other what he himself (sic) needs."[11]

"The right of every man (*sic*) to use them (created material goods) for his (*sic*) own sustenance is prior to all other rights in economic life, and hence is prior even to the right of private ownership."[12]

"The right to private property is not absolute and unconditional. No one may appropriate surplus goods solely for his (*sic*) own private use, when others lack the basic necessities of life."[13]

Rerum Novarum of Pope Leo XIII (1891) and *Quadragesismo Anno* of Pope Pius XI (1931) upheld the right to private property as fundamental and prior to all other rights. But Pope Pius XII (1942) and Vatican II (GS) emphasize the common purpose of created goods and say that the right to use created goods is prior to right to possess.

No to Exclusion and Inequality; Yes to Inclusion, Equality & Ecological Concerns

"No to an economy of exclusion, No to the inequality which spawns violence…..until exclusion and inequality are reversed, it will be highly impossible to eliminate violence."[14]

"Today, however, we have to realize that a true ecological approach always becomes a social approach, it must integrate questions of justice in debates on the environment so as to hear both the cry of the earth and the cry of the poor."[15]

---

[11] GS, No. 69.

[12] Allocution in a broadcast, June, 1941 by Pope Pius XII on the occasion of the 50th anniversary of *Rerum Novarum* of Pope Leo XIII.

[13] Pope Paul VI, *Populorum Progressio (Development of People)*, 1967, No. 23.

[14] Pope Francis, *Evangelii Gaudium (Joy of the Gospel)*, 2013, Nos. 53-54, 57-60.

[15] Pope Francis, *Laudato Si*, 2015, No. 49.

Political Involvement and Participation

"The need is felt to pass from economics to politics... in the social and economic field, both national and international, the ultimate decision rests with political power.... It must have as its aim the achievement of the common good."[16]

"Unless combated and overcome by social and political action, the influence of the new industrial and technological order favors the concentration of wealth, power and decision-making in the hands of a small public or private controlling group. Economic injustice and lack of social participation keep a man from attaining his (*sic*) basic human and civil rights."[17]

Roughly 25 to 30% of Indians, according to international standard, live in abject poverty and destitution. Should theology not address this man-made poverty which is diminishing and destroying human dignity and which is waging a war against God's image in the marginalized poor in our country? When traditional theology comes out from its narrow confines to address such social issues in the 'public sphere', then it becomes public theology.

As of now, the social teachings of the Catholic Church, an extension of theology in today's context – does address social issues as we just saw above. But it does it in closed religious circles and Christian communities often isolated from public life of society. Even the much appreciated charity and development works done in Christian social service centres all over our country are carried out as a parallel government without addressing the root cause of poverty. They do not make a prophetic critique of the unjust structures in public.

Once again more than 22% of the educational institutions are run by Christians in our country. Discipline, punctuality, competition, success, etc., are given priority rather than the Gospel-based public values of social concern for the poor. As a result these institutions make less impact on the political life of the poor. But

[16] Pope Paul VI, *Octogesima Adveniens (Politics, Ideology and Social Commitment)*, 1971, Nos. 46-47.

[17] Pope Paul VI, *Justitia in Mundo (Justice in the World)*, 1971, No. 9; cf. also GS, No. 43.

some radical Christians, inspired by the Gospel and the social teaching of the church, get involved at the grassroots struggles of the poor together with various secular and new social movements, and make some impact in public sphere.

The World Council of Churches (WCC)

Origins: The Commission of the Churches on International Affairs (CCIA) was born for the cooperation of the Churches in the twentieth century. It felt that it must organize the Churches in order to exert some worthwhile influence on the problems of international life.[18] The origins of the WCC may be traced back to the 1910 Conference of Edinburg on 'Evangelization of the world in this Generation'. It was followed by several efforts and discussions between CCIA and International Missionary Council (IMC). In the meantime two world wars broke out. The Second World War affected world peace. Against this historical background the commission of the WCC was officially constituted at the First Assembly in Amsterdam in 1948. It is a council of autonomous Churches. Its Constitution says: "The World Council shall offer counsel and provide opportunity for united action in matters of common interest."[19]

Social Teachings

Once again only a few main themes are cited here without their historical context and other details related to the themes.

The first Assembly of Amsterdam (1948)- No to injustice & yes to justice

"We have to ask God to teach us together to say 'No' and to say 'Yes' in truth. No to… the defenders of injustice in the name of order, to those who sow the seeds of war or urge war as inevitable; yes to all that conforms to the love of Christ, to all who seek for justice, to the peace-makers, to all who hope, fight and suffer for the cause

[18] Cf. Ans J. Van der Bent, *Christian Response in a World of Crisis* (Geneva: World Council of Churches, 1986), 1.

[19] Cf. George H. Dunme, S.J., *Introduction to Church Communication Development: A SODEPAX Report* (Geneva: SODEPAX, 1970), 5.

of man, to all who – even without knowing it – look for new heaven and a new earth wherein dwelleth righteousness."[20]

"Justice... demands that economic activities be subordinated to social ends... ownership is not an unconditional right; it must, therefore, be preserved, curtailed or distributed in accordance with the requirements of justice.[21] It says further that persons must never be made mere means for political or economic ends. The Churches in all lands must work for responsible just society.

The Second Assembly of Evanston (1954)- Social Justice and Responsible Society

"It is not enough that Christians should seek peace for themselves. They must seek justice for others. Great masses of people in many parts of the world are hungry for bread and are compelled to live in conditions which mock their human worth. Does your church speak and act against such injustice?"[22]

Justice demands political institutions to be human and provide protection by law against the arbitrary use of power. It encourages responsible participation by all citizens.

The Third Assembly of New Delhi (1961) - Identification with the oppressed & Struggle for justice

"Where oppression, discrimination and segregation exist, the Churches should identify themselves with the oppressed race in its struggle to achieve justice. Christians should be ready to lead in this struggle."[23]

The Ultimate loyalty of the Church is for biblical justice; Churches must be prepared for conflicts with the State in any nation and under any political system.

---

[20] W. B. Visser't Hooft (ed), *The Assembly of the WCC Official Report* (London: SCM Pres, 1949), 10.

[21] Ibid, 76-77.

[22] Ibid, 3.

[23] Ibid, 42

The Geneva Conference (1966) – Christians in the Technical and Social Revolutions of our Time

"Churches have too often attached themselves to the status quo, resenting and resisting change.... Sometimes they have fallen into the theological error of identifying existing structures with an external divine order, thus overlooking the dynamic character of God as revealed in Scripture."[24]

Christians should seek opportunities to cooperate with non-Christians in promoting social justice.

The Fourth Assembly of Uppsala (1968) – Behold! I make all things new!

This assembly highlights four ways in which God challenges the Churches to make things new: 1) Fellowship with all men, 2) Trusteeship over Creation, 3) Building of a just world Community and 4) Ecumenical worship and dialogue.

Complacency at the face of injustice is a practical heresy.

Between the Geneva World Conference in 1966 and the Fourth WCC assembly in Uppsala in 1968, the ecumenical movement recognized the need of deep changes in world economics and political structures, if global human justice is to be achieved. A new concept of "a just participatory and sustainable society" emerged. The Vancouver Assembly in 1983 started interlinking justice and peace saying, there can be no peace without justice. There was also an increasing stress on the Gospel – based bias towards the oppressed poor and the political necessity of their participation in decision-making processes.[25]

The Fifth Assembly of Nairobi (1975) – Justice and Service

"It becomes increasingly clear that service can only be rendered effectively when it is related to the question of Justice."[26]

---

[24] Ibid, 69.

[25] Cf. Ans J. van der Bent, *Christian Response in a World of Crisis*, 8.

[26] Uppsala to Nairobi-1968-1975, *Report of the Central Committee to the Fifth Assembly of the WCC*, ed. Johnson (New Work: Friendship Press, 1975), 123.

"The Church's unity is lived in the tension of political struggle.... It is frequently tempted to remain silent in order to preserve 'Unity' or to divide in a crusading spirit for or against some particular cause."[27]

"To work for human rights, therefore, also means to work at the most basic level towards a society without unjust structures.... The basic causes for these violations are to be found in the unjust social order, the abuse of power, the lack of economic development and in unequal development."[28]

The Nairobi assembly asked the Churches "to stimulate public discussion and initiate research on the root causes and driving forces behind militarism and the armament dynamics."[29]

The Post Nairobi Teachings (1977) - Dialogue with People of living Faiths and Ideologies

"In an age of World – Wide struggle of humankind for survival and liberation, religions and ideologies have their important contributions to make which can only be worked out in mutual dialogue. Dialogue should be pursued in common enterprises."[30]

Some Observations and Assessments:

WCC, RCC and SODEPAX

It is indeed praiseworthy that in 1948 the World Council of Churches (WCC) came together to raise a unified voice to defend human dignity and rights of all people. The Second Vatican Council (1962-1965) opened the way for cooperation between the Roman Catholic Church (RCC) and the World Council of Churches (WCC). In 1965 a joint working group was established. From then on WCC and RCC – represented by the Pontificial commission for Justice and Peace have had formal consultations and joint action whenever and wherever possible. In 1968 - twenty years after the formation

---

[27] Ibid, 11.

[28] Ibid, 12, 31.

[29] Ibid, 11.

[30] Dialogue in Community Statements and Reports of a Theological Consultation (Chiang Mai, Thailand, 1977), 41.

of WCC and three years after the closure of Vatican Council – the Committee on Society, Development and Peace (SODEPAX), a joint venture of RCC and WCC was created. Its mandate was to "arouse (people) everywhere to a sense of responsibility for the problems of social injustice in the world."[31] Unfortunately, even after making significant progress for 12 years, SODEPAX was disbanded in 1980. It was due largely to circumstances, beyond its control, thus it was said.

I think that it is the need of our time to resurrect the SODEPAX experiment. It can serve as a model for contemporary ecumenical cooperation, as it was a grassroots organization with a bottom-up approach. It provided the first opportunity for Christian ethicists and social scientists to come together and freely discuss the many challenges facing the world community. The social teachings of RCC and WCC would carry more weight if both organizations were to come together again to offer unified ecumenical responses to contemporary social problems.

Social Teachings of the Church (STC) – An Extension of the Gospel

The STC is only an extension of the Gospel interpreted historically, scrutinizing the signs of the times in the concrete context. "At all times the Church carries the responsibility of reading the signs of the times and of interpreting them in the light of the gospel, if it is to carry out its tasks."[32] Pope John Paul II said that to teach and to spread the social teaching of the Church pertains to the Church's evangelizing mission. It points out the direct consequences of the Gospel message in the life of the present society to be witness to Christ.

---

[31] Cf. Ans J. Van der Bent, *Christian Response in a World of Crisis*, 10; Cf. George H. Dunne, SJ, *Introduction to Church Communication Development*, 5.

[32] Vatican II , GS No. 4; cf. also *Oetogesima Advenience*, Pope Paul VI , 1971, no. 4; *Centesimus Annus*, Pope John Paul II, 1991, No. 5.

The STC and Christian Faith

The STC often contains valuable insights on the relationship between Christian Faith and social issues. For example:

- Human dignity rooted in God's image demands equality and participation among humans.
- Love and justice are inseparable dimensions of evangelization.
- The right to use created goods is prior to the right to possess them.
- Authentic church is of the poor, with the poor and for the poor.
- Struggles in solidarity with the exploited victims to change economic and political policies towards common good is a must.
- Ecological - environmental concern is the need of the hour to save the world.
- Political involvement with social movements is needed for structural and systemic change.
- Dialogue with people of living faiths and ideologies should become a way of life.

STC- Inspiration for Social involvement

The STC has inspired some of their members (both RCC and WCC) to make relevant and timely social interventions. It has further inspired some others to get involved in socio-political-economic and cultural issues. It has helped Christians to defend and justify their social commitment in the face of criticism against their involvement with radical and revolutionary groups and movements. As seen before, some radical Christians, who distance themselves from institutional Christianity, inspired by the STC are engaged in action in public sphere / political society.

STC – Church related Institutions

STC is communicated mostly within the Church related institutions, houses of religious formation and seminaries that train the clergy.

Thus it has suffered a strong clericalization says Fr. Felix Wilfred. By and large it has not yet reached the laity who form 98% of the Christian population. Peter Henriot says that the STC is the best kept secret in the Church. Bishops too give more importance to the liturgical guidelines and instructions coming from Rome, and not to the STC, coming from the teaching Roman Magisterium, for reasons known to them. Hence, the STC has not yet reached out to the larger public.

STC-Dialogue and Public Discussion

The fifth Assembly of Nairobi in 1975 asked the Churches 'to stimulate public discussion' on social issues.[33] 'Dialogue with people of living faiths and ideologies' was the main theme of discussion in the post Nairobi teaching. "Religions and ideologies have their important contributions to make which can only be worked out in the mutual dialogue. Dialogue should be pursued in common enterprises."[34]

Vatican II has one whole document on Inter-Religious dialogue. The Church opens up to dialogue with the world, religions and cultures. "Through loyalty to conscience Christians are joined to other men in the search for truth and for the right solution to so many moral (social) problems which arise both in the life of individuals and from social relationships."[35] One can't possess truth. One can only search and seek truth together with others of good will and seekers of truth.

Though both RCC and WCC recommend dialogue, they have a long way to go towards dialogue in public sphere.

The social teachings of both RCC and WCC do address topics like political involvement and participation of the poor, solidarity with the poor, identification with the oppressed and struggles for justice, etc. The so-called public sphere of public theology is mostly occupied by the rich and the powerful in collaboration with the corporate companies. The emerging upper middle class also joins

---

[33] *Uppsala to Nairobi Report*, 123.

[34] *Dialogue in Community*, 41.

[35] GS, No. 16.

them through their upward mobility. The market and media are at the service of these people. Hence the burning social issues of starvation, death, and lack of medical help, honour-killing of the Dalits by caste fanatics, the violent displacement of the tribals from their life resources in the name of development, etc., of the subaltern people will not find a serious consideration in the public sphere.

There is hence a need to look for *political society* as Felix Wilfred suggests: political society is where the poor and the subaltern grapple with their life-issues, waging struggles and protests, and thus exercise their agency. Asian (Indian) public theology will respond to this situation rather than address the question of public sphere.[36] And people of good will and those interested in the wellbeing of the subaltern people will be in solidarity with them to bring about a just and humane society.

In today's unjust India, public theology will take on a definite prophetic stand together with the oppressed and exploited poor to defend their human dignity and rights from the tyranny of the corporate and their market economy. To defend the tribals in particular is the most effective way of protecting the environment as their cry and that of the earth are intimately interrelated. Likewise the dream and struggles of the Dalits for a just and egalitarian society has to be openly upheld by public theology.

The Future of STC is to Go Public in Theologizing

Privatized social teaching is a contradiction. Social problems of male domination or environmental hazards concern all human beings. Hence, social teaching about such issues has to reach out to the public as David Tracy points out. He speaks about three distinct but interrelated social locations of theology. What is said of theology applies also to social teaching, as STC is an extension of theology in the concrete historical situations in a particular context. According to him the three locations are society, church

---

[36] Cf. Felix Wilfred, "Asian Pluralism and Higher Education" in *East Asian Pastoral Review*, 46 (2009), pp. 33-45; also *Asian Public Theology: Critical Concerns in Challenging Times* (New Delhi: ISPCK, 2010), xx.

and academy.[37] Accordingly STC should become a public discourse as the social issues are public, going beyond any particular religion, creed, ethnicity, language, culture, etc.

As of now the STC comes from above, from the Catholic point of view. It comes from the Magisterium- the teaching church and not so much from the learning church. It will pave the way for public theologizing provided it comes down to a bottom up methodology in the articulation of its teaching. For the voice and cries of the crucified people of our society – Dalits, Tribals, women of the lower castes and class, marginalized farmers, fisher folk, etc - will not otherwise be adequately heard. These are the ones who are in touch with the ground realities which are harsh and hard. The articulation of their experience will not only be intellectual but also emotional, appealing more to people towards praxis.

The STC to become public theologizing should work along with people of other discipline such as sociology, history, anthropology, humanities, etc. Since factual realities are highly complex – multi-religious, multi-cultural, multi-linguistic, multi-ethnic, multi-caste, etc., these realities are more important than ideas. Those who articulate social teaching and those who theologize must allow these realities to speak to them, question them, disturb them, challenge them, etc., for adequate and relevant response. They should not impose their conceptual clarity on realities and enclose them; rather clarity should emerge from realities. It is tested again in society for its transformation.

If theologizing is the articulation of the faith praxis in relation to others in a given community, the theologian needs to be involved and take a stand like Jesus who was in struggle-solidarity with the oppressed poor. The victims of economic globalization are the poor, and the victims of Hindutva's exclusive nationalism are the minorities. The victims of structural injustice are these categories of people. The victims of Jesus' time almost decided the nature of Jesus' ministry, his lifestyle and his preaching and teaching. The theologian needs to be a partner with non-governmental social movements in civil society

[37] Cf. David Tracy, *Analogical Imagination: Christian Theology and Culture of Pluralism* (New York: Crossroad Publishing Company, 1982).

to uphold human dignity, right to participate in the public space as citizens. Struggle is the language of the crucified people for the right to speech and action and against all forms of marginalization and discrimination.

Conclusion

The floated idea /concept of public theologizing is of recent origin and it is in the process of gradual making in India. Religion in secular India is not merely private but also public with its impact on society. Besides, public theology further wants the believers to enter into public sphere concerning common social issues, using a very secular language understandable to the common public beyond their religions, creed, ideology, ethnicity, etc. An alienated and insulated theology from the realities of the subaltern people in the public sphere of the socio-economic-political and cultural areas will be of no use to anyone.

Church is one of the civil institutions. Christians are not only the members of the Church but also the citizens of the country. Public theology calls the much divided Christians on the basis of castes, rites, language, ideology, political allegiants, etc., to come together in order to assert their citizenship and their constitutional rights together with all other citizens. Public theology through multifarious dialogue and encounters at various levels should influence public policies in accordance with its biblical-theological vision to secure the common good of all, especially that of the victims. This common good is, in fact, God's will.

Bibliography

Amalorpavadass, D. S. (ed.) *The Indian Church in the Struggle for a New Society.* Bangalore: NBCLC, 1981.

De Berri, Edward P. & others. *Catholic Social Teaching - Our Best Kept Secret.* New York: Orbis Books, 2004. (Fourth Revised and Expanded Edition).

De Souza, Donald H. R. *Final Statements of the General Body Meetings of Catholic Bishops' Conference of India* (C. B. C. I.) (1966-2002). New Delhi: CBCI Centre, 2000.

Desrochers, John. *The Social Teaching of the Church in India*. Bangalore: NBCLC/CSA, 2006.

Door, Donald. *Option for the Poor – A Hundred Years of Catholic Social Teaching*. New York: Orbis Books, 1992 (Revised Edition).

Pontifical Council for Justice and Peace. *Compendium of the Social Doctrine of the Church*. Mumbai: Pauline Publication, 2005.

Therukaattil, George. *Compassionate Love – Ethics (Vol. 2 Social Justice)*. Kochi: Karunikan Books, 2015.

Walsh, Michael & Brian Davies (ed.). *Proclaiming Justice and Peace – Documents from John XXIII to John Paul II*. Bangalore: TPI, 1985.

10

Inter-relationality between Indian State and Church: An Analysis

Peter Susaimanickam
Professor, Sacred Heart College, Poonamallie, Chennai

The relation between the Church and the State will rest on certain fundamental values which we have begun to respect in the modern democratic world namely, equality, liberty and fraternity and other values that proceed from them. A State or society which does not value them cannot provide, in theory, a government of the 21st century. If one takes a survey of the contemporary democratic States, these values are enshrined, at least, in their Constitutions. The Church in the same way is a Church that is historically rooted or indigenous Church in communion with the universal Church that respects democratic values. Hence, the underlying factor in the relation between the two is the respect for the democratic values.

This article, based on the nature of the State and the Church, will analyze the possibility of relationship between the two and the implications of it for a democratic society.

The Context

The social media carry everyday at least one incident against Christians in India, either a comment against Christian institutions or attack on churches. People belonging to different religions other than Hinduism are seen to be anti-nationals just because they do not belong to the religion of the majority. Not only at the global level,[1] but at Indian level too religious persecutions are on the rise.[2] Since, Christians are the targets of the fundamentalists in India, Cardinal Baselios Cleemis, the then president of CBCI, said on 21 December 2017: "The anxiety of the religious minorities is increasing because of the lack of confidence in the administration. So the onus is on the government to bring back the confidence of religious minorities."[3]

On the one hand, the Indian Church seems to be gripped with *unconscious Anxiety* and *fear*. Hence, the discourse of the Christians often invokes the safety of the minority religions. The believing community uses the language of safety and security expecting the State to protect them because they are minorities in this country. On the other hand, the State seems to be silent about what happens around. The silence helps the BJP members to come up with

---

[1] "More than 215 million Christians suffer from intolerance in the world (about 1 every 12 or 8.6%), 3060 Christians were killed, 1922 imprisoned, 793 churches targeted: these are the figures of the 2018 Report published yesterday [January 11 2018] by Ong Portes Ouvertes /Open Doors (reference period November 1, 2016-31, October 2017)." Accessed on 26 February 2018 in the following website: http://www.lastampa.it/2018/01/12/vaticaninsider/eng/documents/christian-persecution-is-growing-million-worldwide-qL2EuMOR8fxeAV0luroCbK/pagina.html.

[2] "According to a report from Persecution Relief, last year 736 incidents of attacks occurred throughout India compared to the 348 that happened in 2016. Most of these are "daring physical attacks," the report said, but the victims of these attacks were also accused of sedition, discrimination, and destruction of religious property." "Attacks against India's Christians Doubled in 2017, published on 21, February 2018: available in the following website: https://www.catholicnewsagency.com/news/attacks-against-indias-christians-doubled-in-2017-55262: accessed on 26 February 2018.

[3] Ritu Sharma, "Christians Lack Confidence in Modi Government, Cardinal," published on 21 December 2017: available in the following website: https://www.ucanews.com/news/christians-lack-confidence-in-modi-government-cardinal/81134: accessed on 5 February 2018.

unsubstantiated hate speeches against Christianity. Recently for example, Bharat Singh, one of members of the Parliament belonging to the BJP said that "the democracy in the north eastern states of the country has 'weakened' due to the 'conversion of people there into Christianity."[4]

It would be wide of the mark to blame the State alone for the anxiety and insecurity of the Christian religious minority. The context leads us to understand that the Church in India also is partly responsible for the State to behave like this, since the Church has not been deeply rooted in the Indian soil.

Reality Check

The reality check shows the strength and weaknesses of both the Church and the state and invites the reader to assess their functions in the society.

The Indian Church

In spite of the presence of Christianity in India for two millennia, it has neither grown numerically nor has become influential in *public* life. In other words, it has neither been adequately a missionary church[5] nor a prophetic Church.[6] The initial observation suggests

---

[4] "Christian missionaries a threat to unity of the country: BJP's Ballia MP," *The Indian Express* 22 April 2018. Available in the following website: http://indianexpress.com/article/india/christian-missionaries-a-threat-to-unity-of-the-country-bjps-ballia-mp-5147341/. Accessed on 24 April 2018.

[5] India Christians have never grown over 2.4 percent in Indian population in spite of their presence for 2000 years. But the Hindu population out of India is growing enormously. "And mind you, the Hindu figures for the UK are on the way up, not down. And the UK is no exception. Here are some other figures—New Zealand: 2 per cent, Canada: 1.6 per cent, Australia: 1.28 per cent, Malaysia: 6.3 per cent and Indonesia: 1.69 per cent. This is without even considering our immediate neighbours such as Sri Lanka or Bhutan, or countries such as Fiji or Mauritius, where the figures are, of course, much higher." Tony JOSEPH, "Why Christianity Failed in India," *Outlook* 13 April 2015. He concludes his article showing the decline of the number of Christians that if at all there is a religion that should worry about its future it is not Hinduism but Christianity.

[6] The Bishops' conference has not come out with open statements on social justice in the earlier phases. "However, the CBCI, from its inception in 1944 until

that in spite of her contribution to Indian society at various levels, the Church has not taken serious measures to fight social injustice. While not undermining the prophetic and liberative works undertaken by the Church both in the past and the present, I only claim that our works have not been *proportionate* to the duration of its presence in India. The Church has been like a Fig tree without fruits.

The Indian Democratic Secular State

The Indian State suffers in understanding the Constitution. Further, it functions against the spirit of unity in diversity. Without accepting plurality as a value of a democratic country, the State attempts to initiate efforts that would eliminate the presence of different religions, languages and cultures in India. Article 14 states that "The State shall not deny to any person equality before the law and equal protection of laws within the territory of India." Article 15 (1) says that "The State shall not discriminate against any citizen on grounds only of religion, race, caste, sex, place of birth or any of them." It should keep in mind the intention of the founding fathers of the nation to establish and respect plurality and promote equality, liberty and fraternity.

Not just it is in the Constitution, but respecting plurality and exhibiting tolerance is the distinctive mark of Indian secularism which is rooted in its cultural milieu. Historical studies will reveal how the soil had tolerance towards every religion irrespective of the different rulers it had in the country. The reality check indicates that basically both the Church and the State should go back to the roots – the Indian State to the Constitution and to its history, and the Church to its scriptural/theological roots.

1970, did not approve any comprehensive statements on the question of social justice. CBCI documents emphasized internal Church affairs and the proper maintenance of charitable organizations. In fact, the CBCI standing committee argued in 1952 that the best contribution the Church could make to "the country's welfare" would be through "her educational and social welfare activities"." Mathew N. SCHMALZ, "The Indian Church: Catholicism and Indian Nationhood," in *The Catholic Church and the Nation-State: Comparative Perspectives,* ed., Paul Christopher Manuel, Lawrence C. Reardon, Clyde Wilcox, 209 – 225 (Washington D.C.: Georgetown University Press, 2006), 214.

Identifying the Problems

In order to substantiate the point that both the Church and the State deviate from their original goals, it is mandatory then to identify the problems that take away from the purpose of establishing God's reign and the values of democracy.

The State

There are at least three problems which can be identified that threaten the unity of the country and the values of democracy.

Assimilation / Homogenization

The current Indian State has the tendency to overlook pluralities. We could call it as the forgetfulness of plural ways of being of the past. In combating the diversities, the State attempts to assimilate everything into 'one'. The recent efforts to imagine an Indian nation based on Hinduism is the effort at homogenization. It is moving towards a kind of 'one rule' – one nation, one tax, one election – and eventually one nation and so one religion. In the words of Romila Thaper who rightly says that "Hindutva [ideology of the state which is different from Hinduism] denies diversity and plurality"[7] and absorbs everything into one big bag. Though the government is supposed to be an administration for all the people, it behaves as though the government of one particular religious citizen. The State should not be uprooted from its acceptance of pluralities.

Misconception of Secularism

The second is the misunderstanding of what secularism is. Discussion on Indian secularism has divided people on many scores. It is often complained that Indian secularism is based on the Western model. Therefore secularism is not advocated in India.[8] Definitely

---

[7] Romila THAPAR, "Is Secularism Alien to Indian Civilization?", in *The Future of Secularism*, ed., T. N. SRINIVASAN, 83 – 108 (New Delhi: Oxford University Press, 2010), 87.

[8] For different perspectives on Indian Secularism, cf. Rajeev Bhargava, *Secularism and its Critics* (New Delhi: Oxford University Press, 1998).

the influence of western discourses might have helped, but Indian secularism as such is not purely a western secularism.

The effort to oppose the Indian model of secularism as a western model is a misconception. Indian secularism does accept religion as a positive aspect of human life and admits its presence in the public sphere; however it does not accept the siding of the State with any religion. In the name of opposing Western secularism, the State tends to side with the majoritarian religion. This is purely a misconception of Indian secularism. It confuses the role of religion in politics. Taking side with a religion is a distortion of Indian secularism.

Focusing on Theory of a Nation than Democratic Values

In resolving conflicts that arise between different religions and languages, the State follows the modern western notion of conceiving a national identity of the sameness. It is an irony that while Christianity is considered a western (foreign) religion, the western theoretical framework of building a nation is followed without hesitation. In this line it does not simply oppose the west but follows it, while the west has left the notion of one State and one identity, the Indian State seems to move anachronistically.

In constructing a nation based on one identity of the majority, the State focuses on a stable nation than safeguarding the values of equality, liberty and fraternity which guide the democratic nation. A real democratic State will have to balance equality, liberty and fraternity rather than denying them, in which case, it will cease to be a modern democratic secular state.

The Church

There are three problems that are identified in the Indian Church which hinder her to become truly an Indian Church.

Imitation Church rather than Indigenous Church

The Indian Church, like the State which is guided by the theory of one nation, insists strictly following the western model of the Church. While the dogmas and eternal truths cannot be altered, the

Indian Church is not able to worship Christ as an Indian Church. Even without going to deeper analysis, one can find how the Church in India is an imitation Church; look at the vestments and the candle stands which are being used in the Catholic Church. There is a forgetfulness of the 'incarnation' of Christ – that Christ entered at a particular time in particular history. The Indian Church does not let Christ be rooted in the Indian soil that it may become truly an indigenous Church. It has the tendency to fall into the 'sameness' since it equates it with unity.

Focusing more on Function rather than Performance

The second problem with the Church is that it seems to define its role mostly in a private sphere rather than in the public sphere. The Church is concerned about its cultic dimension rather than its duty to work against social injustice. Referring to Niklas Luhman who makes the distinction between function and performance of religion, Felix Wilfred explains that function means that which is concerned about providing meaning and performing rituals leading the people to an 'other worldly' salvation, as what a religion is expected to function, whereas performance is to play the role of a prophet in solving problems that are generated elsewhere –like poverty, political oppression, etc.[9] The Church seems to be focusing more on the functions rather than that of performance.

Identification with the Structures rather than with the Faithful

The Church clings to structures rather than values – Church buildings have become more important than the faithful, the living bodies of Christ. We often talk in terms of minority safety intending to safeguard the structures that we possess and the properties that we own. This is the problem that makes our discourse one of safety related rather than justice related.

It would be incomplete to be satisfied with identifying a few problems both within the State and the Church. These problems demand that we as the citizens of the country and the faithful of the

---

[9] Cf. Felix WILFRED, *The Sling of Utopia* (Delhi: ISPCK, 2005), 191-192.

Church find reasonable solutions to overcome them. I believe that the right envisioning of the model of the democratic secular State and the model of the Church could help overcome the problems that we have identified. Once we could identify the correct models of the State and the Church, could we really speak of the kind of relationship that can exist between the State and the Church? Therefore, let me discuss about the models of the State and the dimensions of the Church to show which of them is suitable for a meaningful interaction between the two.

Models of a Democratic Secular State

A discussion on the encounter between the two is naturally to evoke an often discussed and a familiar term, namely secularism. Keeping in mind that secularism has been defined differently by different people, we take certain models to understand the relation of the State with religion. Since our focus is on the models, let us have a broader understanding of secularism, which will be sufficient. Anyone who discusses secularism utters that the State should be an independent organization from an external influences to be guided by democratic values of equality, liberty and fraternity. Rajeev Bhargava's explanation is insightful: "The basic constituents of secularism remain the same throughout the world. Broadly speaking, secularism anywhere in the world, means a separation of organized religion from organized political power inspired by a specific set of values."[10]

Based on this general understanding we shall propose certain models of secular State which will be beneficial for the authentic interaction with the Church. The proposed models are neither *strictly* historical and chronological nor exhaustive. The models are presented only to capture the focal points. In order to understand

---

[10] Cf. Rajeev BHARGAVA, "The Distinctiveness of Indian Secularism," in *The Future of Secularism*, ed., T. N. SRINIVASAN, 20 - 53, (New Delhi: Oxford University Press, 2010), 21.Cf. also Thapar, "Is Secularism Alien," 105.

Many define secularism strictly in terms of institutional differentiation, others in terms of neutral public space and others speak in terms of a private secular life which is guided not by religious values but by human values. Cf. Charles TAYLOR, *A Secular Age* (Cambridge, Mass.: The Belknap Press of Harvard University Press, 2007).

better the model of the secular state, let me also specify the value that underlies that particular model.

Antithetical Model – Rigidly Anti-religious

This model typically suggests a 'no relation' to religious organizations in the public sphere. This model can be caricatured as the French model that is totally antithetical to the institutionalized religion. The violent anticlericalism during the time of French revolution can be thought of in this line. The anticlerical attitude is a clear indication that the State ought to be independent and the Church cannot have any influence over the State. The French model thinks that the State is superior to the Church.

What drives this model is the value of *Equality.*[11] The idea is that every citizen of the country, irrespective of one's belonging to any religion or 'non-religion', is equal. Antagonism in a sense is motivated by the value of equality.

However, this model cannot be accepted for reasons that deny liberty of belief in their personal life and the presence of religious organizations.[12] The antagonism may be centered on the notion of equality but if there is no freedom of conscience then it ceases to be a democratic State at all. Martha Nussbaum explains that mere equality cannot guarantee a State to be liberal/secular unless it is accompanied by the freedom of conscience.[13] Even a totalitarian regime that does not allow freedom for its citizens can treat everyone equal. Hence it becomes mandatory for a modern State to allow every citizen, including the religious, the freedom of conscience, because following the directives of conscience is very important to establish

[11] Liberty and fraternity are also present in this model but they are not used as very basic for the construction of the state. Those values are interpreted to suit this construal of state.

[12] For a detailed analysis of how some important values are absent in 'anti-religious' secular state, cf. R. Bhargava, "The Distinctiveness of Indian Secularism," 32.

[13] Cf. J. Maclure and C. Taylor, *Secularism and Freedom of Conscience*, 21; cf. Martha Nussbaum, *Liberty of Conscience: In Defense of America's Tradition of Religious Equality* (New York: Basic, 2008).

the religious identity. A State cannot then play a role of Leviathan to dictate what one has to believe in.

Anti-establishment Model – Rigidly Neutral

This model is closely associated with the former. The difference lies in the attitude: instead of being antagonistic towards religion, it suggests that no fund should be allotted to any religion to establish it. The State in this sense avoids favoritism. This is the anti-establishment model. The State "admits a more general equality between believers and non-believers. It allows freedom for all religions and also freedom from religion itself."[14] This can be probably caricatured as American Model, since it does not support any religion in the public sphere.

The focus here is not necessarily anti-clericalism but one of neutrality – the State will not promote a particular religion or any religious organization. It may in principle allow everyone to have her/his religious practices in a closed campus privately. It can behave both with the religious as well as the non-religious in the same way. Charles Larmore makes the claim that "the distinctive liberal notion is that of the neutrality of the state."[15]

The idea behind the institutional arrangement of neutrality is that the State is not supposed to support one worldview over the other. If a society has theists – Jews, Christians, Muslims, Hindus, atheists, and others, the State cannot extend its alliance with any one of them. By keeping itself to the religious and other worldviews, the State claims that it can establish the freedom of conscience which lacks in the first model. It means that the State will not be concerned about what makes one's life good; rather it would deal with every view with a fair and equal treatment by displaying neutrality. In a positive sense, it means that the State considers every worldview of the conception of the good as something disputable or something that cannot be arrived at a general agreement and therefore it pays only attention to the non-interference of promoting the 'good' of

---

[14] R. Bhargava, "The Distinctiveness of Indian Secularism," 28.

[15] Charles E. Larmore, *Patterns of Moral Complexity* (Cambridge: Cambridge University Press, 1987 [reprint 1992]), 42.

different views.In doing so it respects *the autonomy* of the religious institutions.

What drives this model is the value of *freedom* – freedom of conscience and freedom of expression. The State allows the individual citizen the liberty to follow one's conscience which is hardly to be found in the first model.

However, this model too has problems. Though it insists on the value of neutral treatment, it seems that it is guided by a dominant liberal/ atheistic view of the common good and thus it promotes the good of the liberals. Often neutrality is associated with atheism. I shall show how this model is partialto some world views and thus does not take into consideration the value of equal respect.

Let me give two examples to show that the so-called neutral State is partial in its treatment with religious conception of good.

Refusal of Rocco Buttiglione (b. 1948) as one of the commissioners of European Union is a specimen to show how a neutral state is partial. When asked whether he thought homosexuality is a sin, Buttiglione replied, "'I may think it is a sin,' he said, 'but in politics we may not speak of sin. We should speak of non-discrimination, and I am solidly opposed to discrimination against homosexuals or any type of discrimination.'"[16] However, he was outrageously rejected to be a commissioner. The neutralists may argue that a believer might be biased against some sections of the country. But the point is that the State itself is biased against a religious person. There is no guarantee that a liberal/atheist/neutral person would be impartial in her / his treatment with the citizens.[17]

---

[16] M. Pakaluk, "Religion in a Liberal Democracy: Foundation or Threat?" in *The Naked Public Square Reconsidered: Religion and Politics in the Twenty-First Century*, ed., Christopher Wolfe (Wilmington, Delaware: ISI Books, 2009), 85.

[17] Suppose someone asks me whether I believe that the world is created and if my answer is affirmative, does this belief disqualify me to be part of a scientific venture? My belief about God's creation does not mean that I should treat all the objects of the world as 'sacred' as a pantheist does. There is an 'unthought' of hatredness towards religion and the values supported by them.

To understand the problem further, we could take the dispute related to abortion. Though it is a very complex issue,[18] this explains how a strict secular regime is partial. Some argue that abortion should be left to the personal choice and the decision of an individual and therefore anti-abortion laws violate the fundamentals of the constitutional privacy.[19] If legalization of abortion comes under constitutional privacy, does this mean that the State should intervene in the conscience of the believers who believe that abortion entails a violation of human rights? In the year 2012, the department of Health and Human Services [HHS] of the United States of America issued a mandate that expects all the employers to provide *free of charge* "services and counseling regarding sterilization and contraceptives including those that prevent implantation of the fertilized egg in the womb thus causing abortion."[20] The imposition of one ideology over all institutions is another example of the partiality of the neutral state.

Because of this partiality and the imposition of one conception of good over the other, the society will find it difficult to relate with others in a friendly way.

---

[18] It is very difficult to establish who is ultimately right with regard to 'abortion' without taking into consideration the comprehensive view one holds. It is because, Taylor notes, "Protagonists of each side tend to think that their position is grounded in something self-evident." Charles TAYLOR, "Explanations and Practical Reason," in *The Quality of Life,* ed., M. NUSSBAUM and Amartya SEN (Oxford: Clarendon Press, 1993), 208. One thinks that foetus is not a person and the other thinks that foetus is human and it has life. The idea is that one will have to explain this only based on his metaphysical claim. My point is the stand one takes with regard to issues like these is due to the comprehensive view s/he holds.

[19] "Anti-abortion laws violate principles of constitutional privacy, not because their political advocacy is today led by certain religious groups but because the grounds for such laws are non neutral in the constitutionally forbidden way in an area at the core of the fundamental human right of intimate personal relationships." D. A. J. RICHARDS, *Toleration and the Constitution* (New York: Oxford University Press, 1986), 262.

[20] W. Jerome BRACKEN, "What Should be One's Moral Response to the HHS 'Contraceptive Mandate'," *The Linacre Quarterly* 80, 1 (2013): 63.

Recognition Model – 'Open Acceptance' – [Communitarian]

The two models which were discussed basically flow from the liberal tradition's conception of human person. In its view the individual is seen as an unrelated monad. The third model flows from the communitarian conception of human person which sees that the individual is intimately connected to a community.

Because of its anthropology, first of all, it accepts the multiple ways of being and believing. It considers plurality as a fact of life. Therefore, it does not treat religion in a negative way but accepts and approves every way of being and believing as genuine. The State accepts every religion as something valuable and gives the respect that it deserves.

The idea of equality is understood here in a *broader sense*; that everyone, irrespective of her /his beliefs be equally respected and that everyone has the freedom to follow her/his conscience. Therefore, equal respect is given to all religions, at least, constitutionally. Though there is a dominant religion in a country and may be guided by the cultural orientation of the majority (as in the case of Pakistan), other minority religions are safeguarded. In some countries, the minority religions are given special privileges to feel safe amidst a dominated majority. This can be designated as the Indian Model. I believe that Indian State's distinctiveness lies not only in respecting every religion as equal and offering freedom to all citizens the right to choose one's belief, but also in offering certain privileges to the minority religions.

Taking the notion of Rajiv Bhargava, we could say that '*the principled distance*' is the criterion for the Indian State.[21] The principled distance is an essential aspect of being a democratic Indian state. While there is a distance as per the understanding of secularism, it positively approaches religion, so that the citizens of the State might relate with one another with the sense of recognition appreciating the differences.

What directs this model is *fraternity*. Along with freedom of expression and equality of citizens, the State ensures that despite our differences, the citizens should live as brothers and sisters. It does not mean that there are no problems with this model, but the model

[21] R. Bhargava, "The Distinctiveness of Indian Secularism," 40.

might create and sustain opportunities for amicable dialectical relations. Besides, this model thinks that belief, as non-belief for some, is an element that cannot be separated from the life of its citizens.

Unless and until the State has a right attitude towards religion, how could one speak of a relationship between the two? The recognition model creates a better opportunity to encounter Indian Christianity in the real spirit of harmony. Unless and until the State houses its citizens as its citizens with all their identities, will there be a genuine discourse between the two. The State without supporting one religion has to allow its citizens to be better persons who fraternally relate with everyone, irrespective of the differences. I believe along with many others that the Indian State is distinctive in relating with religions. Hence the State has to be intimated of its distinctiveness. The State in a sense helps its citizens to be better religious, in our case, better Christians. It is only in this model that we can really relate / interact. Because the first two models do not respect religion as an institution that deserves respect, one cannot even think of any type of positive interaction. Hence, I believe that Indian secularism is a distinct and a better model, irrespective of its failures in *following* the Constitution. I believe that it is the duty of the Indian Church to remind the State of its responsibilities in its interaction with the State.

Before discussing about the duty of the Church, it is binding that we should speak of the model of the Church that will be able to establish a relationship with the State.

Dimensions of the Church

Let me speak here of dimensions rather than models, since different dimensions have been emphasized in different periods of time. These dimensions also can co-exist, making it difficult for someone to understand which dimension is dominant. However, we might develop a model out of this. Along with every dominant dimension in the Church, I also would like to show which of the theological virtue that accompanies the development of a dimension. Though the dimensions point to a progressive idea, it only attempts to capture the differences between them so that we could build a better Church that can encounter a secular State properly.[22]

Kingly Dimension

The Church that became powerful in the 4th century[23] gave importance to the dimension of Christ as the King of the Universe. The Church claimed superiority over the temporal kingdom. The kingly dimension of the Church kept the idea of heavenly abode as the eternal world and this world as an unstable and impermanent world. Hence the ruler of the universe has priority over the king of the world. The Pope crowned the kings and in turn the temporal kings safeguarded the representatives of the universal King – the Christ. The Church, Christ's bride, portrays herself as the true and higher kingdom over every kingdom of the world.

What dominated the Church was the idea of heaven as the true abode of the humans and hence the world of humans was subordinated to the transcendental world. This type of thinking is obviously seen in St. Augustine's explication of the two worlds – The city of God and the City of men. What motivates the promotion of this dimension is the phrase – 'My kingdom is not of this world' [Jn 18: 36].

The heavenly kingdom was strengthened by a theological virtue, namely, the virtue of faith. The church insisted on faith which is defined as "the assurance of things hoped for, the conviction of things not seen" [Heb 11:1]. Hence the Church's official teachings were carried out as *the* truth, immutable and indisputable, since she is

---

[22] The dimensions presented here are neither strictly historical nor exhaustive. It is not strictly historical since there is no strict historical line that separates the paradigmatic shift of one dimension to another. It is not exhaustive since there are also other dimensions which can be seen to have been dominant in the understanding of the Church.

[23] "Four hundred years after Jesus' resurrection, then, Christianity had clearly come far from a small group of unorganized followers on the edge of the Roman Empire." Christopher M. BELLITTO, *Ten Ways the Church Has Changed* (Mumbai: St. Paul's, 2006), 16 – 17.

the representative of Christ.[24] She established her rule in every dispute [we could think of the phrase *Roma locuta causa finita*]. Parallel to the virtue of faith is the notion of obedience. Every member who has faith was expected to obey the Church. Obedience was seen to be proper of the faithful in the kingly Church. The members of the Church had no other role than to have faith in its rulers and obey them.

The implication of this thinking in the church also shaped the way we understand ourselves (humans). The dualistic understanding of man might have been dominant in this period where soul is considered to be superior to the body, because the former is imperishable while the latter is not. Therefore, monastic life was probably well appreciated than the life in the world.

Priestly Church

The second dimension of the Church comes to prominence when the Church is challenged by the local kingdoms. The bifurcation of the sacred and the profane takes place because of the insistence of the 'affirmation of the ordinary'.[25] The superiority of the transcendental world and the sacred Kingdom are challenged by the local kingdoms. In this context, the direct rule of the Church comes to an end. The Church then needs to safeguard her kingdom among other kingdoms. Bellitto notes: "The medieval papacy took a series of steps to consolidate its authority and power versus secular governments. At the same time, the Popes made sure that they were seen as the ultimate executive, legislative, and judicial authorities within the body of the Church."[26] Church sees herself as a kingdom that runs a

---

[24] Cf. Isaac PADINJAREKUTTU, *Challenges to Religion: Church and Theology* (Mumbai: St. Paul's, 2008), 95.

[25] Charles Taylor uses this term to refer to awareness and the insistence that the humans take this life seriously. He says, "I believe that this affirmation of ordinary life ... has become one of the most powerful ideas in modern civilization." The issues in politics with the ideas of welfarism, Marxism which insists on understanding the agent as the producer can be cited as specimen for the notion of ordinary. Charles TAYLOR, *Sources of the Self: the Making of the Modern Identity* (Cambridge: Cambridge University Press, 1989), 14.

[26] M. BELLITTO, *Ten Ways the Church Has Changed*, 20.

parallel kingdom along with the temporal. She paid attention both to the temporal as well as the spiritual features of the believers. The best example can be given from the papacy of

> Pope Sixtus V (1585 – 1590), who in 1588 reorganized the papal bureaucracy – the curia – into fifteen congregations. Six congregations dealt with the temporal life of the Church, which chiefly meant the papal states. These congregations administered food supplies, the navy (the Italian coast from pirates), tax relief (what we might call a welfare system), universities, infrastructures, and legal matters. Another nine congregations focused on spiritual matters: the Inquisition, the *signature* (which dealt with legal cases, some of which were also concerned with religious questions), new churches, rites, ...[27]

With strong institutional structures, power is vested with the clergy, which strengthens this dimension of the church. The secular priest becomes the leader of his own parishes [kingdom]. The priest becomes an important person in the secular world. Though the temporal ruler was a different one and yet the clergy were still powerful on establishing their superiority in terms of religious ceremonies and as mediators of peace.

In order to run her spiritual functions properly, she had to struggle with the secular kingdoms.[28] The dictum that is followed here is 'give to Caesar what belongs to Caesar and to Give to God what belongs to God' [Mt 22: 21]. In the struggle with secular kingdoms,

---

[27] M. Bellitto, *Ten Ways the Church Has Changed*, 24 - 25.

[28] "While, despite various obstacles, democracy was putting down roots and sweeping across Europe the Catholic Church was evolving in the *opposite* direction, growing more and more alien from contemporary European civilization. The process of internal constitutional transformation made the Roman Church into an island of absolutism and autocracy among the republican states of the West, increasing the level of its antagonism with an outside world that was largely non-religious and secularized." Andrzej Fliz, "The Catholic Church's War with Democracy," *Pantheon* [*Náboženství a politika*](02/2007), 40 – 61. Available in the following website: http://dspace.upce.cz/handle/10195/35321, 50.

the theological virtue of *hope*[29] offered them great strength. The Scripture says: "Let us hold fast the confession of our hope without wavering, for he who promised is faithful' [Heb 10: 23]." One's faith in the redemption is supported by hope. The priests' power was honored much because of 'celibacy' which became mandatory officially in the 12th century. The vow of chastity is to be seen in relation to celibacy. What is insisted is that we live in the world but we are not of the world.

The human person is still seen dualistically but there is a subtle difference. In the previous understanding, strengthening the soul by spending time in prayer, solitude, contemplation, was seen to be essential even to the extent of neglecting the body. However in this understanding, body and soul exist side by side and the soul is considered like the secular priests who live in the world and yet not of the world. We affirm the ordinary and yet rise beyond the ordinary.

Prophetic Church

Overcoming the dominant dimensions of the kingly and priestly Church, a new shift takes place because of Vatican II and the Medellin Conference and other events that follow. These help conceive the church differently: the foundational members are not the bishops and priests, but the faithful. The Church sees herself not in terms of kingdom but as the living body of Christ - the people of God. *Lumen Gentium* in fact testifies to that. It does not do away with the hierarchy but interprets it as a multilayered Church. The importance given to the Basic Christian Communities would bear witness how the faithful are seen to be the foundation of the Church.

The power of the Church is vested with the people. The role of the church is seen to be more prophetic rather than offering rituals. God is seen as one who is Just. The rise of liberation theologies is an indication of the development of the prophetic dimension of the

---

[29] *CCC* **1817** defines "Hope [as] the theological virtue by which we desire the kingdom of heaven and eternal life as our happiness, placing our trust in Christ's promises and relying not on our own strength, but on the help of the grace of the Holy Spirit." Available in the following website: http://www.vatican.va/archive/ccc_css/archive/catechism/p3s1c1a7.htm : accessed on 26 February 2018.

Church. The local church gains importance and attempts to develop intercultural theology so that the prophetic role of the Church is properly realized. The Church, which considered other ecclesial churches and secular forces as enemies, now recognizes others as true others.

What drives ultimately this dimension is the theological virtue of Love / charity – love understood as the love of God and the love of humanity. God's word 'I desire steadfast love and not sacrifice' [Hos 6: 6] is respected strongly. Christ is seen as the face of the suffering humanity - 'Truly I tell you, just as you did it to one of the least of these who are members of my family, you did it to me' [Mt 25: 40]. Hence wiping out the tears of the suffering humanity becomes mandatory to communicate one's love to Christ. The demand of the love of neighbor becomes essential for one's own salvation. One has to love her / his neighbor so much so that losing one's life for the other becomes an easy way to enter into union with God. Here faith is redefined. Indifference to injustice is seen as inauthentic faith. Love for the people makes the members of the Church to be prophets. In this dimension of the Church, the vow of poverty accompanies the virtue of love.

The human person is seen here holistically. Injustice in the world cannot be ignored because it is not simply injustice done to the body but to the whole person. The idea is that we know ourselves in and through the body. A person is a person. When one physically suffers, the whole person suffers. When one spiritually suffers, the whole person suffers.

Because of the shift in understanding of person, the relationship with others in the public sphere becomes essential. The Church engages in ecumenical relations and interreligious dialogue – an attempt to enter into genuine dialogue with people of other faiths. Recently the Church also joins hands with people of different faiths and 'no faith' to work for justice and peace. The liberation theologies, intercultural theologies, Ashramic theologies and local theologies are a few examples of how the Church explores her various dimensions when the understanding of human person changes.

Learning from Models and Dimensions

Of the three models of the State which we have discussed, the third model which is an accommodative democratic secular State that keeps a 'principled distance' from any religious influence, is the suitable model that can relate with the Church. The choice of this model is based on the flaws of the other two models. The third model values plurality and not rigidly indifferent like other models. In other words, only in the third model, freedom of religion and its publicness is acknowledged by the State.

It does not mean that the third model is the perfect model, but certainly it is a better model. In fact the third model suggests that there can be no perfect model. It gives an option for the interaction of the different world views so that these values may be constantly checked and be balanced in a secular society in an authentic way. In other words, accommodation model suggests that even if the State deviates from the values of constitution, different civil societies can put the State back in its track. In the same way, the third model – the Prophetic Church – gives a better scope of her active role in the *public* sphere and thus in a better position to encounter the State authentically.[30]

In order to substantiate the choice of these models, let us see whether the problems that we had identified initially are overcome.

Keeping a 'principled distance' for the state means accepting the hybridity of contemporary citizenship. The State should accept the plurality of life. Indian nation even before its conception has had always accepted diversities of life. The Hindutva agenda is an attempt to homogenize the nation overriding multiculturalism. Homogenization of one identity over many identities that we have will lead to fanaticism and fundamentalism. The principled distance of the State ensures peaceful and fraternal living of different beliefs in the country.

---

[30] The choice of the third dimension does not mean that only the virtue of love is sufficient to believers. Other theological virtues are also essential for the conception of the Church as the people of God and to encounter people of other faiths in the public sphere. Without faith and hope the Church will cease to exist and it will merely become another non-governmental organization.

The Prophetic Church, on the other hand, to quote Felix Wilfred, will "deconstruct Eurocentric representation of Asian Christianity and recognize its unique character and agency."[31] He makes a further point with regard to the Church's understanding of local or particular church. We used to think that universal doctrines have to be strictly *translated* into another culture. Now the local Church should develop its own narrative. The Postcolonial understanding gives a better view. He says:

> Asian local Church has its own *narrative* wherein its subjectivity is involved which no narration or report can capture. It has its consequences in the field of theology, worship and other faith-expressions. The real co-relate of singularity is not universality but *pluriversality*. In early centuries, the relationship among the Churches, each one very singular in its origin and narrative, was characterized by the spirit of pluriversality, of communion and exchange.[32]

In this way, both the State and the Church overcome the problem of homogenization and imitation of the universal Church.

An accommodative democratic secular State would focus its attention on the *values* that operate the State rather than the *rigid* organizational structures. A Just democratic society that accommodates and values equality, liberty and fraternity is a better State than an oppressive and strong State that does not respect democratic values.

The prophetic Church in the same way concentrates more on the virtue of Love and justice and brings out her prophetic dimension and thus she pays attention to the performative actions to ensure justice in the world. This leads to re-conceive the structures of the Church. This model suggests that worshipping places should become places of encountering equality and fraternity where one experiences inner peace. The prophetic church challenges the kingly dimensions

---

[31] Felix Wilfred, "Asian Christianities and Theologies through the Lens of Postcolonialism," *Concilium* (2018 / 1: [15 – 26], 16.

[32] F. Wilfred, "Asian Christianities and Theologies through the Lens of Postcolonialism," 18-19.

and the priestly dimensions to be interpreted based on the virtues of Love and justice.

A State, which understands secularism whose elemental feature is to keep a principled distance to provide equal respect and opportunity to every citizen of the country, will promote a genuine and public interaction of the different faiths in the public arena so that they can relate with others freely without any anxiety of insecurity. In this sense, we could say that only an accommodative State can offer a secured public space where one becomes truly an Indian and a Christian.

And a Church which values justice and love than structures and organizations, will use the public space that will become the meeting point in which she can exercise her capacity to be a prophet. The encounter is essential because we make other people of faith to interact with us. It can be captured in the words of Ferraro: "The Indian Christians are made, as much as they make other Indians and others in the world. It is through the immersion into the plural ecologies of Indian society that we have the emergence of Indian Christians."[33]

Prophetic dimension has to be understood here – as the one who speaks not for the personal injustice, but for the injustice done to others. Hence the goal of the prophetic dimension is that we raise our voice in support of the 'suffering other'.

The Encounter

In the public space, as the State understands secularity as a principled distance which will create space for its religious citizens, the religious institutions too are expected to confront the secular State in public. The Church too will keep a principled distance from the State and yet will interact with it as a civil society that comprises the citizens of the country belonging to a particular religion. Hence there is a greater transparency in the encounter that takes place in public. It is only through this we shall strengthen the secular character of the

---

[33] Victor Ferrao, "Becoming an Indian Christian," in Becoming *a Nation: Processes and Prospects*, ed., Dolreich Pereira, 93 – 105 (Eluru & New Delhi: ACPI & Christian World Imprints, 2017), 98.

State and will continue to keep the prophetic church alive. Rustom Bharucha says:

> One needs to strengthen secularism as a philosophy and life practice by unearthing and activating its insufficiently mobilized resources and potentialities in the public sphere. Only then would it be possible to shift the secular struggle from its defensive position to a more positive agenda, transcending the innate condescension of 'tolerance,' to arrive at new modes of respecting and living with difference.[34]

Hence the interaction with the state is an essential component of the Church.

Mode of Interaction

The Church cannot relate with the liberal models of the secular state *significantly* since the antagonistic and the anti-establishment models of the State do not respect religion at all. Hence only the third model which respects religion will be a suitable model to relate with. The third model of the State can be confronted by the Church in three different modes according to the dominant dimension of the Church. Since the contemporary Church has all the three dimensions, the interaction can take place in three different ways.

The first mode is the relationship that can exist between the kingly Church and the democratic State. The Indian State and the State of Tamil Nadu have ministries for minorities.[35] Hence the meeting will take place among the rulers of the Church and the ministers of the State. Since the secular State gives certain privileges

---

[34] Rustom BHARUCHA, *In the Name of the Secular* (Delhi: Oxford University Press, 1998), 24. As quoted in Nishanth A. IRUDAYADSON, "Imagining a Nation: Postcolonial Perspectives," in Becoming *a Nation: Processes and Prospects*, ed., Dolreich PEREIRA, 3 – 14 (Eluru & New Delhi: ACPI & Christian World Imprints, 2017), 5-6.

[35] The central government's ministry for the minority religions includes religions like Sikhism, Buddhism, Christianity and Islam. It covers also minority linguists. It also takes care of the minority Hindu Temples in Pakistan. It sets aside 4, 900 crores for the ministry in the annual budget.

to the minority religions, the bishops might request for those rights and to ensure safety for them and their institutions.

In this interaction, only the *officials* of both the institutions will meet. The meeting place would be their offices. The other members of the church or other citizens will not participate in the interaction.

The second mode is the relationship that can exist between the Priestly Church and the democratic State. Since the Church considers herself as an institution that serves as an instrument to receive God's blessings abundantly, the officers of the democratic State might come to meet the priests to receive blessings. Recently Mr. Banwarilal Purohit, the Honorable Governor of Tamil Nadu went to the Shrine Basilica of Vailankanni on 18 February 2018. There was a special blessing given to him by the Rector of the Shrine. The officers of the State or the members of the family likewise might go to meet priests in the Church to receive blessing. The interaction will take place in the churches. Others might witness the interaction but only as viewers.

The third mode is the relationship that can exist between the Prophetic Church and the democratic State in public sphere. The democratic State offers the uninterrupted public space – a space where everyone can meet and interact. The State ensures establishment of justice – to see that everyone is given what is his or her due in the country.

What makes the relationality more emphatic is the mutual respect and recognition. Besides, they share a better vision of who we are. The third model of the State has a communitarian understanding of humans as persons belonging to different cultural communities. The third model of the Church too has a holistic understanding of a person as rooted in a particular history and culture. And thus she insists on the fuller communion of the person– both vertical and horizontal. Both of them share a great deal in common with regard to the understanding of person, which makes the interaction meaningful.

The interaction of the Church and the State in public is rooted and strengthened by the redefined understanding of faith. The prophetic Church insists that taking into consideration the sufferings of the other is 'matter of faith'. If we do not see the suffering of the other, how can we see Christ?[36] From the angle of Christianity – fighting for justice becomes an essential element in the Church which has to appear in public beyond its premises.

Therefore, the Church has a stronger role to play in the democratic society in raising its voices for social justice. It has a stronger role to play as part of the civil society to ensure fraternal and peaceful living with the values of democracy. So much so, Felix Wilfred says, "Christianity becomes the interlocutor in civil society."[37] We could say then that the prophetic Church is the vibrant civil society that will keep democratic values alive.[38]

The Church as member of civil society interacts with the State to make it realize its distinctive character of secularism. The voice of the Church in public will not rise simply for the safety of the minority Christians, but for all the oppressed. It will not simply be a voice for the Christians but for every poor person in the country. It will be a voice against every type of oppression. The Church becomes the voice of the suffering humanity. She would collaborate with those who work to strengthen democratic values, because the prophet does not confront the ruler seeking justice for herself / himself, but for others.

Thus the prophetic Church opens the possibility of interaction with the people beyond the boundaries of her institutions.[39] The Church in its interaction with people of other faiths in the public

---

[36] Cf. Felix WILFRED, *Asian Dreams and Christian Hope: At the Dawn of the Millennium* (Delhi: ISPCK, 2000), 52.

[37] F. WILFRED, *Asian Dreams and Christian Hope: At the Dawn of the Millennium*, 133.

[38] I have argued elsewhere insisting that the Church as a civil society has a stronger role to play in the society. "We insist on the role of the Church because the members of the Church have a stronger *source* to withstand in its prophetic role …" cf. Peter SUSAIMANICKAM, "The Interpenetration of Democracy, Church, and Civil Society: Interpreted through the Prism of Self-Identity" in *Democracy and Religion: A Philosophical Appraisal*, ed., Gnanamuthu V., 51 – 71 (Tiruchirappalli: Thedal, 2018), 66.

[39] Wilfred says: "The realization that the religious experience of our neighbours is related to the mysterious plan of God … This fellowship transcends all kinds of borders and boundaries." Felix WILFRED, *On the Banks of Ganges: Doing Contextual Theology* (Delhi: ISPCK, 2005), 216.

arena for issues on social justice engages in dialogue. This could also be called as 'secular dialogue'.[40]

Of all the three modes of interaction between the State and religions, I believe that this is the most authentic and significant interaction with the State. The meeting here takes place not on the offices, and not on the Church premises, but on the street, on the road, on the public arena. The meeting takes place not between the officials and the representatives of the Church but the members of the Church accompanied by the clergy and the leaders of the Church.

While the other meetings might be well received and cordial – the ministers might welcome us with a smile and the priests may welcome the State officials with a red carpet – the interaction on the road may be blocked by the constables.

The discourse between the church and the State will involve completely a different language – not in terms of financial and security assistance for the minority, but a language that insists on fundamental human rights, rights of the citizens of the country and the rights of equal treatment and the right for human dignity.

In this street interaction, because our language itself is different, the Indian Christians will meet the State on the road in collaboration with the people of other faiths and the people of Good Will. We will not march alone – the Muslims, the Hindus, the Sikhs – the citizens of the country will walk with us, because they are our brothers. There the State will come and meet us. This type of encounter would strengthen the values of democracy and the safety of the citizens. In the establishment of the democratic values in the State, we shall become truly Christians.

On the road the Church will be. On the road, she will contemplate. On the road, she will meet Christ – She will become truly a good Samaritan Church. The content of her theology will emerge from the context. The dogmas will be interpreted from the struggles of the Church. She will truly be a living church which engages in contemplative action.

---

[40] Cf. F. Wilfred, *The Sling of Utopia*, 197.

Pointers for Active Interactions

When the Church is deeply rooted in the Indian soil, she has her role to play in the public sphere. In her protest for social justice and the struggle for the common good, she will display a truly secular face, an Indian face, or so to say, an Indian Christian Face.

In order to do that the Church should speak in public; she should encourage its members to actively engage in the works of justice. An active member of the church is not the one who is inside the premises of the Church but outside the campus in the public sphere. The Church has a greater responsibility to work against any form of injustice and not simply for her safety.

The Prophetic Church has to raise voice against every type of evil that endangers the secular face of the Indian state. We shall offer here some pointers through which the Church can be rooted in Indian soil to be truly a prophetic Church. They are:

1. Corruption
2. Discrimination of Caste
3. Economic Oppression
4. Fundamentalism of every type[41]
5. Gender discrimination
6. The Silence of the media, and
7. Ecological Concerns.[42]

These are some of the Issues which are very prominent through which the Church has to help the citizens, its members to be better

[41] "Every religious leader is called to unmask any attempt to manipulate God for ends that have nothing to do with him or his glory. We need to show, with unremitting effort, that every human life is sacred, that it deserves respect, esteem, compassion and solidarity, without regard for ethnicity, religion, culture, or ideological and political convictions. Adherence to a particular religion does not confer additional dignity and rights upon individuals, nor does non-adherence deny or diminish them." Pope Francis, "Address to the Participants in the International Peace Conference," *Al-Azhar Conference Centre,* Cairo, 28 April 2017. Cf. *L'osservatore Romano* Friday, 09, February 2018, number 6, 4.

[42] It is the right time for the Indian Church to take up the ecological issues and fight for safeguarding the national resources. Pope Francis' *Laudatosi'* should be a great inspiration for the members of the Church.

Indians rather than being silent and secured Indians. That is why we suggest that the Church has to be truly prophetic. Persecutions can be on the rise but it should not bring down the spirit of the Church to actively participate in the public arena of India.

It is only by being rooted in Indian soil, we can exercise our faith in public as citizens of the country, and help the State and put it in the right track to be truly a State that respects every faith in the country. Hence in our voice for justice we become truly Indian and truly Christian. Perhaps this is what meant by Oswald Cardinal Gracias, who said: "The Catholic Church needs our nation and India needs the Church. We will be discussing our role as Indian Christians and be asking our people, also to become better Indian Christians. This is the call of today to be fully Indian fully Christian."[43]

Being fully a Christian can be realized only when the Prophetic Church becomes an extension of the life-giving presence of Jesus in the Indian soil. Becoming fully an Indian can be achieved only when an Accommodative Indian Constitutional Secular State is realized where the State values the interaction of different religions in the public sphere. In such a situation the Prophetic Church will display its public character opting to protest on the road along with people of other faiths. These distinctive characteristics of both, the State and the Church, will enable the state to maintain a principled distance from every religion in order to promote fundamental values. Thus, the aforesaid interactive framework will ensure that we become truly Indians and truly Christians.

---

[43] His Eminence Oswarld Cardinal Gracias, "Inaugural Address of the 30th Plenary Assembly of CCBI," on 5 February, 2018. Cf. https://www.mangalorean.com/fully-indian-fully-christian-cardinal-oswald-gracias/ accessed on 6 February 2018.

Bibliography

Articles and Books

BELLITTO, Christopher M. *Ten Ways the Church Has Changed.* Mumbai: St. Paul's, 2006.

BHARGAVA, Rajeev. "The Distinctiveness of Indian Secularism." In *The Future of Secularism.* Edited by T. N. SRINIVASAN, 20 – 53. New Delhi: Oxford University Press, 2010.

__________. *Secularism and its Critics.* New Delhi: Oxford University Press, 1998.

BRACKEN, W. Jerome. "What Should be One's Moral Response to the HHS 'Contraceptive Mandate'." *The Linacre Quarterly* 80, 1 (2013): 63 – 73.

FERRAO, Victor. "Becoming an Indian Christian," in *Becoming a Nation: Processes and Prospects,* ed., Dolreich Pereira, 93 – 105. Eluru & New Delhi: ACPI & Christian World Imprints, 2017.

IRUDAYADSON, Nishanth A. "Imagining a Nation: Postcolonial Perspectives." In Becoming *a Nation: Processes and Prospects.* Edited by Dolreich PEREIRA, 3 – 14. Eluru & New Delhi: ACPI & Christian World Imprints, 2017.

LARMORE, Charles E. *Patterns of Moral Complexity.* Cambridge: Cambridge University Press, 1987 [reprint 1992].

MACLURE, J. and Charles TAYLOR, *Secularism and Freedom of Conscience.* Translated by Jane Marie TODD. Cambridge, Mass.: Harvard University Press, 2011.

NUSSBAUM, Martha. *Liberty of Conscience: in Defense of America's Tradition of Religious Equality.* New York: Basic, 2008.

PADINJAREKUTTU, Isaac. *Challenges to Religion: Church and Theology.* Mumbai: St. Paul's, 2008.

PAKALUK, M. "Religion in a Liberal Democracy: Foundation or Threat?" In *The Naked Public Square Reconsidered: Religion and Politics in the Twenty-First Century.* Edited by Christopher WOLFE. Wilmington, Delaware: ISI Books, 2009.

Pope Francis, "Address to the Participants in the International Peace Conference," *Al-Azhar Conference Centre,* Cairo, 28 April 2017. Cf. *L'osservatore Romano* 09 February 2018, number 6, 4.

Richards, D. A. J. *Toleration and the Constitution.* New York: Oxford University Press, 1986.

Schmalz, Mathew N. "The Indian Church: Catholicism and Indian Nationhood." In *The Catholic Church and the Nation-State: Comparative Perspectives.* Edited by Paul Christopher Manuel, Lawrence C. Reardon, Clyde Wilcox. 209 – 225. Washington D.C.: Georgetown University Press, 2006.

Susaimanickam, Peter. "The Interpenetration of Democracy, Church, and Civil Society: Interpreted through the Prism of Self-Identity" In *Democracy and Religion: A Philosophical Appraisal.* Edited by Gnanamuthu V. 51 – 71. Tiruchirappalli: Thedal, 2018.

Taylor, Charles. *Sources of the Self: The Making of the Modern Identity.* Cambridge: Cambridge University Press, 1989.

__________. "Explanations and Practical Reason," in *The Quality of Life,* ed., M. Nussbaum and Amartya Sen. 208 – 241. Oxford: Clarendon Press, 1993.

__________. *A Secular Age.* Cambridge, Mass.: The Belknap Press of Harvard University Press, 2007.

Thapar, Romila. "Is Secularism Alien to Indian Civilization?". In *The Future of Secularism.* Edited by T. N. Srinivasan, 83 – 108. New Delhi: Oxford University Press, 2010.

Wilfred, Felix. *Asian Dreams and Christian Hope: At the Dawn of the Millennium.* Delhi: ISPCK, 2000.

__________. *On the Banks of Ganges: Doing Contextual Theology.* Delhi: ISPCK, 2005.

__________. *The Sling of Utopia.* Delhi: ISPCK, 2005.

__________. "Asian Christianities and Theologies through the Lens of Postcolonialism," *Concilium* (2018 / 1): 15 – 26.

E- Sources

"Attacks against India's Christians Doubled in 2017. Published on 21, February 2018. Available in the following Website: https://

www.catholicnewsagency.com/news/attacks-against-indias-christians-doubled-in-2017-55262. Accessed on 26 February 2018.

"Christian missionaries a threat to unity of the country: BJP's Ballia MP." *The Indian Express* 22 April 2018. Available in the following website: http://indianexpress.com/article/india/christian-missionaries-a-threat-to-unity-of-the-country-bjps-ballia-mp-5147341/. Accessed on 24 April 2018.

"The Virtues." In *Catechism of the Catholic Church*. Available in the following website: http://www.vatican.va/archive/ccc_css/archive/catechism/p3s1c1a7.htm. Accessed on 25 February 2018.

Fliz, Andrzej. "The Catholic Church's War with Democracy," *Pantheon* [*Náboženství a politika*](02/2007), 40 – 61. Available in http://dspace.upce.cz/handle/10195/35321.

His Eminence Oswarld Cardinal Gracias, "Inaugural Address of the 30th Plenary Assembly of CCBI." Published on 5 February 2018. Available in the following Website: https://www.mangalorean.com/fully-indian-fully-christian-cardinal-oswald-gracias/ Accessed on 6 February 2018.

Joseph, Tony. "Why Christianity Failed in India," *Outlook* 13 April 2015. Available in the Following Website: https://www.outlookindia.com/magazine/story/why-christianity-failed-in-india/293895 Accessed on 6 February 2018.

Pederiva, Maria Teresa Pontara. "Christian Persecution is Growing, 215 Million Worldwide." Published on 12. 01. 2018. Available at the following Website: http://www.lastampa.it/2018/01/12/vaticaninsider/eng/documents/christian-persecution-is-growing-million-worldwide-qL2EuMOR8fxeAV0luroCbK/pagina.html. Accessed on 26 February 2018.

Sharma, Ritu. "Christians Lack Confidence in Modi Government, Cardinal." Published on 21 December 2017. Available in the following Website: https://www.ucanews.com/news/christians-lack-confidence-in-modi-government-cardinal/81134. Accessed on 5 February 2018.

11

Christianity, Civil Society and Science-Theology Dialogue in India

Binoy Pichalakattu
Director, Loyola Institute of Peace and International Relations, Kochi

Introduction

The concept of civil society has undergone evolutionary changes down the centuries. Civil society is a broader concept encompassing agencies, institutions, movements, cultural forces and social relationships which are not directly under the state. This paper is an attempt to explore the possibility of Christian interactions in the Indian civil society. The role of Christianity in India today is to enter the public forum to converse with the Indian civil society. The paper calls for Christian theological thinking to go beyond binary walls and engage in constructive conversation with the contemporary context and its concerns with special reference to science.

The Notion of Civil Society

Etymologically *civis* means citizens and *civitas* means body of citizens which constitutes the city-state. The Oxford dictionary explains civil society as a community of citizens linked by common interests and collective activity. Different authors have interpreted the notion of civil society differently.[1] The Scottish enlightenment of the eighteenth century (as evident in the writings of Adam Ferguson, Adam Smith, and David Hume) explains civil society as a civilized society in opposition to barbaric society. In the nineteenth century German tradition, Fredrick Hegel places civil society between the family and the state. For Karl Marx (1818-1883), civil society is the realm of private property and market relations. Jurgen Habermas (1991) differentiates civil society from the public sphere. For him, the public sphere is created in and out of civil society. According to the American sociologist Jeffery Charles Alexander (2001), civil society is not merely an institutional realm but a realm of structured, socially established consciousness, and a network of understanding. Thomas Carothers (1999) assumes NGOs as the heart of civil society. However, in his view, it is a mistake to equate civil society with NGOs, but it is a broader concept, encompassing all the organizations and associations that exist outside the state and the market. According to Antony McGrew (1998), the British social scientist, civil society refers to those agencies, institutions, movements, cultural forces and social relationships which are both privately and voluntarily organized and which are not directly controlled by the state.[2] In this paper, I am using the concept of civil society as something which is not part of the state machinery, not of the judiciary, not of the legislature and not of the bureaucracy, but as a reality that has potential to influence governance.

Civil Society in India

The understanding of the word 'civil' in India has its roots in the Vedic period. Vedic hymns mention people's assemblies like *vidath, sabha* and *samiti. Vidath* refers to the general meeting of the whole

---

[1] For detailed explanation of the concept and meaning of civil society see, Vijender Singh, "An Analysis of Concept and Role of Civil Society in Contemporary India," *Global Journal of Human Science*, vol. 12, issue 7, version 1.0, April 2012, pp. 68- 77.

[2] Antony McGrew, "The State in Advanced Capitalist Society," *Global Society*, vol. 12, no. 3, 1998, p. 69.

community with redistributive functions. *Sabha* is a body of village elders who assist the ruler. *Samiti* is an assembly whose main function is to elect the ruler. The concept of civil society in India has developed along with influential religious structures. The numerous religious reform movements during the 19th century such as the Brahmo Samaj, the Ramakrishna Mission, the Theosophical Society in Madras, and the Arya Samaj are a few examples to mention. The post independent India witnessed the emergence of new social movements which include environmental groups, women organizations, and the NGOs. *Narmada Bachao Andolan*, *Chatisgarg Mukti Morcha*, and *Jan Lokpal Bill* are regarded as creative movements of Indian civil society in the recent years. Similar movements/institutes have been a continuous process.

Civil society organizations and networks play important role in the socio-cultural and political context of India. They have the potential to improve governance and transform state-society relations. They have been able to respond to the socio-political and economic problems of the country down the decades and have been able to influence the policies of the government.

Christianity and Civil Society

In the early church, the Christian life was inseparable from the civil life. Whereas, during the middle ages, the religious establishment was controlling every sphere of human society including civil society (e.g. inquisition-the tribunal of the Holy See to combat heresy). By the end of the 19th century we see a change in the Church's approach to civil society especially in the social encyclicals by the Popes and other social teachings of the Church. To name a few we have Pope Leo XIII's encyclical *Rerum novarum* (1891), Pope John XXIII's *Mater et magistra* (Christianity and Social Progress, 1961), Pope John Paull II's *Pacem in terris* (*Peace on Earth, 1963*), Vatican II's *Gaudium et spes* (the Pastoral Constitution on the Church and the Modern World, 1965), and Pope Francis' *Laudato si* (2015).

All these could be seen as an attempt by the Church to engage with the civil sphere. The twentieth century liberation theology can also be seen in this line, a movement in the civil society motivated by Christian ideals of justice. Tracing the historical trajectory, in one sense, Christianity can be counted as part of the civil society, and in the other sense, outside the civil society. How to overcome this ambiguity? This calls for clarity regarding Christianity's relationship with the civil society. Have we got any role in the civil society without having to compromise our core values? If yes, how should Christianity interact with the civil consciousness? Which are the areas that we should necessarily engage in conversation with?

Christianity and Civil Society in India

The Indian civil consciousness, as elsewhere, is rooted in its socio-politico-cultural context and their concerns. The key elements of the contemporary Indian civil society are religion, media, science and literature as they play significant roles in shaping up the cultural perceptions of the civil society. Directly or indirectly they affect the ethical, the mythical and the symbolic elements of society and culture. In the following section, I focus specifically on the impact of science in the Indian civil worldview and affirm the dire need for Christianity to engage in conversation with the scientific realm. The developments of science in India can be classified into three phases: The ancient era, the modern era and the contemporary era. [3]

Ancient Era of Indian Science (-1900)

This phase includes Vedic science and also the sciences of ancient India. Universities were established in India much before the establishment of universities in Europe. Thakshasila, Nalanda, Vikramsila, Vallabhi, Pushpagiri, Odanthapuri and Somapura were our ancient universities. Whereas, the schools of Plato and Aristotle were not universities, Nalanda existed during 427 CE to 1197 CE. Nalanda was the pre-eminent, internationally renowned institution in the field of higher education in India. Mathematics, astronomy, arts, architecture, medicine, politics, philosophy and the strategy of warfare were taught there. Indians could make some priceless

[3] For details refer K. Babu Joseph, "Bahrathiya Satra Paithrukathil Bahvana Kalartharuthu," in *Ezhuthu* Magazine, March 2018, Vol 3, no. 5, pp. 60-63 (independent translation).

contributions in all these areas during the ancient era. How astrology devalued astronomy and architecture is a sad later story.

Along with astronomy, Ayurveda and Veterinary science were also developed. Treatment of diseases was conducted scientifically based on the results of experiments. It was Varahamihira who wrote books on agricultural science. Carpentry, blacksmithy, goldsmithy and metal works were treated as heredity works and they were reserved for particular castes. Technical knowledge in these areas was not known to the public domain. The Indian contribution to the fields of mathematics, physics and chemistry were indeed excellent. In fact, Arabs took the decimal system from India to Europe.[4] In physics, the work of the sage Kanada titled 'Vaiseshika Soothram," is famous world over. Matter, motion, properties, space and time are the main topics dealt in this treatise. The atomic theory of Kanada still remains a beacon in the world of chemical sciences.

Aryabhatan describes pure astronomy in his *Aryabhatiyam* (499 CE) which does not have any astrological aspects. He opines that the universe is infinite with neither beginning nor end. There are also indications of planets moving in elliptical path. In *Aryabhatiyam*, there are 121 stanzas of four lines each. They are presented in the form of formula/riddle. *Aryabhatiyam* was an indication of the direction of Indian mathematics and astronomy in future. The influence of it continued to exist well over for one thousand years in Indian mathematical arena. It had an impact over Kerala's mathematical thinking. There were quite a few great mathematicians in Kerala along the banks of the river *Nila*, who conducted their mathematical pursuit as a solemn duty. Madhava (1360-1430) is rightly considered the founder of *Nila* school. It is he who derived the findings of *Aryabhatiyam* from the properties of a circle. We have every reason to be delighted of the fact that even three hundred years before Newton and Leibnitz, mathematicians of the *Nila* school expounded the basic principles and propositions of the branch of mathematics called calculus. None of the later day Indian mathematicians has written a book on mathematics without

[4] Decimal system is the ingenious method of expressing all numbers by means of ten symbols starting from zero to nine.

offering tribute to the great master Madhava. From all these, it can be inferred that the architect of Indian calculus is Madhava himself.

Modern Era (1900-2000)

India produced several great scientists during this phase. Sir C.V. Raman, known for 'Raman Effect,' carried out a ground breaking work in the field of light scattering. J.C. Bose pioneered investigation in the area of electromagnetic waves, made vital contributions to plant science and laid foundations for experimental research in India. E.K. Janakiyammal was a noted Indian Botanist who conducted scientific research in sugarcane and brinjal. Homi Bhaba is known as the "Father of Indian Nuclear Programme." He is the founder of Tata Institute of Fundamental Research (TIFR), Mumbai. Some of the scientists of the modern era are regarded to be the earliest users of quantum theory expounded by Max Plank in 1900.

Vikram Sarabhai is regarded as the "Father of Indian Space Programme." The establishment of the Indian Space Research Organization (ISRO) is one of his greatest achievements. Subrahmanyan Chandrasekhar (1910-1995) is best known for his discovery of Chandrasekhar Limit. He proved that there is a maximum mass which can be supported against gravity by pressure made up of electrons and atomic nuclei. The value of this limit is about 1.44 times a solar mass. The Chandrasekhar Limit plays an important role in understanding the stellar evolution. Known as the "Missile Man of India" world-wide, Dr. A. P. J. Abdul Kalam was a scientist of great distinction. There are several other names of Indian stalwarts and their contributions to make the volume complete. Thus, the modern era of science in India is adorned by the contributions of many eminent scientists.

Contemporary Era (2000-till today)

India has witnessed remarkable growth in the area of science and technology in the recent decades. The contemporary Indian science is marked mainly by advances in information technology, space research, nuclear physics, electronics and defence. India has the third largest scientific and technical manpower in the world. Indian

Contributions to the science of missile Launching technology is outstanding that our country is among the top five nations of the world. ISRO is the sixth largest space research organization in the world. It has numerous credentials to its merit since its establishment in 1969. It crossed a milestone in June 2016 by launching 20 satellites through a single rocket. India became the only country to orbit Mars in the first attempt with the success of *Mangalyaan* which put India on the elite club of nations to have achieved interplanetary missions. The Council of Scientific and Industrial Research (CSIR), established in 1942, is one of the premier institutions for scientific and industrial research worldwide. It has a network of 40 laboratories, two cooperative industrial research institutions and more than 100 extensions and field centres.

The discovery of Gravitational Waves (GW) is regarded to be one of the greatest discoveries of the twentieth and twenty-first centuries so far. The existence of GW was predicted by Albert Einstein exactly 100 years ago, based on his General Theory of Relativity. For the past 25 years, about 1000 scientists from more than 25 countries were actively involved in this exploration. In this team, there were 37 Indian scientists engaged in various academic and research institutions in India. On 14 September 2015, scientists were able to detect the GW which originated about 1.3 billion years ago, at two Laser Interferometer Gravitational Observatories (LIGO) in the United States.

India is engaged in serious and rigorous research in all branches of sciences. Indian scientists are making incredible researches in the fields of agriculture, medicine, biotechnology, cold regions research, communications, environment, industry, mining, nuclear power, space and transportation. Scientific papers and research publications from Indian institutes are globally appreciated. In spite of the scientific and technological advances, it seems the scientific temper is being lost in the Indian psyche. It is unfortunate that a section of people in India believes and publicize that most of the modern technology and inventions were known to Indians thousands of years ago.

Pseudoscience and Its Impact on Indian Civil Consciousness

Superstitions and pseudoscience are dominating not only the civil society but scientists themselves. Many a scientist of ours do not have the scientific bend of mind and awareness. In 2007, a survey was conducted by the Institute for the Study of Secularism in Society and Culture (ISSSC) of the Trinity College, Connecticut on "The Worldviews and Opinions of Scientists in India."[5] 1100 Indian scientists were surveyed from 130 institutes all over, 69% of them strongly believed in astrology and *Vaasthu*, vast majority of them were strictly following superstitions. It is a fact that the Christians are also not insulated against the influence of astrology and *Vaasthu*. Over and above, the papers presented by the Indian scientists at the Indian Science Congress in Mumbai in 2015 have made ruthless claims regarding the Indian contributions to aviation (*Pushpakavimanam*), plastic surgery, space propulsions since the Vedic times. Most recently, the chief minister of the north-eastern state of Tripura has made some controversial comments at a public function that the internet technology and satellites were invented thousands of years ago by ancient Indians. Such claims are ridiculous and are drastically against modern science as it demands evidence and predictability.

We have, indeed, a great heritage of which we can be proud of. But there is no need for making bogus claims and inviting troubles from various corners. Attempt to connect between the atomic theory of Kanada and Democretes with modern atomic theory is an exercise in futility. Similarly, it is also suicidal to denigrate modern views and theories simply because of the fact that these things have no reference in ancient epics. What is now going on in India is a dialectical conflict between tradition and modernity. The progress in science and its dynamic worldview cannot be chained within the boundaries of a

[5] "The Worldviews and Opinions of Scientists in India Summary Report" gives the highlights of an international, academic web survey conducted by the nonpartisan Institute for the Study of Secularism in Society and Culture (ISSSC) of Trinity College in Hartford, Connecticut. The survey was conducted between August 2007 and January 2008 in cooperation with the Center for Inquiry India. See, https://www.scribd.com/document/17138974/Worldviews-and-Opinions-of-Scientists-India-2007-2008-Summary-Report.

nation behind its faith, rituals, conventions, philosophical doctrines and ideologies. Superstitions and misconceptions, conventional practices and rituals blindly lead vast majority of the Indian civil society. When we examine some of the recent undesirable events that took place in India, we may have the apprehension whether the direction of our progress has taken an about-turn. Unscientific thinking and intolerance is growing day by day and spreading fast like wildfire. In such a dreadful ambience scientific development and cultural enhancement will be weakened and paralyzed. It should be acknowledged that the so-called 'ancient wisdom' is fictional, incapable of making any prediction. Mixing up of speculative thinking with science is not science but a methodological error. What is required is clarity regarding what is genuine science and what is not science.

Since science and technology have powerful impact on humanity, theology should enter into dialogue with science and its concerns for better clarity on issues of science that affect human life every day. I propose, theology has to engage in public discourse (intellectual discourse) using a language that is understandable and intelligible to those particularly from the discipline of science.

Paradigm Shift in the Scientific Worldview

Till the sixteenth century the scientific community upheld a static worldview. The geocentric worldview of Ptolemy, the heliocentric view of Copernicus, the theories of Galileo, Kepler and Newton emphasized a mechanized worldview. This worldview considered scientific knowledge certain, exact, predictable and objective. However, the evolutionary theory of Darwin in the nineteenth century and Einstein's theory of relativity and quantum mechanics in the twentieth century gave birth to a dynamic worldview. The theory of relativity humbled absolutism, quantum mechanics ruled out certainty, theory of chaos disregarded an ordered universe, the detection of Higgs Boson and Gravitational Waves led the scientific world to a mysterious and mystical realm. Scientists realize today that fundamental reality is ever approachable and never attainable. Thus the revolutionary developments in the twentieth century are regarded as the "humbling experience" of science. The humbling experience of science opens the door for engagement with other disciplines.

Paradigm Shift in Theological Worldview

Like science, theology too has undergone a paradigm shift. In this section, I will be focusing on the catholic theological worldview with specific reference to the views of Pope John Paul II as well as the documents of Vatican Council II.

Pope John Paul II on Science-Theology Dialogue

In a path-breaking letter to George Coyne, S.J., the Director of Vatican Observatory, on June 1, 1988, Pope John Paul II expressed his sincere appreciation for the power and impact of science and the need for science and theology to engage in a constructive and mutually respectful dialogue. In his view, such a dialogue is the need of the hour: "We need each other to be what we must, what we are called to be."[6] What is envisaged is an interaction in which "each discipline should continue to enrich, nourish and challenge the other to be more fully what it can be and to continue to contribute to our vision of who we are and who we are becoming."[7] The Pope calls upon theologians to consider the contemporary scientific findings seriously and make the best use of sciences in their theological study and reflection. "Theology must be in vital interchange today with science just as it always has been with philosophy and other forms of learning. Theology will have to call on the findings of science to one degree or another as it pursues its primary concern for the human person, the reaches of freedom, the possibilities of Christian community, the nature of belief and the intelligibility of nature and history."[8] At the same time, the Pope warns that this dialogue is not a one-way monologue, but a mutually enriching process. He says: "[S] cience can purify religion from error and superstition; religion can

---

[6] Robert Russell, William R. Stoger and George V. Coyne, S.J. eds., *Physics, Philosophy and Theology: A Common Quest for Understanding* (Vatican City: Vatican Observatory Publications, 1988), M 14.

[7] Russell, Stoger and Coyne, "Pysics, Philosophy and Theology," M 7.

[8] Russell, Stoger and Coyne, "Pysics, Philosophy and Theology," M 10.

purify science from idolatry and false absolutes. Each can draw the other into a wider world, a world in which both can flourish."[9] Later, the Pope writes in the same line, "faith is not based on reason, it can certainly not dispense with it. At the same time it becomes apparent that reason needs to be reinforced by faith, in order to discover horizons it cannot reach on its own."[10]

Vatican II on Science - Theology Dialogue

Vatican II encourages research in all academic branches and opines that science could serve as instruments in the hands of God:

> Methodological research in all branches of knowledge provided it is carried on in a truly scientific manner and in accordance with moral norms, can never conflict with faith, because the things of the world and things of faith derive from the same God. It can be said, indeed, that one who humbly and perseveringly applies himself to investigating the secrets of nature is being led, even unknowingly, by the hand of God, who holding all things in existence causes them to be what they are (Vat II, *Gaudium et Spes*, no. 36 in Abbot, 234).

The Council emphasizes the need to become aware of the signs of the times in modern cultures to better understand how the spirit of God continues to reach out to humanity and the world through the events and experiences of contemporary times. Such signs of the times in our world must be perceived, interpreted, and eventually understood in terms of the Gospel message. In this sense, the scientific developments and technological advances must be viewed as resources for theology (*loci theologici)*. The theological basis for this is that Christian faith considers the whole universe, all of creation and creative endeavours, as a manifestation of God's glory and goodness.

---

[9] Russell, Stoger and Coyne, "Pysics, Philosophy and Theology," M 13.

[10] Pope John Paul II, *Fides et Ratio*: *The Encyclical Letter of the Supreme Pontiff John Paull II to the Bishops of the Catholic Church of the Relationship Between Faith and Reason* (Washington, D.C., United Sates Catholic Conference, 1998). Para. 67.

The Council is of the opinion that theology is an important beneficiary from the scientific developments because they can "stimulate the mind to a more accurate and penetrating grasp of the faith. For recent studies and findings of science, history and philosophy raise new questions which influence life and demand new theological investigations" (Vatican II, *Gaudium et Spes*, no. 36 in Abbot 268). Hence the Council wants theology to be in constant touch with developments in the sciences. According to the Council:

> Through a sharing of resources and points of view, let those who teach in seminaries, colleges and universities try to collaborate with people well versed in the other sciences. Theological inquiry should seek a profound understanding of revealed truth without neglecting close contact with its own times (Vatican II, *Gaudium et Spes*, no.36 in Abbot 270).

All these and similar statements are indicative of the open and positive attitude Vatican Council II has taken towards science and scientific developments.

Science-Theology Dialogue: The Need of the Hour

In spite of the developments in science and the opening in theology, theology does not seem to have much progress in dialoguing with science. The humbling experience of science and its dynamic worldview must be an inspiration for theology to change its mindset and to have a more open and dynamic worldview. There have been both global and national attempts in promoting science-theology dialogue. The Templeton Foundation, the Centre for Theology and Natural Sciences (USA), the Indian Institute of Science and Religion (IISR, Delhi), the Institute of Science and Religion (ISR, Aluva) are a few among these. However, their reach is limited to academic circles, not reaching the public. Hence, I recommend the following to underline the significance of science-theology dialogue in the contemporary times.

Theological Re-orientation

Theology should provide meaning to humanity in the context of the scientific predictions of the cosmic futility. In spite of radical shifts in the scientific worldviews, materialism and reductionism are prevalent in the contemporary scenario. The impact of materialist reductionism has reached to an extent that amidst the scientific advances, disorientation, hopelessness, and a sense of ultimate meaninglessness of life prevail among the contemporary civil society globally and locally. Scientific predictions on the end of the universe also affirm such a pessimist worldview. Scientific account and philosophical ideologies demonstrate that there is nothing beyond the material reality and thereby reduces all human experience, including mental, the aesthetic, the personal and the spiritual to what dies and decays. Theology can retrieve value bearing components from our religious and cultural perceptions and steer the scientific worldview accordingly.

Interpreting Theology from Scientific Perspective

Faith becomes reasonable and theology becomes intelligible by way of interpreting theological mysteries from scientific perspective. For example the theological concept of *Trinity* can be explained using fuzzy mathematics.[11]

Towards Authentic Narratives

Falsified myths and falsified narratives in theology (Scriptural literalism) can be corrected using scientific accounts so that theological language becomes more comprehensible and reasonable. Similarly, fallacious scientific speculations can be rectified using theological questions.

Revising Theological Syllabus

The revision of theological syllabus/curriculum is the need of the time. Philosophy of science is taught in our institutions. But

---

[11] Binoy Pichalakkattu, *Bridging Mathematics, Philosophy and Theology: Fuzzy Logical Thinking for Science-Religion Dialogue* (Delhi: Christian World Imprints, 2017).

theology of science is not incorporated as a major course in most of the seminaries.

Redefining Theological Publication

Redefining the Nature of Theological Publication is a major concern for the contemporary times. What is the impact of our theological writings? Our writing seldom reaches the boundary of the churches. How to break this isolation? One example could be *Ezhuthu* magazine, a literary-cultural-scientific magazine in the regional language Malayalam.[12] Now entering its third year of publication, *Ezhuthu* is making waves of impact on the secular fabric irrespective of caste, creed and religion. The beneficiaries of the magazine have an extended range of readers covering all sections of society. It implies, a public theological publication must be academic in nature, spiritual in vision and interdisciplinary in approach.

Science-Theology Dialogue for Betterment of Humanity

Science-theology dialogue presupposes that science and theology are complementary. Science seeks knowledge but the theological quest is for wisdom. Knowledge and wisdom are neither coextensive nor mutually exclusive. They overlap, in the sense, science explains; theology reveals, science informs; theology transforms. Science is a study of causes and theology is an inquiry into meaning. So science and theology are like different sorts of maps, and both help us to get a better picture of reality because each in its own way represents that reality more or less faithfully. Science and theology are two sides of reality and they complement each other.

Methodology for Science Theology Dialogue

The methodology, I propose, for science-theology dialogue is both hermeneutical and dialogical. This method takes into account different possible interpretations of data within science and theology, and fuses the horizons by which the meaning of data can be apprehended, which would further give rise to the emergence of

---

[12] *Ezhuthu* magazine is published by Loyola Institute of Peace and International Relations (LIPI), Kochi. For details see, www.ezhuthu.org.

new meaning and interpretations. The emergence of new meaning and interpretations are possible in respective horizons only when the meaning of the data and events in both science and theology interact.

Conclusion

The role of Christianity and theology today is to interact with the civil society. Such an interaction is possible only if theology overcomes its binary thinking. In spite of the radical developments in theology down the centuries/decades, binary thinking still dominates our theological language and thinking. It is a requirement for theology to go public. This is so much in consonance with the call of Pope Francis 'to build bridges, not walls'. The paper specifically calls for bridging science and theology for a better understanding of reality and also for a better enhancement of human life.

Bibliography

Books

Barbour, Ian G. *Issues in Science and Religion* (San Francisco: Harper and Row), 1966.

Knitter, Paul F. *Introducing Theologies of Religions* (Maryknoll, NY: Orbis Books) 2002.

Murphy, Nancey. *Theology in the Age of Scientific Reasoning* (Ithaca, NY: Cornell University Press, 1990).

Panikkar, Raimon. *The Cosmotheandric Experience* (Maryknoll, NY: Orbis Books, 1993).

Pichalakkattu, Binoy. *Bridging Mathematics, Philosophy and Theology: Fuzzy Logical Thinking for Science-Religion Dialogue* (Delhi: Christian World Imprints, 2017).

Polkinghorne, John. *Faith, Science, and Understanding* (New Haven, CT: Yale University Press, 2000).

Russell, Robert John. *Cosmology: From Alpha to Omega* ((Minneapolis: Fortress Press, 2008).

Articles

Joseph, K. Babu. "Bahrathiya Satra Paithrukathil Bahvana Kalartharuthu." In *Ezhuthu: Chinthikkunna Hrudayangalkku-Malayalam* Monthly Magazine. Vol. 3, no. 5 (March 2018): 60-63.

Kozhamathadam, Job. "The Changing Face of Science-Christianity Dialogue: Encouragement, Estrangement, and Encouragement." In *Science, Technology and Values*, ed. Job Kozhamthadam (Pune: ASSR Publications, 2003): 3-34.

McGrew, Antony. "The State in Advanced Capitalist Society." In *Global Society*. Vol. 12, no. 3 (1998): 69.

Murphy, Nancey. "Bridging Theology and Science in a Postmodern Age." In *Bridging Science and Religion*, ed. Ted Peters and Gayman Bennet (Minneapolis: Fortress Press, 2003): 35-46.

Paul II, Pope John, *Fides et Ratio*: *The Encyclical Letter of the Supreme Pontiff John Paull II to the Bishops of the Catholic Church of the Relationship Between Faith and Reason* (Wahisngton, D.C: United Sates Catholic Conference, 1998): Para. 67.

Russell, Robert, William R. Stoger and George V. Coyne, S.J. (eds.) *Physics, Philosophy and Theology: A Common Quest for Understanding* (Vatican City: Vatican Observatory Publications, 1988), M 14.

Singh, Vijender. "An Analysis of Concept and Role of Civil Society in Contemporary India." In *Global Journal of Human Science*. Vol. 12, issue 7, version 1.0 (April 2012): 68-77.

Web Reference

"The Worldviews and Opinions of Scientists in India Summary Report." In https://www.scribd.com/document/17138974/Worldviews-and-Opinions-of-Scientists-India-2007-2008-Summary-Report.

Contributors

T. K. Oommen

Prof. Dr. T. K. Oommen is a Padma Bhushan Awardee and Professor Emeritus at JNU. A renowned sociologist, he has authored books like *Charisma Stability and Change, Social Transformation in Rural India – Mobilization and State Intervention, Protest and Change – Studies in Social Movements, Citizenship Nationality and Ethnicity, Knowledge and Society, Pluralism Equality and Identity, Crisis Contention in Indian Society, The Christian Clergy in India, Nation Civil Society and Social Movements.*

X. D. Selvaraj

Dr. X. D. Selvaraj has a Master degree in Theology, M. A. in Politics and a doctorate in Moral Theology. After teaching moral theology for 18 years, he served in CCBI as Laity Commission National Executive Secretary and now serves as Visiting Professor in few seminaries and institutes.

Varghese Manimala

Dr. Varghese Manimala has been a secretary of the Association of Christian philosophers of India, and has served as the Director of the Henry Martin Institute – International Centre for Research, Inerfaith Relations and Reconciliation, Hyderabad. He has edited and published books like *Being, Person and Community: A Study in Intersubjectivity with Special Reference to Marcel, Sarte and the Concept of Sangha in Buddhism* and *Faith, Reason and Science* and has authored *Toward Mutual Fecundation and Fulfilment of Religions* (2009). An ardent disciple of Raimond Panikkar, Manimala has penned several articles on Panikkkar's philosophy of religion.

Prakash Mallavarapu

Dr. Prakash Mallavarapu is archbishop of the catholic archdiocese of Visakhapatnam, and the Secretary General of the Conference of Catholic Bishops in India. He had his Masters in Philosophy from Jnana-Deepa Vidyapeeth, Pune, from 1974-1976. He took his Ph.D. in philosophy from Jnana-Deepa Vidyapeeth, Pune, in 1985 and took a Masters in theology from Loyola University of Chicago, from 1989-1990.

Moses Manohar

Dr. Moses Manohar is Executive Director of ICSA (Inter-Church Service Association) - Chennai. He is author of *Rights-Based Politics* (ICSA Books, 2014), and *A New Political Paradigm for India* (PROMILLA & Co, Delhi, 2009). He had been the secretary – national issues unit of NCCI, New Delhi, and presently holding a honorary position of Chair, Constitution Committee, NCCI.

S. M. Michael

Dr. Sebastian M. Michael is the Director of Institute of Indian Culture, a Post-graduate Research Centre in Society, Culture and Religion. He is also Professor Emeritus of Cultural Anthropology, University of Mumbai. He is Chairman of Bombay Archdiocesan Commission for Inter-Religious Dialogue. Among his several books, the edited volume "Dalits in Modern India: Vision and Values" (1999) has been translated into several languages. He is also visiting Professor in several academic centres in India and abroad.

P. T. Mathew

Dr. P. T. Mathew is a Jesuit priest who was formerly a member of the Faculty of Theology, Vidyajyoti College, Delhi. He holds a Ph.D. in Christian Studies from the University of Madras, and did his post-doctoral research at the JSTB, Berkeley, USA. His publications include *We Dare the Waters – the World and the Worldview of Mukkuvar* (University of Madras, 2001), and *Human Persons in the World – Explorations in Christian Anthropology* (Anand: Gujarat Sahitya Prakash, 2017).

Gnana Patrick

Dr. Gnana Patrick heads the Department of Christian Studies, and serves as the Chairperson of the School of Philosophy and Religious Thought at the University of Madras. Along with Prof. Elisabeth Schussler Fiorenza, he edited a volume titled, *Negotiating Borders: Theological Explorations in the Global Era*, and has authored *Wings of Faith: Towards Public Theologies in the Indian Context*. He was awarded the Fulbright-Nehru Visiting Lecturer Fellowship and taught a course on *Public Religion* at Harvard University, USA.

Mohan Doss

Dr. Mohan Doss is a member of the Society of the Divine Word (SVD) - an international catholic religious congregation -, and belongs to Mumbai SVD Province. He was ordained a priest on May 4, 1985. He completed his P.G. studies in Sociology from the Jawaharlal Nehru University, New Delhi, in English literature from Osmania University, Hyderabad, and in Systematic Theology from Jnana-Deepa Vidyapeeth (JDV), Pune. He obtained his doctorate in Systematic Theology from Albert-Ludwig University, Freiburg, Germany. He is the author of the book, *Christ in the Spirit: Contemporary Spirit Christologies*. He teaches Systematic Theology in JDV, Pune from June 2000. He was the Rector of the Divine Word Seminary from 2002 to 2008 and was the Dean of the Faculty of Theology in JDV, Pune, from September 2014 to April 2018. He has edited a few books and contributes scholarly articles in theology, sociology and anthropology to national and international journals.

L. Sahayaraj

Dr. L. Sahayaraj is Deputy Secretary General of Tamil Nadu Bishops' Council. He holds a doctorate in Canon law from the

Catholic Institute of Paris and also a doctorate in Civil law from the University of Paris XI, France. He is also serving as the Member of the High Council of AIDOP Commission of Paris (Agence international diplomatie et opinion publique) and as Associate Research Scholar of the Asian Department of Canon law and Culture of the Faculty of Canon Law, Catholic Institute of Paris, France. He has authored 16 books in Tamil, English and French and is contributing articles in Studia canonica, Studies in Church Law, Shepherd's Voice, Vaigarai, etc.

Peter Susaimanickam

Dr. Peter Susaimanickam, a Catholic priest from the diocese of Tanjore, Tamilnadu, completed his licentiate in philosophy in the *Katholieke Universiteit*, Leuven and obtained doctorate in Philosophy from the *Lateran University*, Rome, specializing in Nietzsche and Charles Taylor respectively. The other areas of his expertise include Secularism and Tamil Thinkers. Besides presenting papers in different seminars at the regional and national level, he has written articles on Civil Society, Church, and Democracy in various journals and magazines. Right now he is professor in the department of philosophy at Sacred Heart Seminary, Chennai where he served as the dean of philosophy from 2014 to 2017. He is also the director of Archbishop Louis Mathias Library in Sacred Heart Seminary, Chennai.

Binoy Pichalakkattu

Dr. Binoy Pichalakkattu is a Jesuit of Kerala Province. He holds doctorates in Mathematical Statistics and in Systematic Theology. He is a member of Clavius Group for Mathematicians, U.S.A. Currently he is the Director of Loyola Institute of Peace and International Relations (LIPI), Kochi, and also the Managing Editor of EZHUTHU, a literary – cultural – scientific magazine, published by LIPI. He is a visiting faculty in institutions in India and abroad. Email: binoysj@gmail.com

Index